Mastering Magento Theme Design

Create responsive Magento themes using Bootstrap, the most widely used frontend framework

Andrea Saccà

[PACKT] open source*

PUBLISHING

community experience distilled

BIRMINGHAM - MUMBAI

Mastering Magento Theme Design

First published: April 2014

Production Reference: 2210514

Published by Packt Publishing Ltd.
Livery Place
35 Livery Street
Birmingham B3 2PB, UK.

ISBN 978-1-78328-823-6

www.packtpub.com

Cover Image by John Harkness (jtothem@gmail.com)

Credits

Author

Andrea Saccà

Reviewers

Srikanth AD

Ray Bogman

Andi Mancuso

Fernando J. Miguel

Commissioning Editor

Ashwin Nair

Acquisition Editors

Mary Jasmine

Nikhil Karkal

Content Development Editor

Priya Singh

Technical Editors

Neha Mankare

Menza Mathew

Krishnaveni Nair

Shiny Poojary

Copy Editors

Aditya Nair

Tanvi Gaitonde

Kirti Pai

Project Coordinator

Sanghamitra Deb

Proofreaders

Simran Bhogal

Indexer

Hemangini Bari

Mehreen Deshmukh

Graphics

Ronak Dhruv

Abhinash Sahu

Production Coordinators

Pooja Chiplunkar

Melwyn D'sa

Adonia Jones

Cover Work

Melwyn D'sa

About the Author

Andrea Saccà is a web designer and a frontend developer based in the infamous, central area of Rome, Italy. He is also one of the first **Magento Certified Front End Developers** and he will be speaker to the first Meet Magento Italy 2014.

After his studies in Graphic and Web Design in Rome, he worked for a few renowned web agencies as a web designer, and in 2012, he started his freelance career. After two years of freelancing, he started his own web agency, **1604lab** (www.1604lab.com) in Rome. You can visit the twitter page for his website at @1604lab.

He is a multiskilled web designer and a developer who specializes in creating an effective online presence for all kind of businesses, start-ups, and individuals, for customers all over the world.

Andrea is a passionate and hard-working individual with a strong ambition, and yes, he's a bit of a geek too! In his free time he likes snowboarding, playing guitar, going to the cinema, and drinking some beer with his friends.

You can follow Andrea on twitter at @andreasacca, and on his personal blog at www.andreasacca.it.

A special thanks to my mother and family, who always supported me; my girlfriend, Ilaria, who supported and endured me in this adventure; Gaia, who believed in me from the beginning; Paolo, who introduced me to Magento from the earlier versions; Mihai, who taught me the PHP basics; and Antonio, who bought me my first computer. I would also like to thank my friends, Silvia and Andrea e Riccardo, who helped me with English, and all my friends and people who believe in me.

Last but not least, I would like to thank Magento Commerce, who created this awesome CMS, and the community, who support the open source environment.

About the Reviewers

Srikanth AD is a Magento Certified Front End Developer passionate about developing and optimizing websites for a better user experience and search engine visibility. He is particularly interested in adapting content management systems to develop structured and scalable websites. Find out more about him at `http://srikanth.me` and get in touch via Twitter `@Srikanth_AD`.

Ray Bogman is an IT professional and a Magento evangelist from the Netherlands. He started working with computers as a hobby in 1983. In the past, he worked for KPN, a large Dutch Telecom company, as a senior security officer.

He has been the CTO of Wild Hibiscus, Netherlands, since 2010; the CTO of Jira ICT since 2005, and the CTO of SupportDesk B.V, which he co-founded in 2011. He is also the co-founder and creator of Yireo.

At SupportDesk B.V, he is a Magento, Joomla, web/server/mobile performance specialist, and a security evangelist. At work, he focuses on business development and on training webmasters and consultants in Magento, from the basics up to an advanced level. He has trained over 1000 Magento and 750 Joomla experts worldwide since 2005.

In Magento events such as Magento Developers Paradise and Meet Magento, he has been a regular speaker since 2009.

Besides work, his hobbies are snowboarding, running, going to the movies and music concerts, and loving his wife Mette and daughter Belize..

He has participated in reviewing *Mastering Magento, Bret Williams, Packt Publishing; Mastering Magento [VIDEO], Franklin Strube, Packt Publishing*; and *Joomla! templates ontwerpen, Jisse Reitsma, Van Duuren Media*, a Dutch book that covers Joomla template tutorials.

I would like to thank my loving wife, Mette, and daughter, Belize, for their constant support.

Andi Mancuso is a web designer and Internet marketer with a wide range of skills including CMS management and theme customization. She has an experience of over a decade in creating unique, branded websites and professional blogs, and she has worked in both corporate and small business environments with e-commerce and/or informational online presences. Her primary focus in web designing is user experience, employing deep knowledge of visual psychology and a written voice to optimize a visitor's usage and impression of a website. She currently works for a global company as a marketing manager, accepting independent editing and design work in her free time.

Fernando J. Miguel has been working on the backend development of Content Management System (CMS) since 2004. He has a bachelor's degree in Information System and is a postgraduate in Health Informatics at Universidade Federal de São Paulo, Brazil. He has experience in PHP, JSP, Java, Objective C, Zend Framework 2, Yii PHP Framework, jQuery, Node.js, Prototype, Mac OS X, iOS, Android, MySQL, Oracle, PL/SQL, HTML5, CSS3, web services, WordPress, Magento, and Joomla!

Currently, he is working in the company named Origami Web (http://www.origamiweb.com.br) and has also been working with Magento Development, WordPress, and Zend Framework 2, besides working on Android and iOS mobile development. Fernando is also engaged in social projects such as technologically assisting an NGO, Alma Vira-lata from Ubatuba, SP, Brazil (http://www.almaviralata.org.br), which is responsible for the protection of abandoned animals.

Fernando has reviewed the following Packt Publishing books: *Magento 1.4 Theming Cookbook*, *Jose Argudo Blanco*; *Mastering Magento, Bret Williams*; and the *Mastering Magento [VIDEO], Franklin Strube*. He is currently working on revising the *Mastering Magento PHP* book.

I would like to dedicate this work to my beloved grandmother, Mildes, and my mother, Ednéia, who are no longer with me, and the love of my life, my dear wife, Elizabete. These women will always continue to inspire my work.

www.PacktPub.com

Support files, eBooks, discount offers, and more

You might want to visit `www.PacktPub.com` for support files and downloads related to your book.

Did you know that Packt offers eBook versions of every book published, with PDF and ePub files available? You can upgrade to the eBook version at `www.PacktPub.com` and as a print book customer, you are entitled to a discount on the eBook copy. Get in touch with us at `service@packtpub.com` for more details.

At `www.PacktPub.com`, you can also read a collection of free technical articles, sign up for a range of free newsletters and receive exclusive discounts and offers on Packt books and eBooks.

`http://PacktLib.PacktPub.com`

Do you need instant solutions to your IT questions? PacktLib is Packt's online digital book library. Here, you can access, read and search across Packt's entire library of books.

Why Subscribe?

- Fully searchable across every book published by Packt
- Copy and paste, print and bookmark content
- On demand and accessible via web browser

Free Access for Packt account holders

If you have an account with Packt at `www.PacktPub.com`, you can use this to access PacktLib today and view nine entirely free books. Simply use your login credentials for immediate access.

Table of Contents

Preface

In recent years, Magento has become one of the most important CMS platforms for e-commerce. The e-commerce sector is growing very rapidly and professionals find it a very useful resource to work on. Thanks to its great flexibility, scalability, and optimization, Magento has become a tool that is most used by designers, developers, and web agencies to create an e-commerce website.

Magento is a CMS that is very complex and hard to customize, but with this book, you will learn how to create a customized, responsive Magento theme with custom pages, widgets, and an awesome admin panel.

You will also be able to edit the design of the backend, customize the login panel, and add a new look and feel to the Magento admin panel.

At the end of this book, you will know how to create a customized, professional, and fully responsive Magento theme.

You can improve your development skills with the best practices and tips, adding new skills to your portfolio/resume, and expanding your target customers.

What this book covers

Chapter 1, *Introducing Magento Theme Design*, introduces the basic information that you need to create a customized Magento theme with all the required files, and a review about the files' structure.

Chapter 2, *Creating a Responsive Magento Theme with Bootstrap 3*, guides you to create the base for a responsive design of the theme with the integration of the famous frontend framework, Bootstrap 3.

Chapter 3, Customizing Our Custom Theme, guides you to develop a customized home page by adding the Bootstrap carousel as the main slider, a custom vertical navigation menu on the left sidebar, and a products grid.
We will also learn how to customize the other main pages of the theme.

Chapter 4, Adding Incredible Effects to Our Theme, helps you to insert awesome animations and CSS3 and jQuery effects into the theme, improving the aesthetics, usability, and graphic appeal to create a great visual impact.

Chapter 5, Making the Theme Fully Responsive, guides you in the optimization of the theme for mobile and tablet devices, solving the most commons problems related to the responsive design.

Chapter 6, Making the Theme Socially Ready, explains how to integrate social plugins in your theme to enable social sharing of the contents in some sections of the theme.

Chapter 7, Creating a Magento Widget, introduces the base of the Magento widgets and helps you learn how to create a customized module that provides a simple customized widget.

Chapter 8, Creating a Theme Admin Panel, explains how to create a custom Magento module that adds a control panel for the theme with configuration options to customize the theme from the backend.

Chapter 9, Customizing the Backend of Magento, explains how to improve the look and feel of the design of the Magento backend, and create a custom theme for the backend that will customize the administration area from the login page to the admin backend.

Chapter 10, Packaging and Selling the Theme, explains how to pack the theme with all the necessary files, for it to be sold on the most popular theme marketplaces.

Appendix, Conclusions and Credits, contains the useful links, resources, and credits mentioned in the book.

What you need for this book

To start creating the advanced theme described in this book, you will need the following:

- A Magento 1.8.0.0 CE installation with sample data
- One graphic theme mockup PSD to develop the themes

Prerequisites

To start this project, you need basic knowledge of Magento CMS and the file structure. An advanced knowledge of programming languages such as HTML, PHP, CSS, and JavaScript are needed to proceed rapidly through all the chapters.

The prerequisites include knowledge in the following fields:

- HTML, CSS, PHP and JavaScript
- jQuery
- Magento CE (Community Edition)
- Magento files structure
- The Bootstrap 3 framework (non-essential)

Who this book is for

If you are a designer, developer, or web agency who is already familiar with Magento designing, but want to create a complex template, this book is for you.

Among the potential readers of this book, there are also backend developers who want to learn how to create themes for the frontend.

So, if you want to learn how to create fully customized Magento themes, this is the right book for you.

Conventions

In the book we have used the following typographic conventions including: *Italic* for emphasis, and `Monospace` for indicating paths and filenames.

A block of code, indicating HTML, PHP, or jQuery snippets of code and other code blocks are set as follows:

```
<a href="
  <?php echo Mage::helper('adminhtml')->getUrl(
    'adminhtml/index/forgotpassword',
      array('_nosecret' => true)) ?>">
  <?php echo Mage::helper('adminhtml')->__(
    'Forgot your password?') ?>
</a>
```

When we wish to draw your attention to a particular part of a code block, the relevant lines or items are set in bold:

```
<topheader_color1 translate="label">
<label>Top Header Background: </label>
   <comment>Comment...</comment>
   <frontend_type>text</frontend_type>
   <validate>color</validate>
   <sort_order>02</sort_order>
   <show_in_default>1</show_in_default>
   <show_in_website>1</show_in_website>
   <show_in_store>1</show_in_store>
   <depends>
      <topheader_enable>1</topheader_enable>
   </depends>
</topheader_color1>
```

New terms and **important words** are shown in bold. Words that you see on the screen, in menus or dialog boxes for example, appear in the text like this: "To make a donation, click on the **Contribute** button and make your offer."

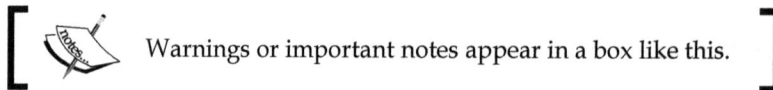

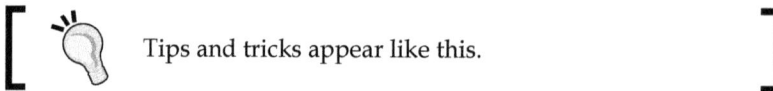

> Warnings or important notes appear in a box like this.

> Tips and tricks appear like this.

Reader feedback

Feedback from our readers is always welcome. Let us know what you think about this book—what you liked or may have disliked. Reader feedback is important for us to develop titles that you really get the most out of.

To send us general feedback, simply send an e-mail to feedback@packtpub.com, and mention the book title via the subject of your message.

If there is a topic that you have expertise in and you are interested in either writing or contributing to a book, see our author guide on www.packtpub.com/authors.

Customer support

Now that you are the proud owner of a Packt book, we have a number of things to help you to get the most from your purchase.

Downloading the example code

You can download the example code files for all Packt books you have purchased from your account at http://www.packtpub.com. If you purchased this book elsewhere, you can visit http://www.packtpub.com/support and register to have the files e-mailed directly to you.

Errata

Although we have taken every care to ensure the accuracy of our content, mistakes do happen. If you find a mistake in one of our books—maybe a mistake in the text or the code—we would be grateful if you would report this to us. By doing so, you can save other readers from frustration and help us improve subsequent versions of this book. If you find any errata, please report them by visiting http://www.packtpub.com/submit-errata, selecting your book, clicking on the **errata submission form** link, and entering the details of your errata. Once your errata are verified, your submission will be accepted and the errata will be uploaded on our website, or added to any list of existing errata, under the Errata section of that title. Any existing errata can be viewed by selecting your title from http://www.packtpub.com/support.

Piracy

Piracy of copyright material on the Internet is an ongoing problem across all media. At Packt, we take the protection of our copyright and licenses very seriously. If you come across any illegal copies of our works, in any form, on the Internet, please provide us with the location address or website name immediately so that we can pursue a remedy.

Please contact us at copyright@packtpub.com with a link to the suspected pirated material.

We appreciate your help in protecting our authors, and our ability to bring you valuable content.

Questions

You can contact us at questions@packtpub.com if you are having a problem with any aspect of the book, and we will do our best to address it.

1
Introducing Magento Theme Design

Creating a Magento theme can be more complicated than any other **CMS** (**Content Management System**). This is because Magento has a complex structure and the files are located in multiple directories.

In this chapter, we will analyze the concepts and basic information that you need to know about the design of Magento, how to create the structure of a new theme, and how to activate it.

At the end of this chapter, you will be able to create the foundation of your theme, ready to be developed.

The following topics will be covered in this chapter:

- The basic concepts of a Magento theme
- The structure of a Magento theme
- Structural blocks and content blocks
- CMS blocks and pages
- Variables
- Widgets
- Creating and activating a theme
- Tips and tricks

The basic concepts of a Magento theme

Before you begin to create your theme, there are some basics you need to know that will help you. This is supposed to be a review of the basic concepts and techniques that you should already know, which will speed up the development of the theme.

The Magento base theme

The base theme was introduced in the **CE** (**Community Edition**) Version 1.4 and **EE** (**Enterprise Edition**) Version 1.8. The main difference between the CE and EE is the price and support.

In fact, the CE is open source and anyone can download and use it as an e-commerce platform. The EE has an annual fee of $12,000, and it has the same base of the community edition but it is aimed to companies that needs special customizations, additional functionality, and the support of the Magento team.

It's very important to understand that the base theme of Magento is essential to make the other themes work correctly, which in fact will depend on it. The base theme is the core of the Magento frontend.

The following are the frontend base theme directories:

- `app/design/frontend/base`
- `skin/frontend/base/`

The hierarchy of files and the fall-back system

The frontend of Magento has been structured in such a way that it allows the designers to create themes based on the basic theme, without changing its structure. This fall-back system allows us to create only the files that are necessary for the customization of our theme. All other files, if any, will be taken from the base theme.

In order to create the theme's files, we can proceed in the following two ways:

- Create the empty files in the appropriate directories and write all the code by hand. You can choose this option if you are an advanced developer who knows how to get the information in the right way from the database.
- Copy the files from the base theme and edit them accordingly. You can use this option to analyze and study the code, and learn how to retrieve the information of the products, blocks, and so on.

In this book, we will use the second option, which is easier and faster. In the theme you need to create/duplicate only the strictly necessary files for its customization. This allows you to have a theme that is much lighter and with fewer files.

For example, let's say we want to change the `header.phtml` file that is the block of the theme header. You can copy the `header.phtml` file from the `app/design/frontend/base/default/template/page/html/` path to the `app/design/frontend/custom_package/custom_theme/template/page/html/` path.

> It is absolutely important to know that you must not create a theme under the `base` package; you should create a custom package and place the themes inside it.

The structure of a Magento theme

The files in a Magento theme are divided into two main directories: `app` and `skin`, as shown in the following screenshot:

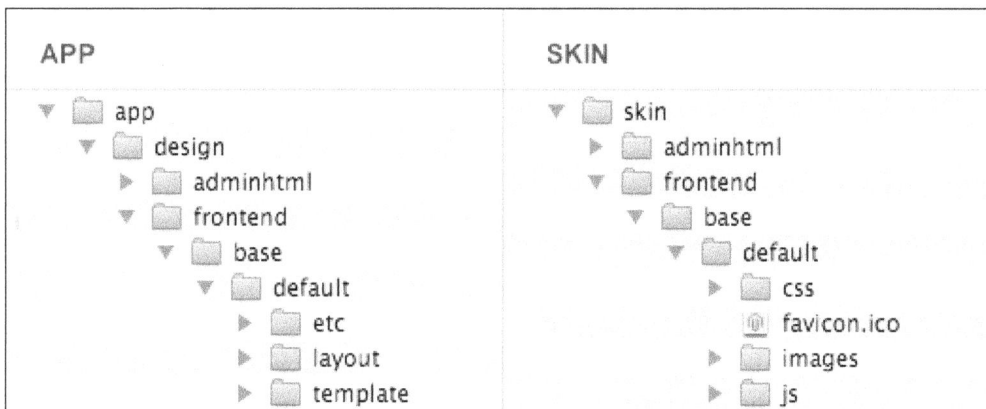

```
APP                          SKIN

▼ 📁 app                      ▼ 📁 skin
  ▼ 📁 design                   ▶ 📁 adminhtml
    ▶ 📁 adminhtml              ▼ 📁 frontend
    ▼ 📁 frontend                 ▼ 📁 base
      ▼ 📁 base                     ▼ 📁 default
        ▼ 📁 default                  ▶ 📁 css
          ▶ 📁 etc                    📄 favicon.ico
          ▶ 📁 layout                 ▶ 📁 images
          ▶ 📁 template               ▶ 📁 js
```

The following is the description of the two directories:

- `app`: The `app/design/frontend/base/default/` directory contains the layout, translation, and template files
- `skin`: The `skin/frontend/base/default/` directory contains the images, CSS, and JavaScript files

Design packages and design themes

Magento allows you to incorporate the themes in design packages. This provides greater flexibility to manage the graphics and design of a store.

The following screenshot shows the `base` package and the `default` theme:

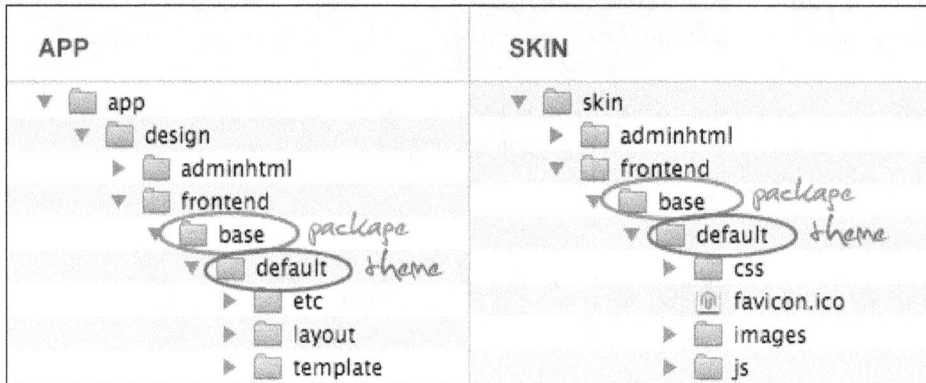

The main advantage of packages is very simple: we can create a default theme and endless themes with the graphic variants for the same store without having to change the entire theme.

Directory 1 – app

This directory contains the layout, translation, and template files.

The layout subdirectory

The `layout` subdirectory allows you to define the structure of the pages through the XML files. Various page types and blocks within each page type are defined in respective XML files. Using XML, you can also incorporate CSS files or JavaScript either to be loaded throughout the site or for specific pages.

There are layouts for page types such as a catalog and category, but not for CMS pages; for them you can define custom XML directly from the admin.

Each page, part, and block of the theme is defined by an XML file. Every page is defined by a handle. To understand better how they work, we need to have an overview of the handles.

The following are the two main handles:

- Default handles that manage the whole site
- Non-default handles that handle specific parts of the site

A handle is a reference name that Magento uses to refer to a particular page. For example, the `<cms_page>` handle is used to control the layout of the pages in your Magento store created through the **CMS (Content Management System)**. Another example is the `<catalog_product_view>` handle used to control the layout of the product view page.

The XML files are located in `app/design/frontend/base/default/layout/`. For the curious, the following is a piece of code of the XML file `page.xml`:

```xml
<?xml version="1.0"?>
<layout version="0.1.0">
<!--
Default layout, loads most of the pages
-->

    <default translate="label" module="page">
        <label>All Pages</label>
        <block type="page/html" name="root" output="toHtml" template="page/3columns.phtml">

            <block type="page/html_head" name="head" as="head">
                <action method="addJs"><script>prototype/prototype.js</script></action>
                <action method="addJs"><script>lib/ccard.js</script></action>
                <action method="addJs"><script>prototype/validation.js</script></action>
                <action method="addJs"><script>scriptaculous/builder.js</script></action>
                <action method="addJs"><script>scriptaculous/effects.js</script></action>
                <action method="addJs"><script>scriptaculous/dragdrop.js</script></action>
                <action method="addJs"><script>scriptaculous/controls.js</script></action>
                <action method="addJs"><script>scriptaculous/slider.js</script></action>
                <action method="addJs"><script>varien/js.js</script></action>
                <action method="addJs"><script>varien/form.js</script></action>
                <action method="addJs"><script>varien/menu.js</script></action>
                <action method="addJs"><script>mage/translate.js</script></action>
                <action method="addJs"><script>mage/cookies.js</script></action>

                <block type="page/js_cookie" name="js_cookies" template="page/js/cookie.phtml"/>

                <action method="addCss"><stylesheet>css/styles.css</stylesheet></action>
                <action method="addItem"><type>skin_css</type><name>css/styles-ie.css</name><params/><if>lt IE 8</if></action>
                <action method="addCss"><stylesheet>css/widgets.css</stylesheet></action>
                <action method="addCss"><stylesheet>css/print.css</stylesheet><params>media="print"</params></action>
```

In this example, we see in action the `<default>` handle that defines the generic JavaScript and CSS for the whole theme.

For the layout, there is no need to duplicate every single XML file to change the appearance of a block; just insert a JavaScript file or CSS file. In fact, with the exception of template files, we can create a single XML file where we can declare all the information that will add or override information of the basic theme.

For example, if we want to insert a new custom JavaScript `test.js` file in the head for the whole site (where all the main JS are defined), we don't need to duplicate the `page.xml` file, and declare the new JavaScript file there. Overrides should go in the `local.xml` file of our theme.

So, we can insert the new custom JavaScript `test.js` file in the header for the whole site by performing the following steps:

1. Open the `page.xml` file from `app/design/frontend/base/default/layout/page.xml` (we open that file only for reference). Check how the JavaScript is declared in the base theme. In this case, we will see that the generic JavaScript is declared in the `<default>` handle in the following way:

   ```
   <action method="addJs">
   <script>varien/js.js</script></action>
   ```

   Please note that this directory is typically used by third-party extensions to store JS files. The JS loaded from themes is expected to be stored in `/skin/frontend/package/theme/default/js` and they are declared similarly using the following way:

   ```
   <action method="addItem">
   <type>skinJs</type><script>js/test.js</script></action>
   ```

2. In the `layout.xml` file, insert the action in our default handle, and change it.

3. Create the JS file in the specified folder in `[magento_root]/skin/frontend/package/default/js/test.js`.

Templates

The template files are the PHTML files, a mix of HTML and PHP. These files contain the code of the various blocks and are located at `app/design/frontend/base/default/template/`.

The following screenshot shows a piece of code of the `header.phtml` file located at `app/design/frontend/base/default/page/html`:

```
<div class="header-container">
    <div class="header">

        <?php if ($this->getIsHomePage()):?>
        <h1 class="logo">
            <strong><?php echo $this->getLogoAlt() ?></strong>
            <a href="<?php echo $this->getUrl('') ?>" title="<?php echo $this->getLogoAlt() ?>" class="logo">
                <img src="<?php echo $this->getLogoSrc() ?>" alt="<?php echo $this->getLogoAlt() ?>" />
            </a>
        </h1>
        <?php else: ?>

        <a href="<?php echo $this->getUrl('') ?>" title="<?php echo $this->getLogoAlt() ?>" class="logo">
            <strong><?php echo $this->getLogoAlt() ?></strong>
            <img src="<?php echo $this->getLogoSrc() ?>" alt="<?php echo $this->getLogoAlt() ?>" />
        </a>

        <?php endif ?>

        <div class="quick-access">
            <?php echo $this->getChildHtml('topSearch') ?>
            <p class="welcome-msg"><?php echo $this->getWelcome() ?> <?php echo $this->getAdditionalHtml() ?></p>
            <?php echo $this->getChildHtml('topLinks') ?>
            <?php echo $this->getChildHtml('store_language') ?>
        </div>

        <?php echo $this->getChildHtml('topContainer'); ?>

    </div>
</div>
<?php echo $this->getChildHtml('topMenu') ?>
```

Locales

Locales contain the files of localization and translation of the theme. The folder that contains translation files of the theme is `app/design/frontend/base/locale`.

The file that handles the translations must be named `translate.csv`, and within it, we're going to insert the original lines of text that are defined in the translations, or of the new text that we created in the PHTML file.

To find the default Magento localizations lines of text, you can explore the files at `app/locale/en_US`. If you open this folder, you can see that the translations are organized in various CSV files. Each of them represents a specific section of the site. For example, the `Mage_Catalog.csv` file includes all the text about the catalog pages of the site.

The `locale` folder contains many folders, as there are translations that we want provide, and the `translate.csv` file must be placed inside the language folder. For example, `app/design/frontend/base/locale/en_US/translate.csv`.

`en_US` is the name of the folder that indicates the language of the localization (en) and the country or region of the language (US).

For example, if we want to create an Italian version of the theme, we have to duplicate the `translate.csv` file from `app/design/frontend/base/locale/en_US/` to `app/design/frontend/base/locale/it_IT/`.

This will be very useful to those who use the theme and will have to translate it in the future.

As I said before, we can change some existent translations or create a new one for the custom text that we insert in the PHTML files. To change the existent translation, we have to proceed in this way. For example, let's suppose that we want to change the text of the **Add to Cart** button from the default **Add to Cart** to **Buy**. We have to write in our two CSV columns. In the first column, the original text, and in the second column, the translated text: **Add to Cart, Buy**.

Alternatively, you can use the inline translation that will be stored in the database and is the final fallback. However, for theming the method described previously, it is better to have the theme localized.

Creating new translatable entries

Let's suppose that you want to add a new title or a new text line into a block. Inside the PHTML file, to make the line translatable, you must incorporate the text into the PHP code in the following way:

```php
<?php echo $this->__('New text') ?>
```

Now, put the following in the default CSV file: `"New text","New text"`.

When I say "the default CSV file", I mean the English version of the `translate.csv` file.

Directory 2 – skin

The `skin` folder contains CSS and `.js` files and images of the theme and is located at `skin/frontend/base/default/`.

Structural blocks and content blocks

The following screenshot shows **Reference Blocks** and **Content Blocks**:

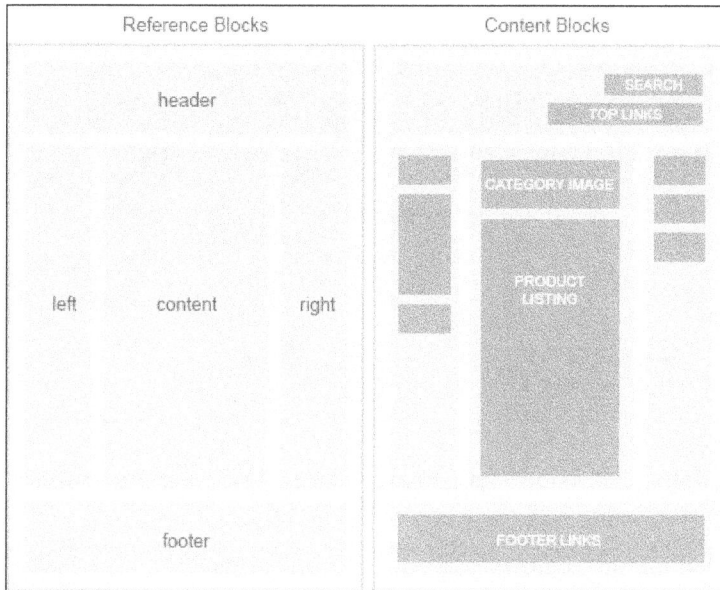

The reference blocks or structural blocks are the blocks that precisely define the container of the content blocks. For example, the header, the footer, the left and right sidebar, and the main content are a part of structural blocks. These blocks are defined in the layout XML files and the source files in the template files.

The content blocks are the blocks that hold the content. The structural blocks hold these blocks. For example, the logo, the links at the top, and the search are "content blocks" that are placed inside the reference block "header".

CMS blocks and page

CMS (**Content Management System**) pages and blocks are static pages and blocks that you can manage through the admin panel. Both CMS pages and CMS blocks can contain the HTML code and Magento variables (check the next topic for more information).

CMS blocks

CMS blocks are blocks that you can create from the admin panel. They are useful for allowing the end user to customize some parts of the theme without modifying the files directly by the admin.

To create a CMS block, navigate to **Admin Panel | CMS | Static Blocks** as shown in the following screenshot:

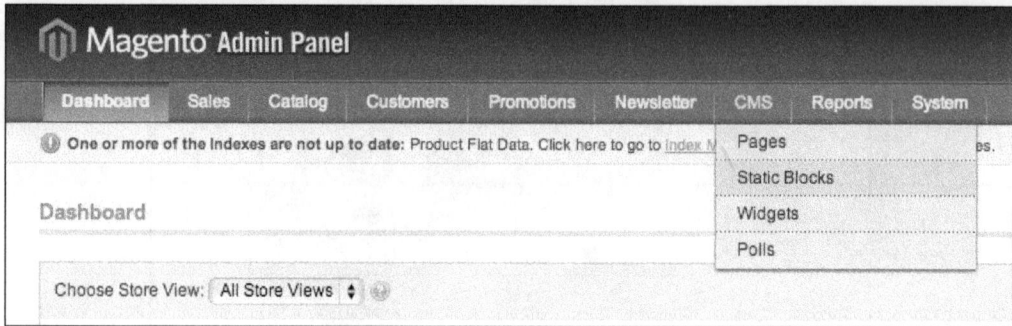

Let's say, a customer needs to insert a banner independently, but hasn't HTML or other programming knowledge. We can create a link to a specific CMS block into an XML file that the customer can directly edit by admin, using the editor to insert text or an image.

CMS pages

CMS pages are the pages that can be created directly from the admin panel. CMS pages are static pages such as **Homepage**, **About Us**, and **Customer Service**. They are available via their own URL address that can be defined with his content from the admin as well.

You can create new pages by navigating to **Admin Panel | CMS | Pages**, as shown in the following screenshot:

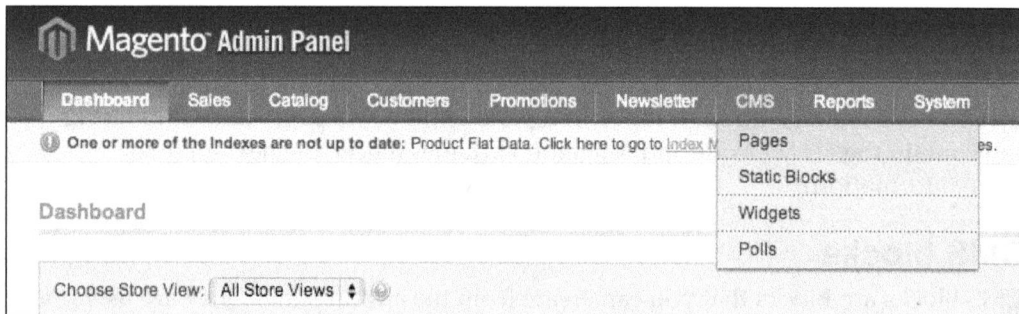

CMS pages can contain html code and Magento variables. You can also customize the page aspect through the **Design** tab, where you can choose the layout of the page, and add additional **Layout Update XML** that will overwrite the `local.xml` file as shown in the following screenshot:

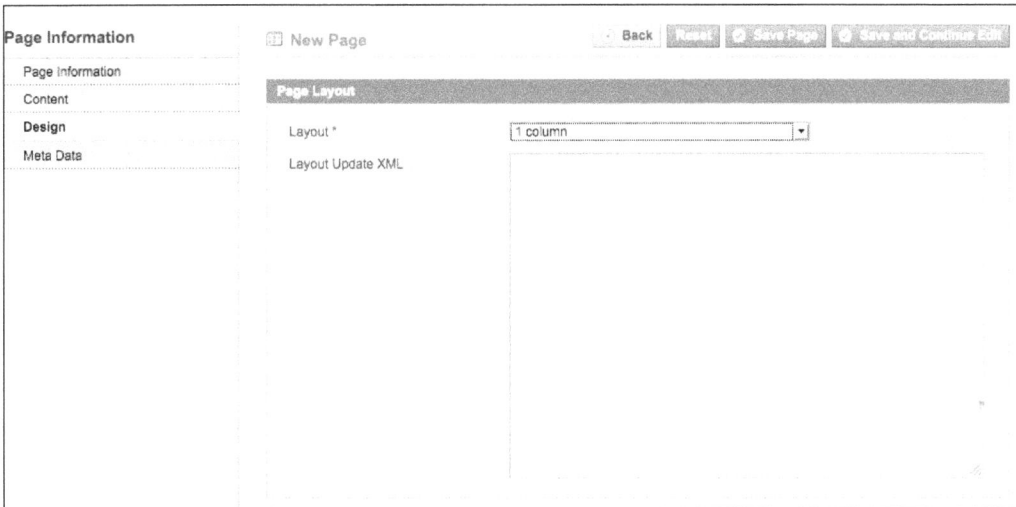

Magento variables

Magento variables, which were mentioned in the previous topic, are moveable pieces of plain text or HTML content that are great for adding to transactional e-mails, or adding a constant copy and designs to your store with static blocks and CMS pages.

By doing so, custom text and design can be created once and applied to multiple areas to save the merchant time.

Magento comes with some system variables such as `{{store url=""}}` (stores the website address), `{{var logo_url}}` (URL of the store logo), and many others. For a full reference about Magento variables, check the Magento blog at `http://www.magentocommerce.com/knowledge-base/entry/defining-transactional-variables`.

We can also create a new custom variable from the admin panel. To create a custom variable, perform the following steps:

1. In the backend, navigate to **System | Custom Variable** as shown in the following screenshot:

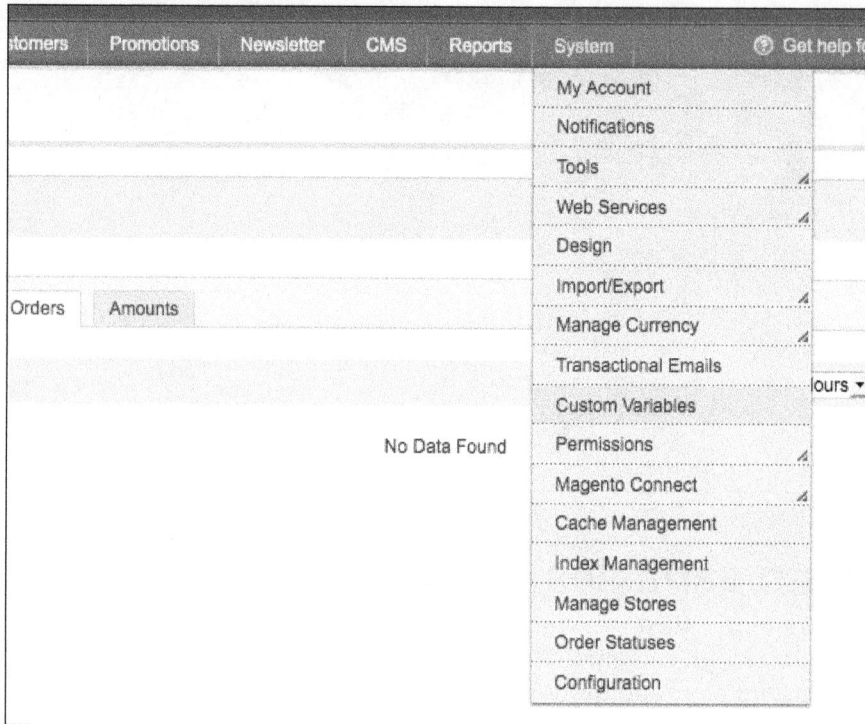

stomers	Promotions	Newsletter	CMS	Reports	System		⑦ Get help fo
					My Account		
					Notifications		
					Tools	◢	
					Web Services	◢	
					Design		
					Import/Export	◢	
Orders	Amounts				Manage Currency	◢	
					Transactional Emails		ours ▾
					Custom Variables		
			No Data Found		Permissions	◢	
					Magento Connect	◢	
					Cache Management		
					Index Management		
					Manage Stores		
					Order Statuses		
					Configuration		

2. Click on the **Add New Variable** button.

3. In the **Variable Code** field, enter the variable identifier only in lowercase and with no spaces, for example, `store_city`, as seen in the following screenshot:

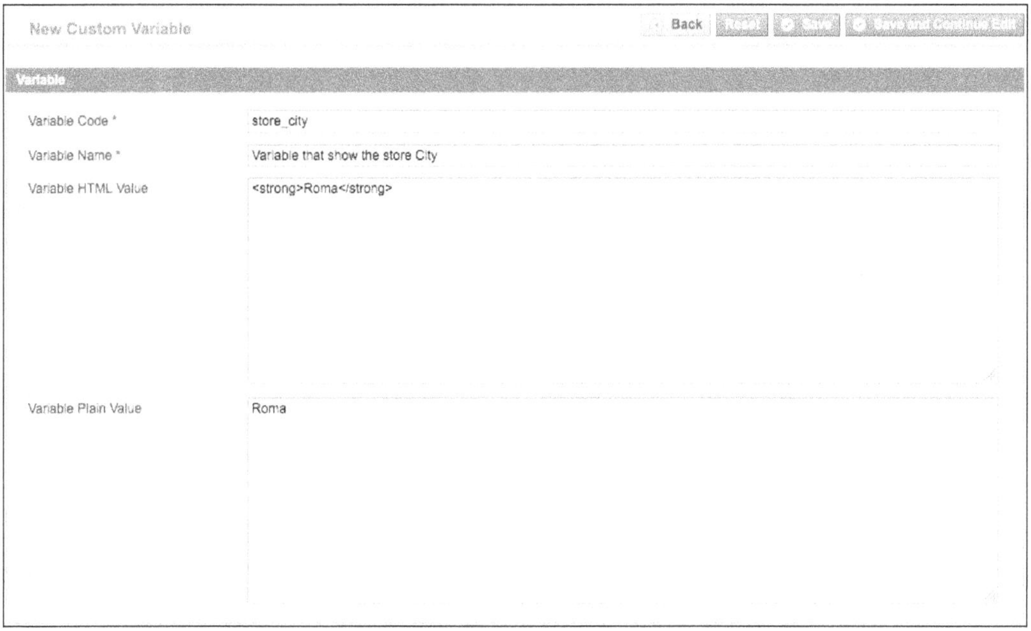

4. Enter **Variable Name**, only for internal purposes.
5. Enter the HTML code or plain text in one of the relative text areas and save it.

> The html code of this new variable that you created will be `{{CustomVar code="store_city"}}`. It is important to insert it with the editor hidden, or the editor will change the code.

Now, you can use this variable in the transactional e-mail, or in CMS pages, or also in CMS blocks. For example, insert the custom variable in the About Us page by performing the following steps:

1. Open the CMS **About Us** page (this page is present only if you are working on Magento with sample data).
2. Hide the editor and insert the following line:

```
<p>Our store Location: {{CustomVar code="store_city"}}</p>
```

This is shown in the following screenshot:

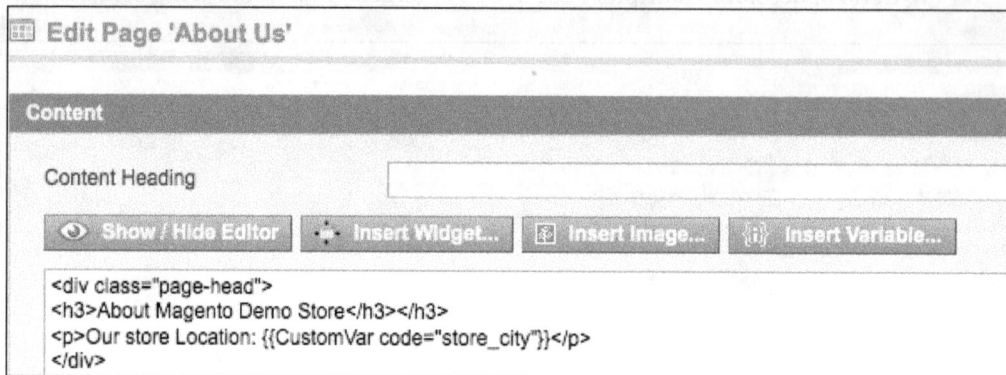

⊞ **Edit Page 'About Us'**

Content

Content Heading

| ◉ Show / Hide Editor | ✦ Insert Widget... | ▦ Insert Image... | {i} Insert Variable... |

```
<div class="page-head">
<h3>About Magento Demo Store</h3></h3>
<p>Our store Location: {{CustomVar code="store_city"}}</p>
</div>
```

3. Save the page and go to the frontend at `http://path_to_magento/about-magento-demo-store`; the following will then appear:

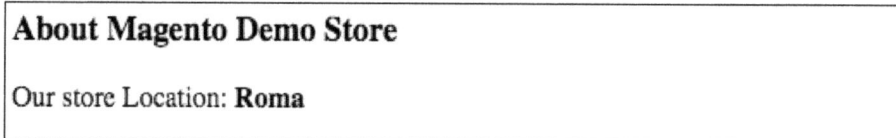

About Magento Demo Store

Our store Location: **Roma**

You can also add the custom variable through the **Insert Variable** button, which is visible when the editor is hidden.

Widgets

Magento widgets are frontend blocks with a predefined set of configuration options. These configuration options are displayed in a special edit form in the backend panel when a widget is being added or edited by a store owner. The ability to easily set widget configuration options allows store owners the full control of widget placement on a page.

Magento widgets allow users with no technical knowledge to easily add dynamic content (including product data, for example) to pages in Magento stores. This allows the user to create informational and marketing content through administrator tools with some easy steps. Some examples of widgets are as follows:

- CMS blocks (yes, you can add a CMS block in a page as a widget)
- Recently viewed items
- Catalog product link

The same options can also be seen in the following screenshot:

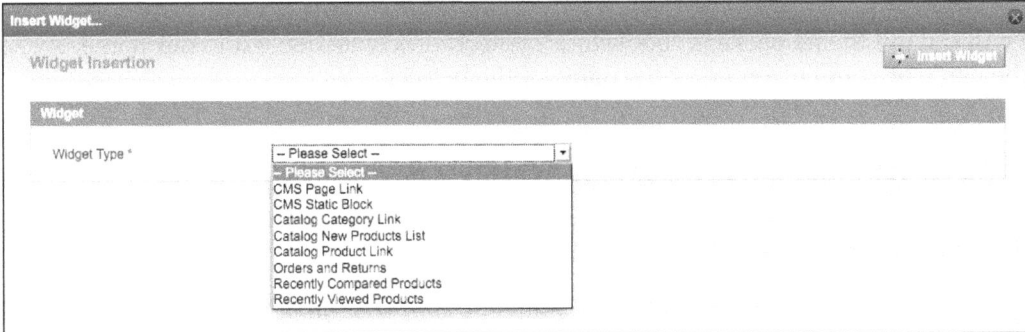

We will discuss more about this topic in the chapter dedicated to creating a widget.

Creating the theme

Once you understand the hierarchy of themes and know the basic information, you are ready to create your own custom theme. But, before you put your hands on the code, I will always recommend that you already have a mock-up to be developed, rather than designing as you go.

This will allow you to have a clear idea of what you will achieve without wasting unnecessary time to decide the position of the blocks. In this case, I have prepared the following custom layout for a hypothetical store selling books online:

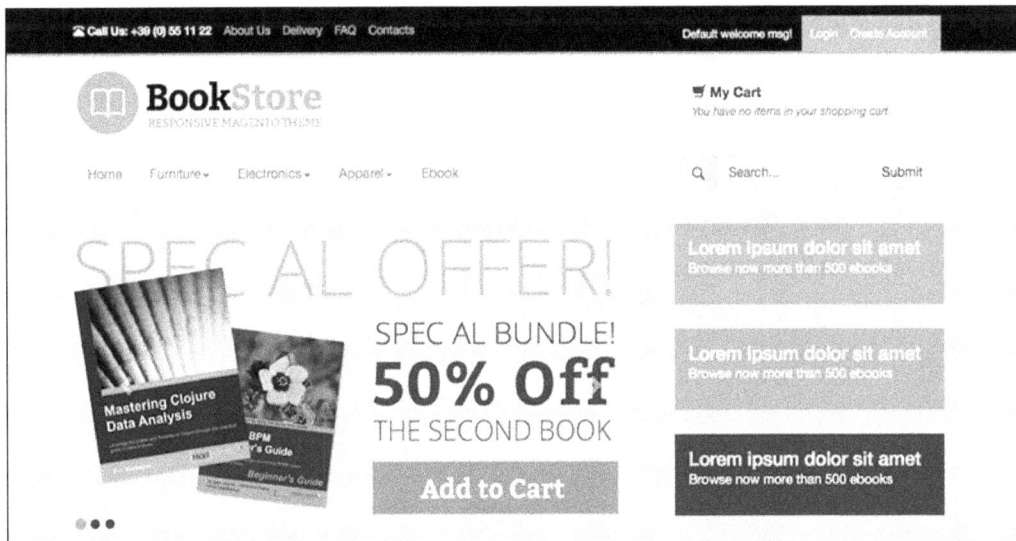

Now that we a mock-up ready to be transformed into a Magento theme, you have to decide the name of the package to create and use that for the whole project.

I will call my theme package "bookstore"; you could create one with your name, the name of your customer, or the name of the project.

Starting with the app folders

Now let's see how to begin the creation of our new theme, starting from one of the main folders, the app folder .

1. Create the `bookstore` package folder at `app/design/frontend/`, so you will have `app/design/frontend/bookstore`.

2. Create the child theme folder `default` at `app/design/frontend/`, so you will have `app/design/frontend/bookstore/default`.

3. Create all the necessary subfolders inside the default theme:

    °   `app/design/frontend/bookstore/default/template`

    °   `app/design/frontend/bookstore/default/layout`

    °   `app/design/frontend/bookstore/default/locale`

Creating the skin folders

Once we have created the app, let's create the `skin` folder. This folder contains the static files of the theme such as images, JSS, and CSS files.

1. Create the `bookstore` package folder at `skin/frontend/`, so you will have `skin/frontend/bookstore`.

2. Create the `default` theme folder at `skin/frontend/`, so you will have `skin/frontend/bookstore/default`.

3. Create all the necessary subfolders inside the default theme:

    °   `skin/frontend/bookstore/default/images`

    °   `skin/frontend/bookstore/default/css`

    °   `skin/frontend/bookstore/default/js`

To sum up, we will have the structure as shown in the following screenshot:

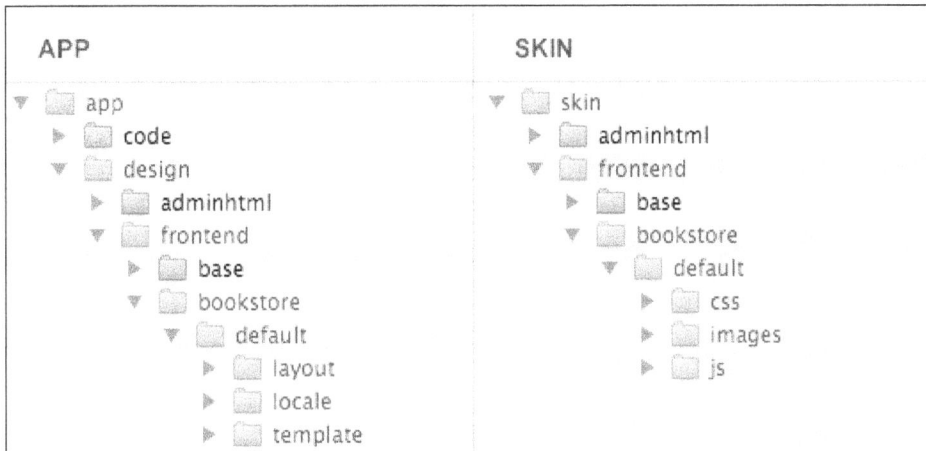

```
APP                                SKIN

▼  📁 app                          ▼  📁 skin
   ▶  📁 code                         ▶  📁 adminhtml
   ▼  📁 design                       ▼  📁 frontend
      ▶  📁 adminhtml                    ▶  📁 base
      ▼  📁 frontend                     ▼  📁 bookstore
         ▶  📁 base                         ▼  📁 default
         ▼  📁 bookstore                        ▶  📁 css
            ▼  📁 default                        ▶  📁 images
               ▶  📁 layout                      ▶  📁 js
               ▶  📁 locale
               ▶  📁 template
```

Creating the necessary files

Now that our theme structure is ready, we have to create the main files we need. As I said before, we can create empty files or copy the files from the base theme. I recommend that you copy the files from the base theme, so you already have blocks and blocks of code that we can keep and edit as you wish.

We start by creating the main files in the app folder, by performing the following steps:

1. Copy the template files. Only copy the following ones, and not everything, and only use what needs to be changed; less is more! Copy the files from `app/design/frontend/base/default/template/` and paste them to `app/design/frontend/bookstore/default/template/`:

    ° `/page/1column.phtml`: This is the file that handles the structure of the page with one column

    ° `/page/2columns-left.phtml`: This is the file that handles the structure of the page with two columns, with the sidebar on the left

    ° `/page/2columns-right.phtml`: This is the file that handles the structure of the page with two columns, with the sidebar on the right

    ° `/page/2columns-left.phtml`: This is the file that handles the structure of the page with three columns (main content and two sidebars)

- ° `/page/html/head.phtml`: This is the file for the head of the theme
- ° `/page/html/header.phtml`: This is the building block of the file header of the theme
- ° `/page/html/footer.phtml`: This is the file of the footer structural block of the theme

2. Create the `layout.xml` file at `app/design/frontend/base/default/layout/`. This basic structure of the local XML file is similar to the following code:

```xml
<?xml version="1.0" encoding="UTF-8"?>
<!--
/**
 * local.xml
 * Local layout modifications for our local theme
 * @category    design
 * @package     bookstore
 * @copyright   Copyright (c) 2013 Andrea Saccà.
 */
-->
<layout version="0.1.0">
<default>

</default>
```

In the next chapter, we will see how to override specific positions, insert JavaScript, CSS files, and other cool stuff.

3. Copy the template files present at `skin/frontend/bookstore/default/css/`, where `styles.css` is the main stylesheet and `print.css` is the style sheet used for printing.

Disabling the cache

Now that we have the basis of the theme ready, before activating it, we have to disable the caching system of Magento throughout the development phase to avoid any inconsistencies during the development process by performing the following steps:

1. Navigate to the Admin Panel, **System | Cache Management**; the following page opens:

Cache Type	Description	Associated Tags	Status
Configuration	System(config.xml, local.xml) and modules configuration files(config.xml).	CONFIG	ENABLED
Layouts	Layout building instructions.	LAYOUT_GENERAL_CACHE_TAG	ENABLED
Blocks HTML output	Page blocks HTML.	BLOCK_HTML	ENABLED
Translations	Translation files.	TRANSLATE	ENABLED
Collections Data	Collection data files.	COLLECTION_DATA	ENABLED
EAV types and attributes	Entity types declaration cache.	EAV	ENABLED
Web Services Configuration	Web Services definition files (api.xml).	CONFIG_API	ENABLED
Web Services Configuration	Web Services definition files (api2.xml).	CONFIG_API2	ENABLED

2. Select all the items and in the **Actions** dropdown, select **Disable,** and click on the **Submit** button to save. After doing this, you should see the success message and the page looks similar to the following screenshot:

Cache Type	Description	Associated Tags	Status
Configuration	System(config.xml, local.xml) and modules configuration files(config.xml).	CONFIG	DISABLED
Layouts	Layout building instructions.	LAYOUT_GENERAL_CACHE_TAG	DISABLED
Blocks HTML output	Page blocks HTML.	BLOCK_HTML	DISABLED
Translations	Translation files.	TRANSLATE	DISABLED
Collections Data	Collection data files.	COLLECTION_DATA	DISABLED
EAV types and attributes	Entity types declaration cache.	EAV	DISABLED
Web Services Configuration	Web Services definition files (api.xml).	CONFIG_API	DISABLED
Web Services Configuration	Web Services definition files (api2.xml).	CONFIG_API2	DISABLED

Activating the theme

Ok we are ready! Now that we have our theme and have disabled the cache, let's activate the theme. To activate the theme, go to **System** | **Configuration** | **Design tab**.

> Keep in mind that the scope of the default configuration is a single website/store view. You can check this configuration on the left-hand side of this page. If you are using a multistore, and you want to have different designs for different stores, you should define the design package or theme by switching first to the configuration scope on the left, selecting the appropriate store view.

Inside the **Package** box, insert the name of the package you created before in the **Current Package Name** option. In this case, we insert `bookstore`, and then click on the **Save Config** button, as shown in the following screenshot:

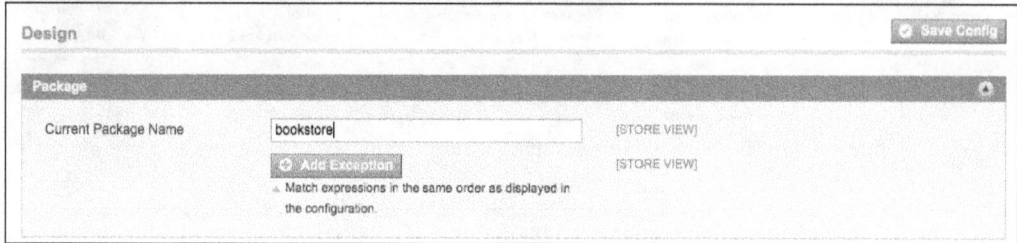

In this way, we are telling Magento to use our `bookstore` package for the current configuration.

Our theme is now ready and active. Let's go to the frontend and see what happens. If you have done everything right, you should see the following page:

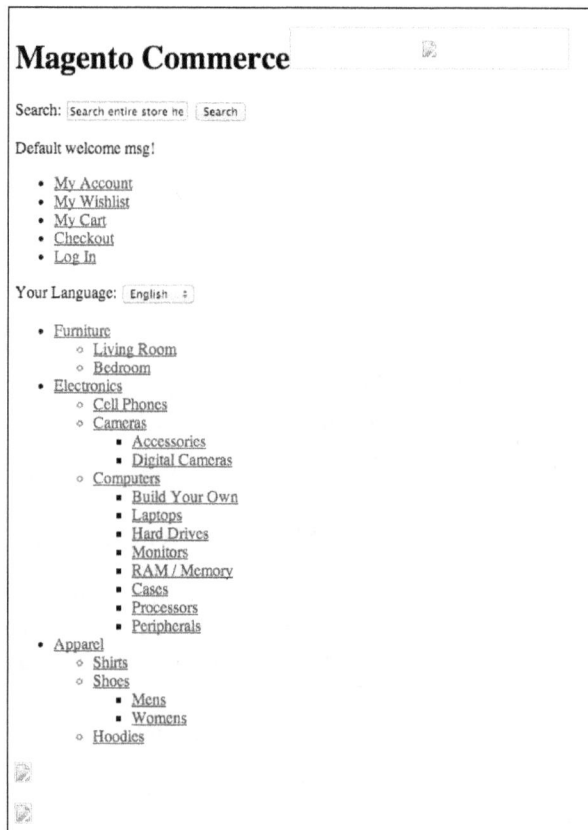

As you can see, it is a blank page with no style, but don't worry about that. Now we have created our theme that is ready to be customized!

Tips and tricks

There is some stuff that you must know while creating a theme. The following tips will help you in cases of extreme necessities, particularly when you are looking for a specific file to override.

Template path hint

The `app/design/frontend/base/default` path contains a lot of files, all divided into many folders. It's a bit hard to remember the path and name of every file. In order to find the path of a file in the base theme, we need to customize and then copy our theme; Magento comes to us with the **Template Path Hints** option.

This feature will help you a lot if you don't know the position of any file and will help you to speed up the theme creation.

To enable this feature, perform the following steps:

1. In the Admin panel, navigate to **System | Configuration**.
2. On the left side at the bottom in the **Advanced** box, click on **Developer**.
3. On the left side in the **Current Configuration Scope** box, select the **Main Website**, option or your own website.
4. Now, in the **Debug** box to the right, select **YES** to **Template Path Hints**.

5. Save the configuration.

Current Configuration Scope:	Developer			
Default Store View				
Manage Stores				
Configuration	**Developer Client Restrictions**			
	Debug			
GENERAL	Profiler	No		☑ Use Website [STORE VIEW]
General	Template Path Hints	No	▼	☐ Use Website [STORE VIEW]
Web	Add Block Names to Hints	Yes / No		☑ Use Website [STORE VIEW]
Design				
Currency Setup	**Template Settings**			
Store Email Addresses	Allow Symlinks	No		☑ Use Website [STORE VIEW]
Contacts		Warning! Enabling this feature is not recommended on		
Content Management		production environments because it represents a		
		potential security risk.		
CATALOG	**Translate Inline**			
Catalog	**Log Settings**			
Inventory	**JavaScript Settings**			
Google Sitemap	**CSS Settings**			
RSS Feeds				

Back in the frontend, we can see each block surrounded by a red border, with the PHTML file path that generates it.

In this way, we can copy the files from the base theme and paste them to the same location of our theme.

> Alternatively, you can use the *Templates Hints 2* module created by Fabrizio Branca at http://www.fabrizio-branca.de/ magento-advanced-template-hints-20.html.

The following screenshot shows the template path hints in action. As you can see, each block is surrounded by a red border with the path to the file that generates it:

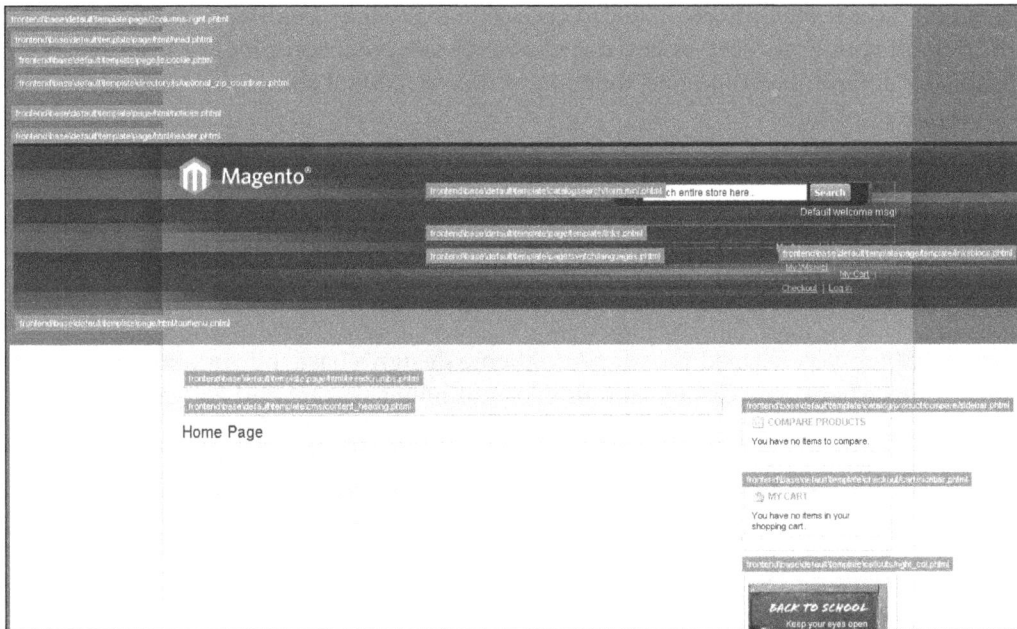

This is an example of what the screen in this program looks like.

Disabling the WYSIWYG editor

Another useful tip is to disable the WYSIWYG text editor. This will save you a lot of time when you have to write the HTML code inside the CMS pages or blocks, and you can prevent the editor from changing the code you've written.

To disable it, navigate to **System | Configuration | Content Management**, as shown in the following screenshot:

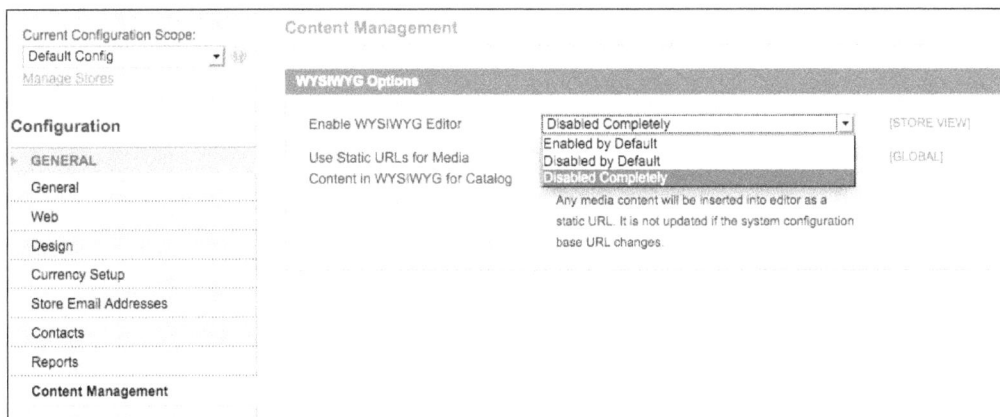

Here you have three options. You can choose to leave it as **Enabled by Default** (the default configuration), or you can choose to disable it completely, or to disable by default. I recommend that you at least disable it completely in the development phase.

Summary

Now you have all the basic components to create a custom theme for Magento, and all the information you need create the foundation of your new theme.

In this chapter, you learned the Magento theme design's basic information, the difference between package and theme, and how to create and activate a custom package with the main folders and files.

And now? Now it is time to have fun! In the next chapter, you will add the Bootstrap framework to the theme and start customizing it.

2
Creating a Responsive Magento Theme with Bootstrap 3

In the previous chapter, we learned the fundamentals to create a custom Magento theme, and we created the basic structure of our theme. In this chapter, we will learn how to integrate the Bootstrap 3 framework and how to develop the main theme blocks.

The following topics will be covered in this chapter:

- An introduction to Bootstrap
- Downloading Bootstrap (the current Version 3.1.1)
- Downloading and including jQuery
- Integrating the files into the theme
- Defining the main layout design template
- Developing the header
- Developing the footer

An introduction to Bootstrap

Bootstrap is a sleek, intuitive, powerful, mobile-first frontend framework that enables faster and easier web development, as shown in the following screenshot:

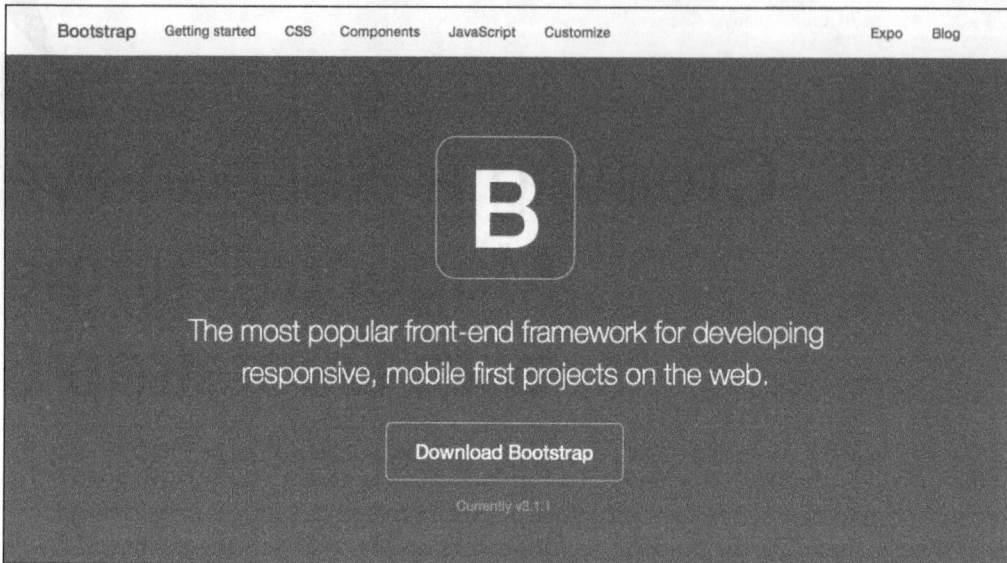

Bootstrap is the most popular frontend framework that is used to create mobile-first websites. It includes a free collection of buttons, CSS components, and JavaScript to create websites or web applications; it was created by the Twitter team.

Downloading Bootstrap (the current Version 3.1.1)

First, you need to download the latest version of Bootstrap. The current version is 3.0. You can download the framework from `http://getbootstrap.com/`.

The fastest way to download Bootstrap is to download the precompiled and minified versions of CSS, JavaScript, and fonts. So, click on the **Download Bootstrap** button and unzip the file you downloaded. Once the archive is unzipped, you will see the following files:

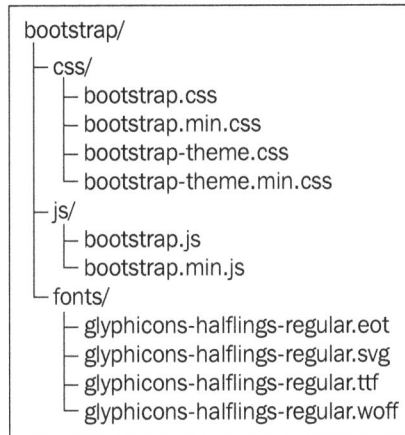

```
bootstrap/
├─ css/
│   ├─ bootstrap.css
│   ├─ bootstrap.min.css
│   ├─ bootstrap-theme.css
│   └─ bootstrap-theme.min.css
├─ js/
│   ├─ bootstrap.js
│   └─ bootstrap.min.js
└─ fonts/
    ├─ glyphicons-halflings-regular.eot
    ├─ glyphicons-halflings-regular.svg
    ├─ glyphicons-halflings-regular.ttf
    └─ glyphicons-halflings-regular.woff
```

We need to take only the minified version of the files, that is, `bootstrap.min.css` from `css`, `bootstrap.min.js` from `js`, and all the files from `font`.

> For development, you can use `bootstrap.css` so that you can inspect the code and learn, and then switch to `bootstrap.min.css` when you go live.

Copy all the selected files (CSS files inside the `css` folder, the `.js` files inside the `js` folder, and the font files inside the `fonts` folder) in the theme skin folder at `skin/frontend/bookstore/default`.

Downloading and including jQuery

Bootstrap is dependent on jQuery, so we have to download and include it before including `boostrap.min.js`. So, download jQuery from `http://jquery.com/download/`.

The preceding URL takes us to the following screenshot:

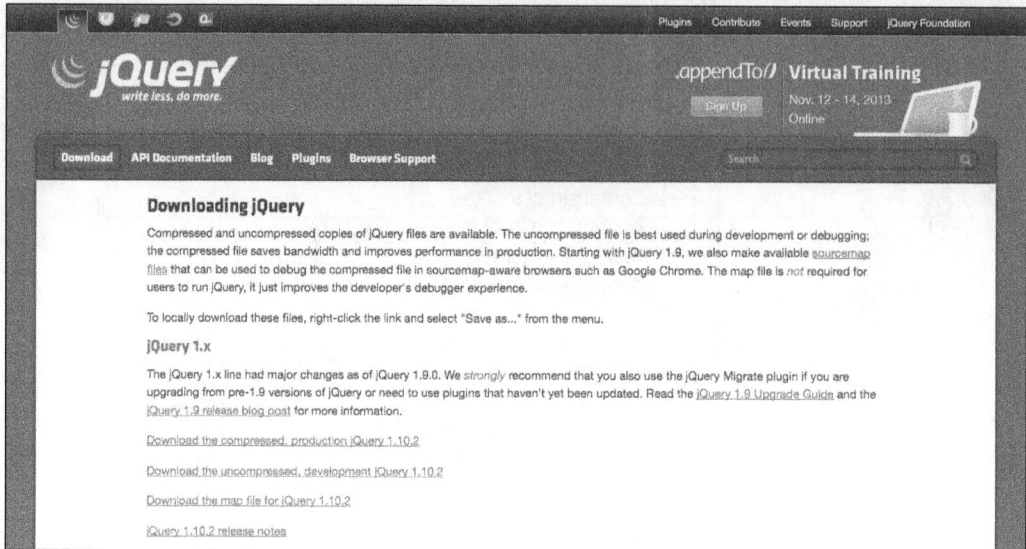

We will use the compressed production Version 1.10.2.

Once you download jQuery, rename the file as `jquery.min.js` and copy it into the `js` skin folder at `skin/frontend/bookstore/default/js/`.

In the same folder, also create the `jquery.scripts.js` file, where we will insert our custom scripts.

Magento uses Prototype as the main JavaScript library. To make jQuery work correctly without conflicts, you need to insert the **no conflict** code in the `jquery.scripts.js` file, as shown in the following code:

```
// This is important!
jQuery.noConflict();

jQuery(document).ready(function() {
    // Insert your scripts here
});
```

The following is a **quick recap of CSS and JS files:**

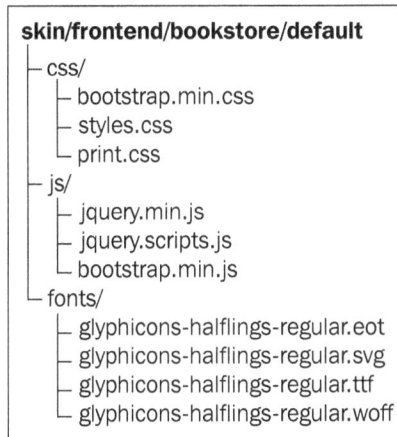

```
skin/frontend/bookstore/default
├─ css/
│     ├─ bootstrap.min.css
│     ├─ styles.css
│     └─ print.css
├─ js/
│     ├─ jquery.min.js
│     ├─ jquery.scripts.js
│     └─ bootstrap.min.js
└─ fonts/
      ├─ glyphicons-halflings-regular.eot
      ├─ glyphicons-halflings-regular.svg
      ├─ glyphicons-halflings-regular.ttf
      └─ glyphicons-halflings-regular.woff
```

Integrating the files into the theme

Now that we have all the files, we will see how to integrate them into the theme.

To declare the new JavaScript and CSS files, we have to insert the action in the `local.xml` file located at `app/design/frontend/bookstore/default/layout`.

> As explained in the previous chapter, all the overrides of the base theme should go in the `local.xml` file and we are going to use it to add new CSS and JavaScript files.

In particular, the file declaration needs to be done in the default handle to make it accessible by the whole theme.

The default handle is defined by the following tags:

```
<default>
   . . .
</default>
```

The action to insert the JavaScript and CSS files must be placed inside the reference `head` block. So, open the `local.xml` file and first create the following block that will define the reference:

```
<reference name="head">
...
</reference>
```

Declaring the .js files in local.xml

The `action` tag used to declare a new `.js` file located in the `skin` folder is as follows:

```
<action method="addItem">
  <type>skin_js</type><name>js/myjavascript.js</name>
</action>
```

In our `skin` folder, we copied the following three `.js` files:

- `jquery.min.js`
- `jquery.scripts.js`
- `bootstrap.min.js`

Let's declare them as follows:

```
<action method="addItem">
  <type>skin_js</type><name>js/jquery.min.js</name>
</action>
<action method="addItem">
  <type>skin_js</type><name>js/bootstrap.min.js</name>
</action>
<action method="addItem">
  <type>skin_js</type><name>js/jquery.scripts.js</name>
</action>
```

Downloading the example code

You can download the example code files for all Packt books you have purchased from your account at http://www.packtpub.com. If you purchased this book elsewhere, you can visit http://www.packtpub.com/support and register to have the files e-mailed directly to you. Repeat this action for all the additional JavaScript files that you want to add.

Declaring the CSS files in local.xml

The `action` tag used to declare a new CSS file located in the `skin` folder is as follows:

```
<action method="addItem">
  <type>skin_css</type><name>css/mycss.css</name>
</action>
```

In our `skin` folder, we have copied the following three `.css` files:

- `bootstrap.min.css`
- `styles.css`
- `print.css`

So let's declare these files as follows:

```
<action method="addItem">
  <type>skin_css</type><name>css/bootstrap.min.css</name>
</action>
<action method="addItem">
  <type>skin_css</type><name>css/styles.css</name>
</action>
<action method="addItem">
  <type>skin_css</type><name>css/print.css</name>
</action>
```

Repeat this action for all the additionals CSS files.

> All the JavaScript and CSS files that you insert into the `local.xml` file will go after the files declared in the base theme.

Removing and adding the style.css file

By default, the base theme includes a CSS file called `styles.css`, which is hierarchically placed before the `bootstrap.min.css`.

One of the best practices to overwrite the Bootstrap CSS classes in Magento is to remove the default CSS files declared by the base theme of Magento, and declare it after Bootstrap's CSS files.

Thus, the `styles.css` file loads after Bootstrap, and all the classes defined in it will overwrite the `boostrap.min.css` file.

To do this, we need to remove the `styles.css` file by adding the following `action` tag in the `xml` part, just before all the `css` declaration we have already made:

```
<action method="removeItem">
  <type>skin_css</type>
  <name>css/styles.css</name>

</action>
```

Hence, we removed the `styles.css` file and added it again just after adding Bootstrap's CSS file (`bootstrap.min.css`):

```
<action method="addItem">
  <type>skin_css</type>

  <stylesheet>css/styles.css</stylesheet>
</action>
```

If it seems a little confusing, the following is a quick view of the CSS declaration:

```
<!-- Removing the styles.css declared in the base theme -->
<action method="removeItem">
  <type>skin_css</type>
  <name>css/styles.css</name>
</action>


<!-- Adding Bootstrap Css -->
<action method="addItem">
  <type>skin_css</type>
  <stylesheet>css/bootstrap.min.css</stylesheet>
</action>

<!-- Adding the styles.css again -->
<action method="addItem">
  <type>skin_css</type>
  <stylesheet>css/styles.css</stylesheet>
</action>
```

Adding conditional JavaScript code

If you check the Bootstrap documentation, you can see that in the HTML5 boilerplate template, the following conditional JavaScript code is added to make Internet Explorer (IE) HTML 5 compliant:

```
<!--[if lt IE 9]>
  <script
src="https://oss.maxcdn.com/libs/html5shiv/3.7.0/html5shiv.js">
  </script>
  <script src="https://oss.maxcdn.com/libs/respond.js/1.3.0/respond.
min.js">
  </script>
<![endif]-->
```

To integrate them into the theme, we can declare them in the same way as the other `script` tags, but with conditional parameters. To do this, we need to perform the following steps:

1. Download the files at `https://oss.maxcdn.com/libs/html5shiv/3.7.0/html5shiv.js` and `https://oss.maxcdn.com/libs/respond.js/1.3.0/respond.min.js`.

2. Move the downloaded files into the `js` folder of the theme.

3. Always integrate JavaScript through the `.xml` file, but with the conditional parameters as follows:

```xml
<action method="addItem">
    <type>skin_js</type><name>js/html5shiv.js</name>
    <params/><if>lt IE 9</if>
</action>


<action method="addItem">
    <type>skin_js</type><name>js/respond.min.js</name>
    <params/><if>lt IE 9</if>
</action>
```

A quick recap of our local.xml file

Now, after we insert all the JavaScript and CSS files in the .xml file, the final `local.xml` file should look as follows:

```xml
<?xml version="1.0" encoding="UTF-8"?>
<layout version="0.1.0">
  <default translate="label" module="page">
    <reference name="head">
    <!-- Adding Javascripts -->
    <action method="addItem">
      <type>skin_js</type>
      <name>js/jquery.min.js</name>
    </action>
    <action method="addItem">
      <type>skin_js</type>
      <name>js/bootstrap.min.js</name>
    </action>
    <action method="addItem">
      <type>skin_js</type>
      <name>js/jquery.scripts.js</name>
    </action>
    <action method="addItem">
      <type>skin_js</type>
      <name>js/html5shiv.js</name>
```

```
      <params/><if>lt IE 9</if>
    </action>
    <action method="addItem">
      <type>skin_js</type>
      <name>js/respond.min.js</name>
      <params/><if>lt IE 9</if>
    </action>

    <!-- Removing the styles.css -->
    <action method="removeItem">
      <type>skin_css</type><name>css/styles.css</name>
    </action>
    <!-- Adding Bootstrap Css -->
    <action method="addItem">
      <type>skin_css</type>
      <stylesheet>css/bootstrap.min.css</stylesheet>
    </action>
    <!-- Adding the styles.css -->
    <action method="addItem">
      <type>skin_css</type>
      <stylesheet>css/styles.css</stylesheet>
    </action>
    </reference>
  </default>
</layout>
```

Defining the main layout design template

A quick tip for our theme is to define the main template for the site in the default handle.

To do this, we have to define the template into the most important reference, `root`. In a few words, the `root` reference is the block that defines the structure of a page.

Let's suppose that we want to use a main structure having two columns with the left sidebar for the theme To change it, we should add the `setTemplate` action in the `root` reference as follows:

```
<reference name="root">
   <action method="setTemplate">
      <template>page/2columns-left.phtml</template>
   </action>
</reference>
```

You have to insert the `reference name "root"` tag with the action inside the default handle, usually before every other reference.

Defining the HTML5 boilerplate for main templates

After integrating Bootstrap and jQuery, we have to create our HTML5 page structure for the entire base template.

The following are the structure files that we created in the previous chapter and are located at `app/design/frontend/bookstore/template/page/`:

- `1column.phtml`
- `2columns-left.phtml`
- `2columns-right.phtml`
- `3columns.phtml`

The Twitter Bootstrap uses scaffolding with containers, a row, and 12 columns. So, its page layout would be as follows:

```
<div class="container">
  <div class="row">
    <div class="col-md-3"></div>
    <div class="col-md-9"></div>
  </div>
</div>
```

This structure is very important to create responsive sections of the store. Now we will need to edit the templates to change to HMTL5 and add the Bootstrap scaffolding.

Let's look at the following `2columns-left.phtml` main template file:

```
<!DOCTYPE HTML>
<html>
  <head>
    <?php echo $this->getChildHtml('head') ?>
  </head>
  <body
    <?php echo $this->getBodyClass()?' class="'.$this-
>getBodyClass().'"':'' ?>>
    <?php echo $this->getChildHtml('after_body_start') ?>
    <?php echo $this->getChildHtml('global_notices') ?>
    <header>
      <?php echo $this->getChildHtml('header') ?>
    </header>
    <section id="after-header">
    <div class="container">
      <?php echo $this->getChildHtml('slider') ?>
```

```
        </div>
      </section>
        <section id="maincontent">
      <div class="container">
      <div class="row">
        <?php echo $this->getChildHtml('breadcrumbs') ?>
        <aside class="col-left sidebar col-md-3">
        <?php echo $this->getChildHtml('left') ?>
          </aside>
      <div class="col-main col-md-9">
      <?php echo $this->getChildHtml('global_messages') ?>
  <?php echo $this->getChildHtml('content') ?>
  </div>
  </div>
  </div>
  </section>
  <footer id="footer">
  <div class="container">
  <?php echo $this->getChildHtml('footer') ?>
  </div>
  </footer>
  <?php echo $this->getChildHtml('before_body_end') ?>
  <?php echo $this->getAbsoluteFooter() ?>
  </body>
  </html>
```

You will notice that I removed the Magento layout classes col-main, col-left,
main, and so on, as these are being replaced by the Bootstrap classes.

I also added a new section, after-header, because we will need it after we
develop the home page slider. In the next chapter, we will gain more information
on this topic.

> Don't forget to replicate this structure on the other template files
> 1column.phtml, 2columns-right.phtml, and 3columns.phtml,
> changing the columns as you need.

Now, we will see how to develop the main sections of the theme header and footer.

Developing the header

The header of our theme will look as shown in the following screenshot:

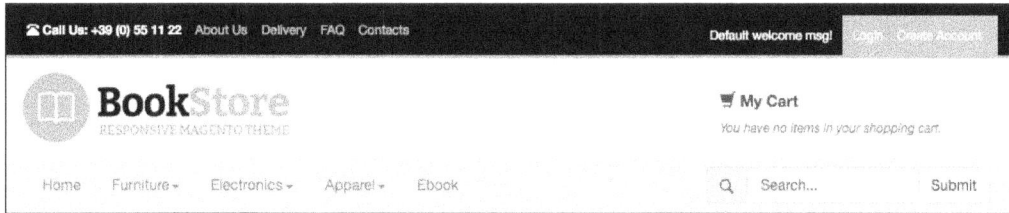

As you can see, there are three main sections that I will call the top header (the black line on the top), the main header (the white one), and the navigation bar.

To customize our header, open the `header.phtml` file located at `app/design/frontend/bookstore/default/page/html` and create the basic structure with the Bootstrap scaffolding. Our header file code will look as follows:

```
<!-- TopBar -->
<div id="topbar">
<div class="container">
<div class="row">
...
</div>
</div>
</div>

<!-- Header -->
<div id="header">
<div class="container">
<div class="row">

</div>
</div>
</div>

<!-- Navigation -->
<nav>
. . .
</nav>
```

Let's discuss the preceding code in detail:

- In the first block, inside the top header div element, we put some custom links or custom text in the left, and the user area in the right
- In the second block, we have the main header with the logo and the cart
- In the third block, we will have the navigation bar with the menus and the search form

Now we will see how to customize each block of the header.

Creating the top header

The top header `div` element, will include:

- A CMS block with custom links on the left
- A user area

CMS block links

To put CMS custom links on the left, we have to perform the following steps:

1. Create a custom CMS block.
2. Declare it in `local.xml`.
3. Finally, declare the block with a PHP statement in the `header.phtml` file.

Creating the CMS block with the links

From the admin panel, navigate to **CMS | Static Blocks** and create a new block with the following information:

- **Block ID**: `topbar_cmslinks`
- **Block Html Code**:

```
<ul class="list-inline">
<li><span class="glyphicon glyphicon-phone-alt"></
span> <strong>Call Us: +39 (0) 55 11 22</strong></li>
<li><a href="{{store_url=''}}">About Us</a></li>
<li><a href="{{store_url=''}}">Delivery</a></li>
<li><a href="{{store_url=''}}">FAQ</a></li>
<li><a href="{{store_url=''}}">Contacts</a></li>
</ul>
```

> We are using a predefined Bootstrap class, `list-inline`, in the `ul` tag to display inline links.

Declaring the CMS block in the local.xml file

Open the `local.xml` file and in the default handle add the following:

```xml
<reference name="header">

  <block type="cms/block" name="topbar_cmslinks" as="topbar_cmslinks">
    <action method="setBlockId">
      <block_id>topbar_cmslinks</block_id>
    </action>
  </block>
</reference>
```

> We insert the block into the reference name `header`.

The `as=""` statement is by which a template calls the block. In PHP, you will see `<?php echo $this->getChildHtml('topbar_cmslinks') ?>`, which indicates that it correlates to `<block . . . as='topbar_cmslinks'>` in `local.xml`.

Declaring the CMS block with a PHP statement in header.phtml

We can declare the CMS block with a PHP statement in `header.phtml`, as shown in the following code:

```html
<!-- Top Bar -->
<div id="topbar">
<div class="container">
   <div class="row">
     <div class="col-md-8">
         <?php echo $this->getChildHtml('topbar_cmslinks') ?>
       </div>
</div>
</div>
</div>
```

To explain better what `$this->` is, I quote Nick Jones's explanation:

> *"All Magento templates have a corresponding block instance. The $this statement exposed to us is the block instance, as if we were inside a method of the object."*

See `Mage_Core_Block_Template::fetchView`. More details and sources are available at `http://www.nicksays.co.uk/magento-this/`.

The `getChildHtml('topbar_cmslinks')` statement loads the block defined in `local.xml`.

The left section is now completed.

The right part of the top header

Now let's work on the right part, the user area.

About this block, please note that we will not use the default Magento top links, but a custom piece of code that will display only the conditional links for the user.

The idea is to display the welcome message and two links, **Register** and **Login**, for the users who are not logged in, and two links, **My Account** and **Logout links**, for the users who are logged in. To do this, Magento has a function that checks the status of the user's session. We will replace the **User Area** text that we used before in the header code with the following condition:

```
<!-- Top Bar -->
<div id="topbar">
<div class="container">
   <div class="row">
     <div class="col-md-8">
         <?php echo $this->getChildHtml('topbar_cmslinks') ?>
       </div>
<div class="user-links col-md-4">
  <span class="welcome pull-left">
    <?php echo $this->getLayout()->getBlock('header')->getWelcome() ?>
  </span>
  <ul class="list-inline pull-left">
  <?php if ($this->helper('customer')->isLoggedIn()): ?>
    <li>
     <a title="<?php echo $this->__('My Account') ?>" href="<?php echo
$this->getUrl('customer/account') ?>">
   <?php echo $this->__('My Account') ?>
    </a>
    </li>
    <li>
```

```
        <a title="Log Out" href="<?php echo $this->getUrl('customer/
account/logout') ?>">
        <?php echo $this->__('Logout') ?></a>
        </li>
    <?php else: ?>
        <li><a href="<?php echo $this->getUrl('customer/account/
login/')?>">
        <?php echo $this->__('Login') ?></a></li>
        <li><a href="<?php echo $this->getUrl('customer/account/
create/')?>">
        <?php echo $this->__('Create Account') ?></a></li>
        <?php endif;?>
    </ul>
</div>
</div>
</div>
</div>
```

Now, add a little bit of CSS to customize it a little. Insert the following CSS code in your styles.css file in the skin folder (skin/frontend/bookstore/default/css/):

```
/* TopBar */
#topbar {
 background:none repeat scroll 0 0 #000;
 color:#FFF;
 font-size:12px;
 padding:10px 0 0;
 border-bottom:3px solid #FA9221;
}
#topbar ul {
 margin:5px 0 0;
}
#topbar a {
color:#9F9F9F;
}
#topbar a:hover {
color:#f89223
}
#topbar .user-links .welcome {
padding:10px;
}
#topbar .user-links ul {
  background:none repeat scroll 0 0 #FA9221;
  margin:0;
```

```
    padding:10px;
}
#topbar .user-links a {
 color:#fff;
}
```

Creating the main header

The main header `div` element, will include:

- A logo
- A top cart

Logo

The default logo image is `logo.gif` and is located in the `images` folder at `skin/frontend/bookstore/default/images/logo.gif`. The filename can be changed by navigating to **System | Configuration | Design | Header**, as shown in the following screenshot:

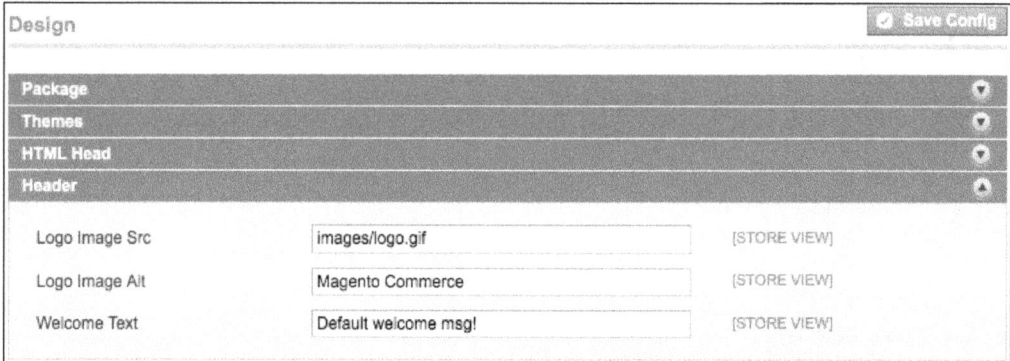

The following code generates the logo URL and the link to the home page:

```
<div class="col-md-4">
<a href="<?php echo $this->getUrl('') ?>" title="<?php echo $this->getLogoAlt() ?>" class="logo">
<img src="<?php echo $this->getLogoSrc() ?>" alt="<?php echo $this->getLogoAlt() ?>" />
</a>
</div>
```

> The logo link's `title` attribute and the logo image's `alt` attribute will be filled in with the **Logo Image Alt** field of the configuration that you can set in the same section of the admin, as shown in the preceding screenshot.

The top cart

We want to put the cart to the right of the header. We can do this in the following two ways:

- By adding a class pull-right to the cart div, but in this way we lose the responsiveness of the block (that we can fix with a media query)
- By adding an empty div, `col-md-4`, between the logo `div` element and the cart `div` element

Therefore, we will have three boxes of four columns where the latest box, the cart `div` element, will be placed at the end of the row.

I will use this method because in future, we can use the intermediate `div` element to insert some additional information or banner in the header after the logo.

The following is the `div` class that contains the cart in the `header.phtml` file, located at `app/design/frontend/bookstore/default/template/page/`:

```
<div class="col-md-4">
  <?php echo $this->getChildHtml('top_cart') ?>
</div>
```

The base theme doesn't include a top cart, but we can duplicate the sidebar mini cart and place it in the header by performing the following steps:

1. Duplicate the `sidebar.phtml` file. You can find it at `app/design/frontend/base/default/template/checkout/cart` in your theme folder in the same path, and call it in the `topcart.phtml` file. Then change the code with the following simplified version of the file:

```
<?php if ($this->getIsNeedToDisplaySideBar()):?>

<div class="block block-cart block-topcart">
<?php $_cartQty = $this->getSummaryCount() ?>
 <div class="block-title"><span class="glyphicon glyphicon-
shopping-cart"></span><strong><span><?php echo $this->__('My
Cart') ?></span></strong>

<?php if ($_cartQty>0): ?>
```

```php
    <div class="summary">

    <?php if ($_cartQty==1): ?>
     <p class="amount"><?php echo $this->__('There is <a href="%s">1
item</a> in your cart.', $this->getUrl('checkout/cart')) ?> <?php
echo Mage::helper('checkout')->formatPrice($this->getSubtotal())
?></p>

    <?php else: ?>

    <p class="amount"><?php echo $this->__('There are <a
href="%s">%s items</a> in your cart.', $this->getUrl('checkout/
cart'), $_cartQty) ?> <?php echo Mage::helper('checkout')-
>formatPrice($this->getSubtotal()) ?></p>

    <?php endif ?>

    </div>

    <?php else: ?>
     <p class="empty"><?php echo $this->__('You have no items in your
shopping cart.') ?></p>
    <?php endif ?>
     </div>
    <!-- // block-title -->
    <div class="block-content">
    <?php if($_cartQty && $this->isPossibleOnepageCheckout()): ?>
     <div class="actions">
    <?php echo $this->getChildHtml('extra_actions') ?>
     <button type="button" title="<?php echo $this->__('Checkout')
?>" class="button" onclick="setLocation('<?php echo $this-
>getCheckoutUrl() ?>')"><span><span><?php echo $this->__
('Checkout') ?></span></span></button>
    </div>
    <?php endif ?>
     <?php $_items = $this->getRecentItems() ?>
     <?php if(count($_items)): ?>
     <p class="block-subtitle"><?php echo $this->__('Recently added
item(s)') ?></p>
    <ol id="cart-sidebar" class="mini-products-list">
    <?php foreach($_items as $_item): ?>
     <?php echo $this->getItemHtml($_item) ?>
     <?php endforeach; ?>
     </ol>
    <script type="text/javascript">decorateList('cart-sidebar', 'none-
```

```
recursive')</script>      <?php endif  ?>
 </div>
</div>
<?php endif;   ?>
```

2. Declare the top cart in the `local.xml` file, in the reference header as follows:

```
<block type="checkout/cart_sidebar" name="top_cart"
template="checkout/cart/topcart.phtml" before="-">
<action method="addItemRender"><type>simple</type><block>checkout/
cart_item_renderer</block><template>checkout/cart/sidebar/default.
phtml</template></action>

<action method="addItemRender"><type>grouped</
type><block>checkout/cart_item_renderer_grouped</
block><template>checkout/cart/sidebar/default.phtml</template></
action>

<action method="addItemRender"><type>configurable</
type><block>checkout/cart_item_renderer_configurable</
block><template>checkout/cart/sidebar/default.phtml</template></
action>
<block type="core/text_list" name="cart_sidebar.extra_actions"
as="extra_actions" translate="label" module="checkout">

<label>Shopping Cart Sidebar Extra Actions</label>
</block>
</block>
```

Now, you should be able to see the top cart in your theme header.

3. Add a little bit of CSS code to customize it. Insert the following CSS code in your `styles.css` file in the `skin` folder (`skin/frontend/bookstore/default/css/`):

```
/* Header */
#header {
  padding-top:10px;
}
#header .logo {
  display:block;
  margin-bottom:20px;
}
#header .block-topcart {
  margin-top: 5px;
  padding: 14px 20px 10px;
}
#header .block-topcart .block-title {
  font-size: 15px;
```

```
     margin-bottom: 5px
   }
   #header .block-topcart p.empty {
     font-size: 12px;
     color: #666;
     font-style: italic
   }
   #header .block-topcart .block-content {
     display: none
   }
```

Now the header block is complete and will look as shown in the following code:

```
<!-- Main Header -->
<div id="header">
<div class="container">
<div class="row">
<div  class="logo col-md-4">
   <a href="<?php echo $this->getUrl('') ?>" title="<?php echo $this-
>getLogoAlt() ?>"><img src="<?php echo $this->getLogoSrc() ?>"
alt="<?php echo $this->getLogoAlt() ?>" /></a>
</div>
<div class="col-md-4"></div>
<div class="col-md-4">
<?php echo $this->getChildHtml('top_cart') ?>
</div>
</div>
</div>
</div>
```

Creating the navigation bar

For the navigation bar, we can use the `<nav>` tag to wrap it up and make it
responsive and ready with some tricks. Bootstrap helps us with the navigation
component that we can integrate with a little help from jQuery.

In the `header.phtml` file, the navigation block looks as follows:

```
<!-- Navigation -->
<nav class="navbar navbar-default navbar-main" role="navigation">
<div class="container">
<div class="row">
<div class="navbar-header">
<a class="navbar-brand visible-xs" href="#">
<?php echo $this->__('Categories') ?>
```

```
</a>
<button type="button" class="navbar-toggle" data-toggle="collapse"
data-target=".navbar-main-collapse">
<span class="sr-only"><?php echo $this->__('Toggle Navigation') ?></
span>
<span class="icon-bar"></span>
<span class="icon-bar"></span>
<span class="icon-bar"></span>
</button>
</div>
<div class="collapse navbar-collapse navbar-main-collapse">
<?php echo $this->getChildHtml('topMenu') ?>
 <?php echo $this->getChildHtml('topSearch') ?>
</div>
</div>
</div>
</nav>
```

The top menu bar

The `topmenu.phtml` file is the navigation file that you can copy from `app/design/frontend/base/default/template/page/html/`.

The final code of this file is as follows:

```
<?php $_menu = $this->getHtml('level-top') ?>
<?php if ($_menu): ?>
<ul class="nav navbar-nav">
<li><a href="<?php echo $this->getUrl('') ?>" title="<?php echo $this-
>getLogoAlt() ?>">Home</a></li>
<?php echo $_menu ?>
</ul>
<?php endif ?>
```

Unfortunately, the Bootstrap menu has some classes that we cannot add in this file. To solve this problem, we can add the Bootstrap classes with some jQuery scripts.

So open the `jquery.scripts.js` file that you created before and add the following code just after `jQuery(document).ready(function() {`:

```
jQuery('.navbar .parent').addClass('dropdown');
jQuery('.navbar a.level-top').addClass('dropdown-toggle');
jQuery('.navbar li.parent ul').addClass('dropdown-menu');
jQuery('.navbar li.level1 ul').wrap('<li class="dropdown-submenu"
/>');
jQuery('.navbar ul.nav li.level0.dropdown').hover(function() {
```

```
jQuery(this).find('.level0.dropdown-menu').stop(true, true).fadeIn();
}, function() {
jQuery(this).find('.level0.dropdown-menu').stop(true, true).fadeOut();
});
```

Now add the following CSS code to hide the submenu that will be displayed only on the mousehover event with the jQuery described before:

```css
/* Navbar */
.navbar {
  border:0 none;
  border-radius:0;
  margin:0;
  border-bottom:3px solid #E7E7E7;
}
.navbar .navbar-form {
  padding-right:10px;
}
.navbar-nav {
}
.navbar-default .navbar-nav > li:hover > a {
 background:#fff;
 box-shadow:0 6px 12px rgba(0,0,0,0.176);
}
.navbar ul.level0,.navbar ul.level1 {
  display:none;
  text-align:left;
}
.navbar .dropdown-menu {
border:0;
}
.navbar ul.level1 {
 left:150px;
 top:0;
}
.navbar-nav > li {
display:inline-block;
}
```

Search

The search file `form.mini.phtml` is the one you can copy from `app/design/frontend/base/default/template/catalogsearch/`.

As usual, we will change the code with the Bootstrap class and the final code will be as follows:

```php
<?php $catalogSearchHelper =  $this->helper('catalogsearch'); ?>
<form id="search_mini_form" class="navbar-form navbar-right"
role="search" action="<?php echo $catalogSearchHelper->getResultUrl()
?>" method="get">
<div class="form-group">
<div class="input-group">
<span class="input-group-addon"><div class="glyphicon glyphicon-search
pull-left"></div></span>
<input id="search" type="text"  name="<?php echo $catalogSearchHelper-
>getQueryParamName() ?>" value="<?php echo $catalogSearchHelper-
>getEscapedQueryText() ?>" class="form-control" maxlength="<?php echo
$catalogSearchHelper->getMaxQueryLength();?>" placeholder="<?php echo
$this->__('Search...') ?>" />
<span class="input-group-btn">
<button type="submit" class="btn btn-default">Submit</button>
</span>
</div>
</div>
<div id="search_autocomplete" class="search-autocomplete"></div>
</form>
<script type="text/javascript">
//<![CDATA[
var searchForm = new Varien.searchForm('search_mini_form', 'search',
'<?php echo $this->__('Search...') ?>');
searchForm.initAutocomplete('<?php echo $catalogSearchHelper-
>getSuggestUrl() ?>', 'search_autocomplete');
//]]>
</script>
```

The header is now completed and we can now proceed to develop the footer.

Developing the footer

The footer I designed for this theme is made up of two rows and two main columns in the first row. We will put the static contents such as the footer company's description, footer links, social links, and card image in CMS static blocks.

Hence, the user who manages the store can easily manage the footer from the admin panel. The final result will be similar to what is shown in the following screenshot:

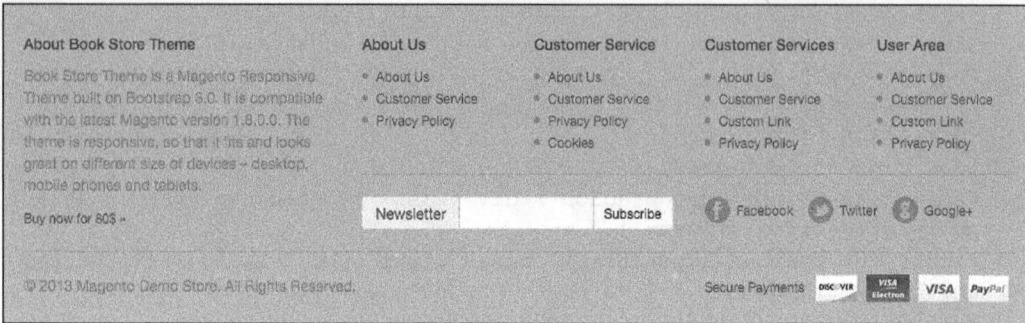

All the links and the text in the footer are made of CMS blocks, so let's see the HTML structure. The footer file `footer.phtml` is located at `app/design/frontend/bookstore/default/template/page/html/` like the header file.

The HTML code of the footer will look as follows:

```
<div class="row">
<div class="col-md-4">
<?php echo $this->getChildHtml('footer-company') ?>
</div>
<div class="col-md-8">
<div class="row">
<?php echo $this->getChildHtml('footer-cmslinks') ?>
<hr>
</div>
<div class="row">
<div class="col-md-6">
<?php echo $this->getChildHtml('footer-newsletter') ?>
</div>
<div class="col-md-6">
<?php echo $this->getChildHtml('footer-social') ?>
</div>
</div>
</div>
</div>
<div class="row">
<div class="col-md-12">
<hr>
</div>
<div class="col-md-8">
```

```php
<?php echo $this->getCopyright() ?>
</div>
<div class="col-md-4">
<?php echo $this->getChildHtml('footer-cards') ?>
</div>
</div>
```

We will have the following blocks:

- **CMS block**: footer-company
- **CMS block**: footer-cmslinks
- **CMS block**: footer-social
- **CMS block**: footer-cards
- The newsletter block
- The copyright block

Let's define the blocks in the local.xml file in the name="footer" reference as follows:

```xml
<reference name="footer">
</reference>
```

And now, we will define the CMS block in the name="footer" reference of the local.xml file as follows:

```xml
<block type="cms/block" name="footer-company" as="footer-company">
<action method="setBlockId"><block_id>footer-company</block_id></action>
</block>
<block type="cms/block" name="footer-cmslinks" as="footer-cmslinks">
<action method="setBlockId"><block_id>footer-cmslinks</block_id></action>

</block>
<block type="cms/block" name="footer-social" as="footer-social">
<action method="setBlockId"><block_id>footer-social</block_id></action>
</block>
<block type="cms/block" name="footer-cards" as="footer-cards">
<action method="setBlockId"><block_id>footer-cards</block_id></action>
</block>
```

Creating the CMS blocks from the admin panel

Now we will create the CMS blocks from the admin panel.

- The `footer-company` CMS block can be created as follows:

```
<h4>About Book Store Theme</h4>
<p>Book Store Theme is a Magento Responsive Theme built on
Bootstrap 3.0. It is compatible with the latest Magento version
1.3. This theme is responsive, so it adapt with the screen. Try to
open this page with your smartphone.</p>
<a href="http://www.themeforest.net/">Buy now for 80$ »</a>
```

- The `footer-cmslinks` CMS block can be created as follows:

```
<div class="col-md-3">
<h4>Column Name</h4>
<ul>
<li><a href="{{store_url=''}}about-magento-demo-store">About Us</
a></li>
<li><a href="{{store_url=''}}customer-service">Customer Service</
a></li>
<li class="last privacy"><a href="{{store_url=''}}privacy-policy-
cookie-restriction-mode">Privacy Policy</a></li>
</ul>
</div>
<div class="col-md-3">
<h4>Column Name</h4>
<ul>
<li><a href="{{store_url=''}}about-magento-demo-store">About Us</
a></li>
<li><a href="{{store_url=''}}customer-service">Customer Service</
a></li>
<li class="last privacy"><a href="{{store_url=''}}privacy-policy-
cookie-restriction-mode">Privacy Policy</a></li>
</ul>
</div>
<div class="col-md-3">
<h4>Column Name</h4>
<ul>
<li><a href="{{store_url=''}}about-magento-demo-store">About Us</
a></li>
<li><a href="{{store_url=''}}customer-service">Customer Service</
a></li>
<li class="last privacy"><a href="{{store_url=''}}privacy-policy-
cookie-restriction-mode">Privacy Policy</a></li>
```

```
</ul>
</div>
<div class="col-md-3">
<h4>Column Name</h4>
<ul>
<li><a href="{{store_url=''}}about-magento-demo-store">About Us</
a></li>
<li><a href="{{store_url=''}}customer-service">Customer Service</
a></li>
<li class="last privacy"><a href="{{store_url=''}}privacy-policy-
cookie-restriction-mode">Privacy Policy</a></li>
</ul>
</div>
```

- The `footer-social` CMS block can be created as follows:

```
<ul class="list-inline footer-social">

<li><a class="ico-facebook" href="#"><span></span>Facebook</a></
li>
<li><a class="ico-twitter" href="#"><span></span>Twitter</a></li>
<li><a class="ico-google" href="#"><span></span>Google+</a></li>

</ul>
```

- The `footer-cards` CMS block can be created as follows:

```
<a href="#">
<span style="font-size:12px; padding-right:10px;">Secure
Payments</span>
<img src="{{skin_url='images/cards.png'}}">
</a>
```

Adding the newsletter block

Now, as you can see in the `footer.phtml` file, we generate the `newsletter` block
with the following statement:

```
<?php echo $this->getChildHtml('footer_newsletter') ?>
```

If you load the page, the CMS newsletter will not appear, but you will see it in
the left column because, by default, the newsletter is located on the left column.

First, we have to remove it from the left column and add it in the footer of our XML file as follows:

```
<reference name="left">
  <remove name="left.newsletter"/>
</reference>
```

In the reference name `footer`, add the following:

```
<block type="newsletter/subscribe" name="footer.newsletter"
as="footer_newsletter" template="newsletter/subscribe.phtml"/>
```

The newsletter block is present in the `subscribe.phtml` file located at `app/design/frontend/base/default/template/newsletter/`.

So, copy it in the relative path of your theme, and replace it with the following code:

```
<div class="block block-subscribe">

<form action="<?php echo $this->getFormActionUrl() ?>" method="post"
id="newsletter-validate-detail">

<div class="input-group">

<span class="input-group-addon"><?php echo $this->__('Newsletter')
?></span>

<input type="text" class="form-control input-sm required-entry
validate-email" title="<?php echo $this->__('Sign up for our
newsletter') ?>" id="newsletter" name="email">

<span class="input-group-btn">
<button class="btn btn-default btn-sm" title="<?php echo $this->__
('Subscribe') ?>" type="submit"><?php echo $this->__('Subscribe') ?></
button>
</span>

</div>
</form>

<script type="text/javascript">
//<![CDATA[
var newsletterSubscriberFormDetail = new VarienForm('newsletter-
validate-detail');
//]]>
</script>

</div>
```

Here, we changed the default structure of the Magento file with the `input` group class of Bootstrap.

Now that we have all the blocks, let's customize the design of the custom footer with a little bit of CSS as follows:

```
#footer {
 background-color:#FA9221;
 color:rgba(0,0,0,0.3);
 padding:20px 0;
 border-bottom:5px solid #333;
 font-size:12px,;
}
#footer h4 {
 color:rgba(0,0,0,0.6);
 font-size:14px;
}
#footer ul {
 list-style-position:inside;
 padding:0;
 margin:0;
}
#footer a {
 color:rgba(0,0,0,0.5);
 font-size:12px;
}
#footer a:hover {
   color:rgba(0,0,0,0.8);
}
#footer hr {
   border-color:rgba(0,0,0,0.2);
   border-style:dotted;
}
/* Social Icons */
#footer .footer-social a {
   display:inline-block;
   font-size:12px;
   line-height:24px;
}
#footer .footer-social a span {
   background:url(../images/sprite-social.png) no-repeat scroll 0 0
rgba(0,0,0,0);
   display:inline-block;
   float:left;
   height:24px;
   margin-right:6px;
   padding-left:20px;
```

```
    width:24px;
}
#footer .footer-social a.ico-facebook span {
   background-position:0 0;
}
#footer .footer-social a.ico-twitter span {
   background-position:-40px 0;
}
#footer .footer-social a.ico-google span {
   background-position:-80px 0;
}
#footer .footer-social a.ico-facebook:hover span {
   background-position:0 -28px;
}
#footer .footer-social a.ico-twitter:hover span {
   background-position:-40px -28px;
}
#footer .footer-social a.ico-google:hover span {
background-position:-80px -28px;
}
```

> I used a sprite for the social icons. The `social-icons.png` image is a sprite with a width of `104px` and height of `52px`. Each icon is `24px x 24px`.

Summary

OK, now the header and the footer are complete! In the next chapter, we will develop our custom home page with the Bootstrap carousel, products in the home page, and some custom banners.

We've seen how to integrate Bootstrap and start the development of a Magento theme with the most famous framework in the world.

Bootstrap is very neat, flexible, and modular, and you can use it as you prefer to create your custom theme.

However, please keep in mind that it can be a big drawback on the loading time of the page. Following these techniques by adding the JavaScript and CSS classes via XML, you can allow Magento to minify them to speed up the loading time of the site.

In the next chapter, we will learn how to develop the home page with advanced techniques and how to create other custom pages following the basic principles of Magento's fall-back system.

3
Customizing Our
Custom Theme

In the previous chapter, we developed the main theme structure and the main sections that are displayed for the whole theme. In this chapter, we are going to learn how to develop our custom home page by adding the Bootstrap carousel as the main slider, a custom vertical navigation menu on the left sidebar, and a products grid.

Then, we are going to analyze how to customize the other main pages of the theme.

The following is a list of topics that will be covered in this chapter:

- Developing the home page
- Customizing the left sidebar
- Customizing the main content
- Customizing the other pages of the theme
- File paths and handles for the other sections of the theme
- Creating the content row

Developing the home page

Let's start developing our custom home page. The following screenshot shows the final result that we are going to reach:

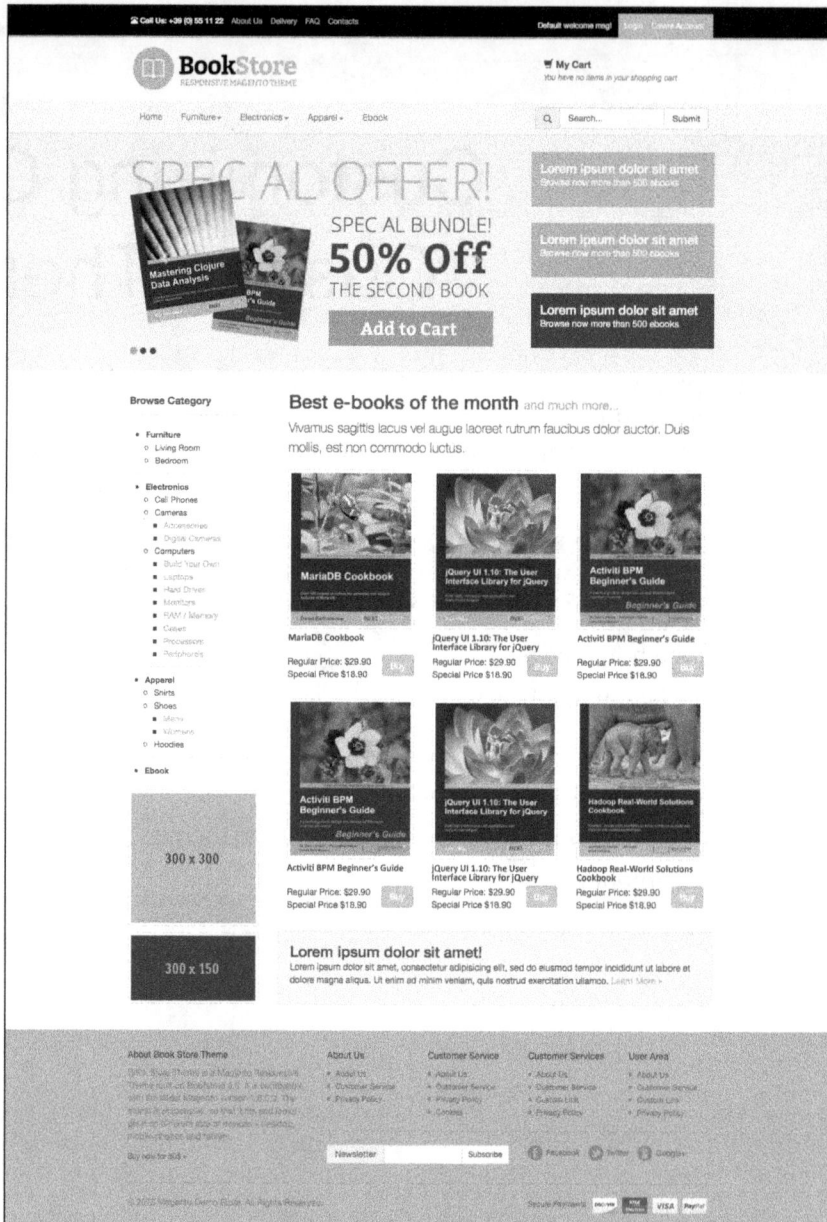

This is an example of what the screen in this program looks like.

Configuring the structure of the home page

The home page structure contains two main blocks that we will call slider block and main content block. As you can see from the design, the slider bar is a full screen bar with a carousel and three text banners on the right.

Under the main slider bar, we have the left sidebar with a vertical navigation, and on the right a simple products list.

We are going to create a home page from the admin panel using the CMS home page, some CMS blocks, and some layout XML updates by using the following steps:

- Creating the slider row
- Creating the CMS block for the carousel
- Creating the CMS block for the text banners
- Creating the CMS home page
- Customizing the look and feel of the home page with CSS

Creating the slider row

First of all, we create all the CMS blocks. Then we display them in the CMS home page. So let's start with the full-width row that we call slider.

This block will contain the carousel and the banners. We wrap these blocks into the CMS static block that we create in the backend from **CMS | Static Blocks**, with the following information:

- **Block name**: Home Block Fullwidth
- **Block identifier**: home-fullwidth

The following is the HTML code to create a responsive row:

```
<div class="row">
  <div class="col-md-8">
    {{block type="cms/block" block_id="home-carousel"
      template="cms/content.phtml"}}
  </div>

  <div class="col-md-4">
    {{block type="cms/block" block_id="home-right-banner"
      template="cms/content.phtml"}}
  </div>
</div>
```

In this way, we have created a responsive row with two main blocks:

- The block with the CSS class `col-md-8` contains the carousel
- The block with the CSS class `col-md-4` contains the three text banners on the right

The `{{block type="cms/block" ... }}` code snippet inserts CMS blocks that can also be created in the admin panel

You can use the same snippet to include a CMS block in a CMS page.

Creating the CMS block for the carousel

Bootstrap includes some nice built-in features that speed up the development process without losing precious time in the research of external components.

The JavaScript carousel, shown in the following screenshot, is very simple to use, and you can find more details in the Bootstrap documentation, under the **Carousel** tab of the **JavaScript** section:

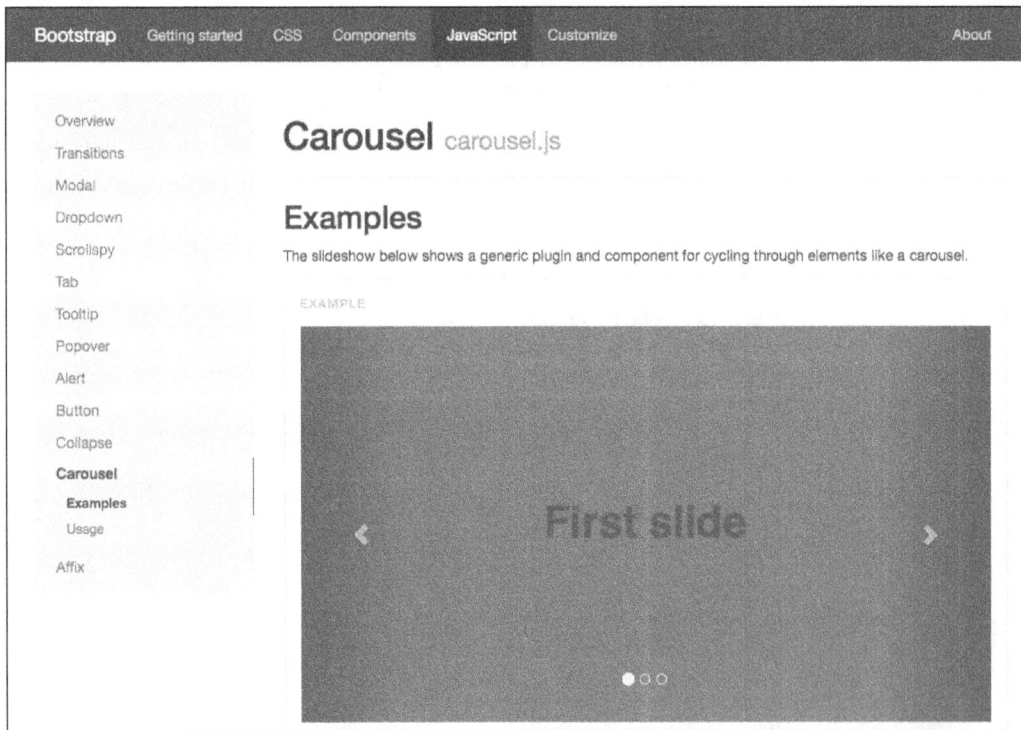

There are two ways to use the carousel: via data attributes and via JavaScript. In this case, we are going to use the data attributes to easily control the carousel and its options without calling a JavaScript.

You can get additional information in the official Bootstrap documentation at http://getbootstrap.com/javascript/#carousel.

Let's start by creating the CMS block from the admin panel with the following information:

- **Block name**: Home Carousel
- **Block identifier**: home-carousel

> The id attribute is the ID present in the code snippet of the previous topic, defined from the following snippet:
>
> ```
> {{block type="cms/block" block_id="home-carousel"
>    template="cms/content.phtml"}}
> ```

The following is the HTML code to create the CMS block:

```
<div data-ride="carousel" class="carousel slide" id="slider-home">

        <ol class="carousel-indicators">
          <li data-slide-to="0" data-target="#slider-home"></li>
          <li data-slide-to="1" data-target="#slider-home"
class="active"></li>
          <li data-slide-to="2" data-target="#slider-home" class=""></
li>
        </ol>

        <div class="carousel-inner">
          <div class="item">
            <img src="{{skin_url='images/slide1.png'}}" alt="Slide 1
Alt Text">
          </div>
          <div class="item active">
          <img src="{{skin_url='images/slide1.png'}}" alt="Slide 2 Alt
Text">
          </div>
          <div class="item">
          <img src="{{skin_url='images/slide1.png'}}" alt="Slide 3 Alt
Text">
          </div>
```

```
          </div>

       <a data-slide="prev" href="#slider-home" class="left carousel-
control">
            <span class="glyphicon glyphicon-chevron-left"></span>
          </a>
          <a data-slide="next" href="#slider-home" class="right
carousel-control">
             <span class="glyphicon glyphicon-chevron-right"></span>
          </a>

     </div>
```

> The `{{skin_url='images/slide1.png'}}` tag looks for the
> image in the theme `skin` folder. You can find the demo image in the
> code bundle given along with the book, or you can change the path
> with an absolute path.

*You can find the following content in the Bootstrap documentation: Use data
attributes to easily control the position of the carousel.* `data-slide` *accepts the
keywords* `prev` *or* `next`, *which alters the slide position relative to its current
position. Alternatively, use* `data-slide-to` *to pass a raw slide index to the
carousel* `data-slide-to="2"`, *which shifts the slide position to a particular
index beginning with 0. The* `data-ride="carousel"` *attribute is used to mark
a carousel as animating starting at page load.*

Creating the CMS block for the banners

Now, we are going to create the CMS block for the banners that will be placed next
to the carousel, with the following information:

- **Block name**: Home Banner
- **Block identifier**: home-right-banner

The `home-right-banner` identifier is the ID present in the code snippet of the previous topic, defined from the following snippet:

```
{{block type="cms/block" block_id="home-right-banner"
    template="cms/content.phtml"}}
```

The following is the HTML code:

```
<div id="banner-home">
  <div class="bg-orange">
    <h3>Lorem ipsum dolor sit amet</h3>
    <p>Browse now more than 500 ebooks</p>
  </div>
  <div class="bg-cyan">
    <h3>Lorem ipsum dolor sit amet</h3>
    <p>Browse now more than 500 ebooks</p>
  </div>

  <div class="bg-darkgrey">
    <h3>Lorem ipsum dolor sit amet</h3>
    <p>Browse now more than 500 ebooks</p>
  </div>

</div>
```

In this section, we have created some text banners. Feel free to replace the content with images or other cool stuff according to your needs.

Creating the CMS home page from the admin panel

Now that we have created the full width bar, we need to display it in the home page. First, we need to have a home CMS page. If you are using a Magento installation with sample data, you already have a default home page that you can edit; if you don't, create the CMS page by navigating to **CMS | Pages** as shown in the following screenshot:

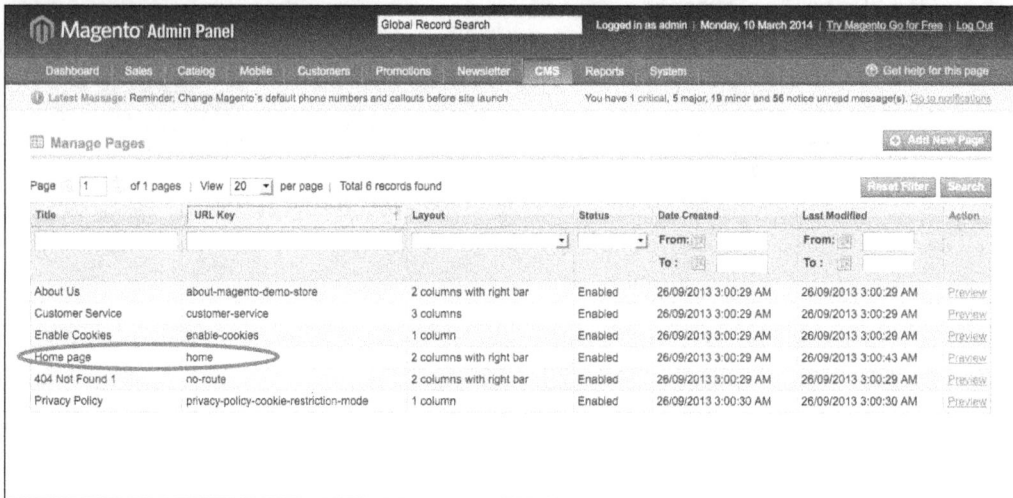

Now, insert a dummy text in the content box. We focus our attention on the slider block, and later we will look at what to insert in the main content.

In the **Design** tab, select the **2 columns with left bar** option for **Layout** as shown in the following screenshot:

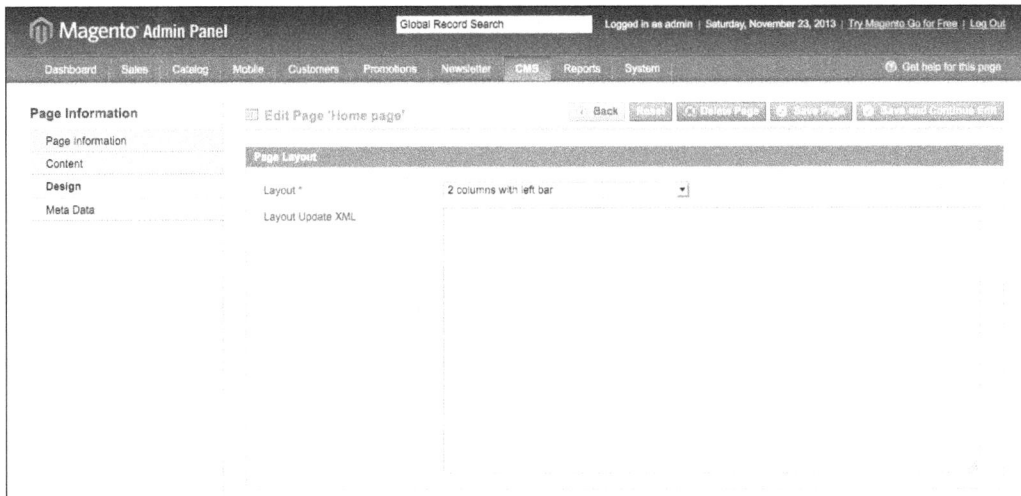

If we try to insert the CMS block `home-fullwidth` in the main content, we will not obtain the expected full-width block because the content inserted in the code block of the CMS pages will be shown in the right-hand part of the layout, in the main content area.

To solve this, we need to create a new section that needs to be displayed before the main page content. To manage this section dynamically, we have to create a new reference.

A reference block is a block that can contain other blocks. To allow this, the block type must be `core/text_list`.

So let's create the new reference block, called slider, with the following steps:

1. Open the file `local.xml` located at `app/design/frontend/bookstore/default/layout/local.xml`.

2. Inside the `<reference name="root">` object, insert the following code that creates the new reference block:

```
<!-- define the reference block slider -->
  <block type="core/text_list" name="slider" as="slider"
  translate="label">
<label>Slider Block</label>
</block>
```

3. Then, we need to specify where to place this new reference block with the following code:

```
<?php echo $this->getChildHtml('slider') ?>
```

Since this block is structural and we can use it in other pages, and not just on the home page, we have to insert it into the template files that control the structure of the pages.

We have already created these files in the previous chapter. Just to remind you, they are located at app/design/frontend/bookstore/default/template/page, such as 2columns-left.phtml.

So, let's place that where you want to make it appear. We have already inserted the code just, before the page container, with the following code:

```
<section id="after-header">
   <div class="container">
       <?php echo $this->getChildHtml('slider') ?> </div>
</section>
```

4. Finally, we only need to update the layout XML of the CMS page with the following code:

```
<reference name="slider">
  <block type="cms/block" name="home-fullwidth" as=
    "home-fullwidth">
    <action method="setBlockId">
      <block_id>home-fullwidth</block_id>
    </action>
  </block>
</reference>
```

> The <block type="cms/block" ... >...</block> piece of code will return the same code of the snippet {{block type="cms/block" }} that we can use in the CMS pages / CMS block content.

5. Save the page; if everything goes well, you will see the full width slider block, including the carousel and the banners.

Customizing the look and feel of the home page with CSS

Now, customize the code a little bit with some CSS added in the `styles.css` file we created in `skin/frontend/bookstore/default/css/styles.css`, as follows:

```css
/* Carousel */

#after-header {
  background-color: #efefef;
}

#slider-home {
  text-align:center;
  padding:40px 0;
}

#slider-home .carousel-control.right,#slider-home .carousel-control.
left {
  background:none;
}

#slider-home .carousel-indicators {
  bottom:20px;
  left:0;
  margin:0;
  text-align:left;
}

/* Carousel Bullets */

.carousel-indicators li {
  border:0;
  background-color:#333;
}

.carousel-indicators li:hover {
  background:#41b7d8;
}

#slider-home .carousel-indicators .active {
  background:#f37541;
  border-color:#f37541;
}


/* 3 Banners */
#banner-home {
}
```

```
#banner-home div {
  color:#FFF;
  height:85px;
  margin:25px 0;
  padding:15px;
  background: #ddd;
}
#banner-home h3 {
  font-size:20px;
  margin:0;
  padding:0;
}

/* Text Banners Background Colors */

#banner-home div.bg-orange {
  background:#f89223;
}

#banner-home div.bg-cyan {
  background:#41b7d8;
}

#banner-home div.bg-darkgrey {
  background:#333;
}
```

And now, if you reload the page, you should see the full width block with banners and carousel, as shown in the following screenshot:

Creating the content row

Now we are going to see how to develop the main content section. The layout we configured for the home page show two columns:

- On the left, a sidebar with a secondary category navigation and sample banners
- On the right, the main content area, which displays the content of our home page text area box

Customizing the left sidebar

By default, Magento includes some blocks on the left sidebar that could be useless; for example, the tags block. Therefore, we are going to replace them. However, before replacing, let's see how to remove the default blocks if we don't need them.

Removing the default blocks from the sidebar

To remove a default block from the left sidebar or from another `core/text_list` block, we can use the `remove` tag in our `local.xml` file. We already used the `remove` tag in the previous chapter when we removed the newsletter block from the sidebar to place it in the footer. The following is a reminder of that line of code:

```
<remove name="left.newsletter"/>
```

Let's suppose that you want to remove the left tags block and the default callouts block; you can do this with the following lines:

```
<remove name="left.permanent.callout"/>
<remove name="tags_popular"/>
```

To find the `name` attribute of each block that you want to remove, explore every single XML file of the base theme. In this case, I found the name `tags_popular` in the `tags.xml` file, and `left.permanent.callout` in the `catalog.xml` file.

As you can see in the `layout` folder of the base/default theme, there are many XML files and each of them is named with a particular name that refers to a particular section.

> Remember to put the `remove` action inside the reference block `left`.

Creating a vertical navigation menu on the sidebar

Now that we removed some blocks from the left sidebar, we create a new vertical navigation that generates some useful links to navigate the Magento store.

What we are going to do is quite easy to implement in three simple steps:

1. Add a new block type in the `local.xml` file.

2. Create a new PHTML file and name it `leftnav.phtml` and place it inside `catalog/navigation`.

3. Add a new block type in the `local.xml` file.

   Let's suppose you want to have the vertical category menu that shows up on every page of the theme. If you want to do this, place the code in the `<default>` handle, inside the `<reference name="left">` block; we want it to always stay on the top, so we add `before="-"` as shown in the following code snippet:

   ```
   <block type="catalog/navigation" before="-" name=
     "leftNav as="leftNav" template=
     "catalog/navigation/leftnav.phtml"/>
   ```

4. Create the `leftnav.phtml` file in `pp/design/frontend/bookstore/default/template/catalog/navigation` with the following code:

   ```
   <div class="block block-leftnav">

     <div class="block-title">

       <strong><?php echo $this->__('Browse Category')
         ?></strong>

     </div>

     <div class="block-content">

       <ul>

       <?php foreach ($this->getStoreCategories() as
         $_category): ?>

         <?php if($_category->name!=""):  ?>

           <?php echo $this->drawItem($_category) ?>

         <?php endif?>

       <?php endforeach ?>
   ```

```
    </ul>

  </div>

</div>
```

This code will return the full category tree with all the classes needed for the customization.

5. Customize the CSS.

   Now, if you take a look at the generated code, you can see that each element has a class, so it's easy to customize it with a little bit of CSS in the following manner:

```
/* Left Menu */
.block-leftnav { margin-top: 35px; }
.block-leftnav .block-title { font-size:16px; border-
  bottom: 1px solid #E1E1E1; padding-bottom:10px;    }
.block-leftnav .block-content { }
.block-leftnav .block-content ul { padding: 0; list-style-
  position: inside;}
.block-leftnav .block-content ul li {      }

.block-leftnav .block-content ul li.active { background:
  #333; color: #fff; padding-left: 10px; }
.block-leftnav .block-content ul li.active a {color:
  #FA9221;   }

.block-leftnav .block-content ul li a { font-size: 13px;
  color: #333    }
.block-leftnav .block-content ul li a:hover { color:
  #FA9221;    }

.block-leftnav .block-content > ul > li.level0 { border-
  bottom: 1px solid #E1E1E1; padding: 10px;}
.block-leftnav .block-content > ul > li.level0:last-child {
  border-bottom: 0; }

.block-leftnav .block-content > ul > li.level0:hover {
  background-color: #efefef}

.block-leftnav .block-content > ul > li.level0 > a { font-
  weight: bold; }

.block-leftnav .block-content ul ul { padding-left: 15px; }
.block-leftnav .block-content ul ul ul a { color: #999 }
```

And the final results will look like the following screenshot:

Browse Category

- **Furniture**
  - Living Room
  - Bedroom

- **Electronics**
  - Cell Phones
  - Cameras
    - Accessories
    - Digital Cameras
  - Computers
    - Build Your Own
    - Laptops
    - Hard Drives
    - Monitors
    - RAM / Memory
    - Cases
    - Processors
    - Peripherals

Customizing the main content

As you can see from the next screenshot, in the main content, we want to display the following points:

- Some text information right at the top
- A block with some products of a specific category
- A block with text information after each product

Best e-books of the month and much more...

Vivamus sagittis lacus vel augue laoreet rutrum faucibus dolor auctor. Duis mollis, est non commodo luctus.

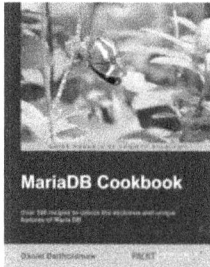

Maria DB Cook Book

Regular Price: $29.90
Special Price $18.90

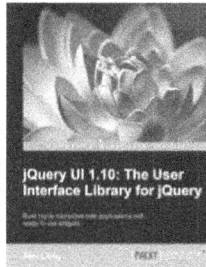

jQuery UI 1.10

Regular Price: $29.90
Special Price $18.90

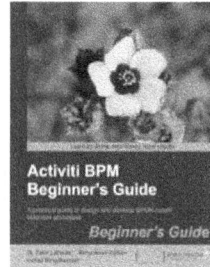

Activity BPM Beginner Guide

Regular Price: $29.90
Special Price $18.90

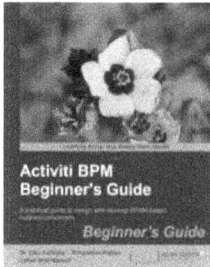

Hadoop Real-World Solutions Cookbook

Regular Price: $29.90
Special Price $18.90

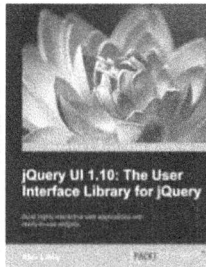

Magento Theme Design

Regular Price: $29.90
Special Price $18.90

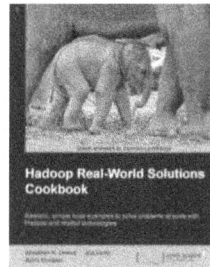

Elephant Js

Regular Price: $29.90
Special Price $18.90

Lorem ipsum dolor sit amet!

Lorem ipsum dolor sit amet, consectetur adipisicing elit, sed do eiusmod tempor incididunt ut labore et dolore magna aliqua. Ut enim ad minim veniam, quis nostrud exercitation ullamco. Learn More »

First, we are going to develop the main block, which contains the products grid. Afterwards, we are going to insert the remaining text blocks.

Adding a block with some products of a specific category

To display some products of a specific category in a CMS page, we need to perform the following steps:

1. Create the custom products list file called `list-home.phtml` in `app/design/frontend/bookstore/default/template/catalog/product` containing the following code snippet:

```php
<?php
$_productCollection=$this->getLoadedProductCollection();
$_helper = $this->helper('catalog/output');
?>
<?php if(!$_productCollection->count()): ?>

<p class="note-msg"><?php echo $this->__('There are no
  products matching the selection.') ?></p>
<?php else: ?>
<div class="category-products">
  <?php $_collectionSize = $_productCollection->count() ?>
  <?php $_columnCount = $this->getColumnCount();

?>
  <?php $i=0; foreach ($_productCollection as $_product):
    ?>
  <?php if ($i++%$_columnCount==0): ?>
  <ul class="products-grid row">
    <?php endif ?>
    <li class="item<?php if(($i-1)%$_columnCount==0): ?>
      first<?php elseif($i%$_columnCount==0): ?> last<?php
      endif; ?> col-md-4"> <a href="<?php echo $_product-
      >getProductUrl() ?>" title="<?php echo $this-
      >stripTags($this->getImageLabel($_product,
      'small_image'), null, true) ?>" class="product-
      image"><img src="<?php echo $this-
      >helper('catalog/image')->init($_product,
      'small_image')->resize(250,310); ?>" alt="<?php echo
      $this->stripTags($this->getImageLabel($_product,
      'small_image'), null, true) ?>" class="img-
      responsive img-thumbnail" /></a>
    <h3 class="panel-title product-name"><a href="<?php
      echo $_product->getProductUrl() ?>" title="<?php
      echo $this->stripTags($_product->getName(), null,
      true) ?>"><?php echo $_helper-
      >productAttribute($_product,
      $_product->getName(), 'name') ?></a></h3>
```

```
            <div class="pull-left"> <?php echo $this-
              >getPriceHtml($_product, true) ?> </div>
            <div class="pull-right">
              <?php if($_product->isSaleable()): ?>
              <button type="button" title="<?php echo $this-
                >__('Add to Cart') ?>" class="btn btn-warning
                btn-cart" onclick="setLocation('<?php echo $this-
                >getAddToCartUrl($_product) ?>')"><?php echo
                $this->__('Add to Cart') ?></button>
              <?php else: ?>
              <p class="btn btn-alert availability out-of-
                stock"><span><?php echo $this->__('Out of stock')
                ?></span></p>
              <?php endif; ?>
            </div>
          </li>
          <?php if ($i==6) break; ?>
          <?php if ($i%$_columnCount==0 || $i==$_collectionSize):
            ?>
        </ul>
        <?php endif ?>
        <?php endforeach ?>
    </div>
    <?php endif; ?>
```

This code is a simplified version of the default file `list.phtml` used for the products list and grid. I have created this custom file to show you how to use Bootstrap classes to set up the products section correctly. Later, we can use this structure for the category page too.

As you can see from the preceding code, we used the CSS class `col-md-4` for the product item so as to be sure it will be correctly displayed with a `float:left` property in all desktop views and be responsive for small devices.

2. Find the category ID. In order to display the products of a specific category, we need to know the category ID; to find the identifier, open the **Manage Categories** section in the admin account and click on the category that you want to show as featured for your home page. The following screenshot shows exactly where you can grab the category ID:

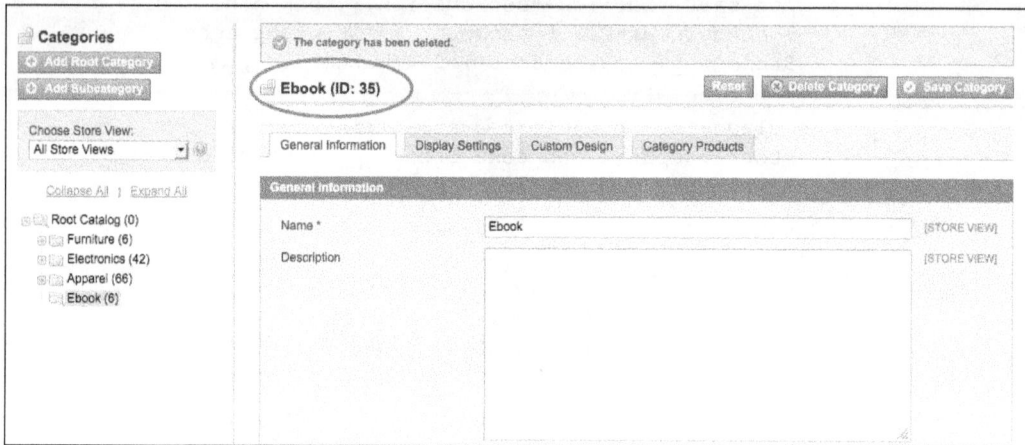

As you can see from the preceding screenshot, next to the category name on the area to the right, there is the category ID that we are looking for. In this case, **Ebook ID: 35**.

3. Insert the products list block into the CMS home content. Now that you have the template file and the category ID, insert the code into the CMS home page within the following code:

```
{{block type="catalog/product_list" category_id="35"
  template="catalog/product/list-home.phtml"}}
```

To insert the text above and after the block as shown in the design layout, add the following code to complete the home page:

```
<div class="col-md-12">
<h2>Best e-books of the month <small>and much
  more...</small>
</h2>

<p class="lead">Vivamus sagittis lacus vel augue laoreet
  rutrum faucibus dolor auctor. Duis mollis, est non
  commodo luctus.</p></div>

{{block type="catalog/product_list" category_id="35"
  template="catalog/product/list-home.phtml"
```

```
column_count="3" products_count="3"}}

<div class="well">
<h3>Lorem ipsum dolor sit amet!</h3>
<p>Lorem ipsum dolor sit amet, consectetur adipisicing
   elit, sed do eiusmod tempor incididunt ut labore et
   dolore magna aliqua. Ut enim ad minim veniam, quis
   nostrud exercitation ullamco. <a href="#">Learn More
   &raquo;</a>
</p>

</div>
```

> Remember to change `category_id="35"` with your category ID.

4. Customize the CSS.

    Now, add some CSS code to customize the page style. You don't need a lot of customization because Bootstrap creates nearly everything for you.

    All you need for the moment is the following CSS code that will be useful to customize the products grid page too:

```css
/* Product List */
.products-grid {
  list-style-type:none;
  margin:0;
  padding:0;
}
.products-grid li.item {
  margin-bottom: 30px;
}
.products-grid .product-name {
  font-size:14px;
  min-height:30px;
  margin:0;
}

.products-grid .panel-footer {
  overflow:hidden;
}

.product-name a {
  color:#333;
}
```

```
.price-box p {
  margin:0;
}

.products-grid .product-image {
  margin-bottom:10px;
  display:block;
}
```

Done! The home page is complete.

Customizing the other pages of the theme

In this topic, we are going to explore quickly how to customize some of the main sections of the theme. Then you will be able to apply this information to personalize any blocks of your awesome theme!

The products grid

To customize the default products grid, duplicate the `list.phtml` file in to your theme. The path of the file is `/app/design/frontend/base/default/template/catalog/product`.

You can use the same structure we used for `list-home.phtml` to make it look like the grid in the home page.

The products category page is managed by two different handles:

- **Layout handle for the default category**: `<catalog_category_default>`
- **Layout handle for the layered category**: `<catalog_category_layered>`

In order to use the `<catalog_category_layered>` handle, the category must have the setting **Is Anchor** set on **Yes**. This option is available on the admin area, under the **Display Settings** tab of the **Manage Categories** section of the category, as shown in the following screenshot:

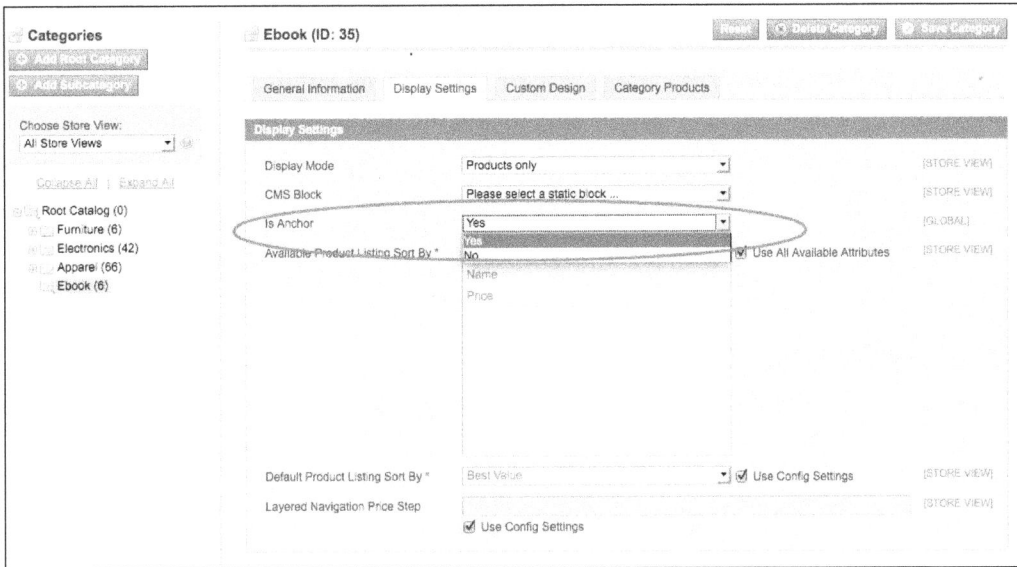

Let's suppose that we want to set the main template for the default category view to one column; in this case, we have to insert the action `setTemplate` into the `catalog_category_default` handle in the following manner:

```
<catalog_category_default>
  <reference name="root">
  <action method="setTemplate">
    <template>page/1column.phtml</template>
  </action>
  </reference>
</catalog_category_default>
```

If we want to set a different template, for example, two columns with the right-hand side sidebar for the layered categories, we will have to set the action in the other handle as follows:

```
<catalog_category_layered>
  <reference name="root">
  <action method="setTemplate">
    <template>page/2columns-right.phtml</template>
  </action>
  </reference>
</catalog_category_layered>
```

In this specific case, we need to move the layered navigation to the right column, because by default it is shown on the left sidebar, and in the 2columns-right layout, we don't have the left sidebar. To do this, add the following code inside the catalog_category_layered handle, inside the reference name right:

```
<reference name="right">
  <block type="catalog/layer_view" name="catalog.leftnav" after=
    "currency" template="catalog/layer/view.phtml" before="-"/>
</reference>
```

The product page

The file that manages the product view page is view.phtml. It's located at /app/design/frontend/base/default/template/catalog/product, and its layout handle is <catalog_product_view>.

The product page default setting is 2 columns with the sidebar to the right. For this theme, you can leave this structure or set the template to 1 column without sidebars.

If you decide to set to 1 column, change the root template to the 1column template as given in the following code:

```
<catalog_product_view>
  <reference name="root">
    <action method="setTemplate">
      <template>page/1column.phtml</template></action>
  </reference>
</catalog_product_view>
```

File paths and handles for the other sections of the theme

In order to customize other theme sections, you will always need to follow the same steps, which includes finding the file path in the base theme and finding the layout handle to set a layout update.

The following table will help you find some useful paths and handles for the main sections that you would like to personalize:

Sections	File path	Layout handle
The cart page	`app/design/frontend/ base/default/template/ checkout/cart.phtml`	`<checkout_cart_index>`
The login area	`app/design/frontend/ base/default/template/ customer/form/login. phtml`	`<customer_account_login>`
The user account registration page	`app/design/frontend/ base/default/template/ customer/form/register. phtml`	`<customer_account_create>`

Summary

In this chapter, we looked at how to develop our custom home page through CMS blocks and layout updates from the admin panel and finally the main layout handle for the other section of the theme.

In the next chapter, we are going to see how to add CSS and JS animations to our theme to improve the usability and to give a great visual impact to the theme.

4
Adding Incredible Effects to Our Theme

In this chapter, we are going to add some lovely animations to the theme to give the end users of the site a better user experience. We will learn how to create a dropdown cart in the header and how to insert jQuery animations and CSS3 transitions.

The following topics will be covered in this chapter:

- Introducing CSS3 transitions
- Creating an animated cart in the header
- Creating a stunning CSS3 3D flip animation
- Creating a custom product images gallery
- Adding custom fonts to our theme
- Adding a custom icon font to our theme

Introducing CSS3 transitions

With CSS3, we can add an effect that allows you to change theme from one style to another without using Flash animations or JavaScripts. As you know, Flash is not supported on Apple devices, so it is recommended that you don't use it for new projects.

You can use jQuery animations that guarantee full browser support to create simple and nice effects, but with CSS3 you can create the same stuff with less code.

You can use CSS3 transitions with all the modern browsers; Internet Explorer 10, Firefox, Chrome, and Opera support the transition property. You can see a full compatibility table at `https://developer.mozilla.org/en-US/docs/Web/Guide/CSS/Using_CSS_transitions#Browser_compatibility`.

Internet Explorer 9 (IE9) and earlier versions do not support the transition property. A best practice to add optional CSS classes, depending on the browser in use, consists of including the JS Modernizr. Modernizr detects the browser being used and appends several classes to the body of the code based on that. In this way, you can target some browsers and add conditional styles for them. For example, if you want to add a different style to a button while hovering for IE9 that doesn't support transition, you can do with Modernizr. You can find out more about this JS at http://modernizr.com/.

To include CSS3 transitions effects, you must specify parameters for the following:

- The CSS property to which you want to add the transition
- The duration of the effect

In the following example, the transition effect is applied to the `opacity` property and the duration is set to 2 seconds:

```
div {
  opacity:0.5;
  transition: opacity 2s;
  -webkit-transition: opacity 2s;
  -moz-transition: opacity 2s;
}
```

The transition effect will show when the specified CSS property changes value. A typical CSS property can be changed by the user hovering the cursor over an element:

In the following example, `div` changes the opacity from `0.5` to `1` when the mouse is hovered over some element.

```
div:hover {
  opacity:1;
}
```

> When we hover the cursor off the element, it gradually changes back to its original style.

Multiple property changes

To add a transitional effect for more than one style, add more properties separated by commas. This can be done as follows:

```
transition: width 2s, height 2s, transform 2s;
```

The CSS3 transition properties

The transition has the following four properties:

- `transition-property`
- `transition-duration`
- `transition-timing-function`
- `transition-delay`

You can specify all the properties, one on each line, as follows:

```
div {
  transition-property: opacity;
  transition-duration: 1s;
  transition-timing-function: linear;
  transition-delay: 2s;

  /* Safari */
  -webkit-transition-property: opacity;
  -webkit-transition-duration:1s;
  -webkit-transition-timing-function:linear;
  -webkit-transition-delay:2s;

/* Mozilla */
  -moz-transition-property: opacity;
  -moz-transition-duration:1s;
  -moz-transition-timing-function:linear;
  -moz-transition-delay:2s;
}
```

> As you can see, we duplicated the properties by adding the vendor-specific tags, for example, `-moz-`, to target Mozilla Firefox browser. You can use these tags to implement new transition features on the browsers that have not standardized them.

Alternatively, you can specify all the properties in a single-line declaration using the shorthand `transition` property in the following way:

```
div {
    transition: opacity 1s linear 2s;
}
```

Now that we understand how the CSS3 transitions work, let's create our custom transition for the dropdown cart in the header.

Creating an animated cart in the header

Let's start from the idea that we want to show the cart content only on hovering the top cart div, combining a fade-in effect with a slide-up transition.

In the *Chapter 2, Creating a Responsive Magento Theme with Bootstrap 3*, we created a new cart block whose file `topcart.phtml` is located in `app/design/frontend/bookstore/default/template/checkout/cart/`.

The file shows a recap of what we placed in the cart in our header. As you can see in the following screenshot, the default status displays **no items** and when a user adds a product to the cart, it will display the items count along with the total price:

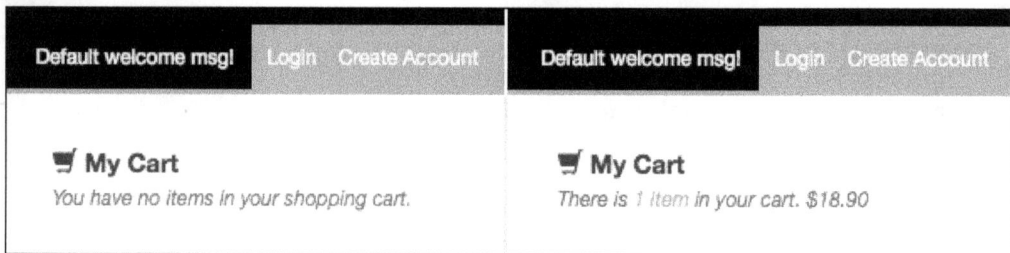

The following code shows the basic file structure of `topcart.phtml`:

```
<div class="block block-cart">
  <div class="block-title"></div>
  <div class="block-content"></div>
</div>
```

The `block-title` attribute is displayed by default and the `block-content` attribute is hidden.

The `block-content` attribute already contains the details of the products added to the cart and now we are going to learn how to display it by hovering over the block.

In the following screenshot, we can see the final result that we want:

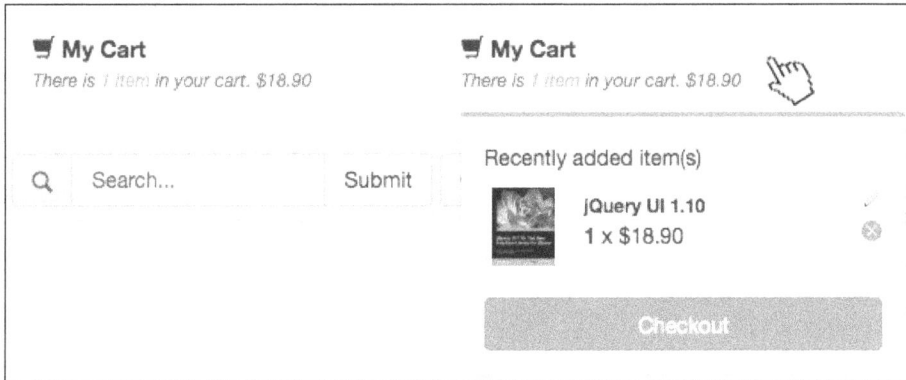

Customizing the topcart.phtml file

First, let's customize the structure of the cart block content a little in the following manner:

```
<div class="block-content">

  <?php $_items = $this->getRecentItems() ?>
  <?php if(count($_items)): ?>
    <p class="block-subtitle"><?php echo $this->__('Recently added
      item(s)') ?></p>
    <ol id="cart-sidebar" class="mini-products-list">
    <?php foreach($_items as $_item): ?>
      <?php echo $this->getItemHtml($_item) ?>
    <?php endforeach; ?>
    </ol>
    <script type="text/javascript">decorateList('cart-sidebar',
      'none-recursive')</script>
    <?php endif ?>

    <?php if($_cartQty && $this->isPossibleOnepageCheckout()): ?>
  <div class="actions">
    <?php echo $this->getChildHtml('extra_actions') ?>
    <button type="button" title="<?php echo $this->__('Checkout')
      ?>" class="btn btn-block btn-success" onclick=
      "setLocation('<?php echo $this->getCheckoutUrl() ?>')"><?php
      echo $this->__('Checkout') ?></button>
  </div>
  <?php endif ?>
</div>
```

Customizing the CSS of the cart

Now, let's customize the CSS with the CSS transition, and that will do the cart content animation, First, we have to customize the CSS of the block content in the following manner:

```
#header .block-topcart .block-content {
    background:none repeat scroll 0 0 #FFF;
    border-top:3px solid #FA9221;
    box-shadow:0 0 3px rgba(0,0,0,0.28);
    padding:15px;
    position:absolute;
    width:100%;
    z-index:0;
    transition:all .5s;
    -moz-transition:all .5s;
    -webkit-transition:all .5s;
    opacity:0;
    top:105px;
    visibility:hidden;
}
```

As you can see in the preceding code, we added the following transitions property to animate all the styles:

```
transition:all .5s;
-moz-transition:all .5s;
-webkit-transition:all .5s;
```

> I used all as the transition property value. Using this as the value, all the properties that change on hovering will have the transition effect.

Now, in the hover status, change the CSS property. In this case, we want to change the top, opacity, z-index, and visibility properties:

```
#header .block-topcart:hover .block-content {
    opacity:1;
    top:65px;
    z-index:999;
    visibility:visible;
}
```

Styling the cart's content with CSS

Now the CSS is complete, and you should see the animation when you hover the cursor over the block cart. Now, let's customize the block cart content a little with the following CSS code:

```css
#header .block-topcart .block-subtitle {
}
#header .block-topcart ol {
  list-style-type:none;
  padding:0;
  overflow:hidden;
}
#header .block-topcart ol li {
  width:100%;
  float:left;
  clear:both;
  position:relative;
  margin-bottom:10px;
}
#header .block-topcart ol li a.product-image {
  display:block;
  float:left;
  width:25%;
}
#header .block-topcart ol li .product-details {
  float:left;
  width:65%;
}
#header .block-topcart .product-details .product-name {
  margin:0;
}
#header .block-topcart .product-details .product-name a {
  font-weight:700;
  font-size:12px;
}
#header .block-topcart a.btn-edit,#header .block-topcart a.btn-remove
{
  position:absolute;
  right:0;
  top:0;
  display:block;
  text-indent:-99999px;
  height:15px;
  width:15px;
```

```
}
#header .block-topcart a.btn-edit {
  background:url(../images/btn_edit.gif) no-repeat center center;
}
#header .block-topcart a.btn-remove {
  background:url(../images/btn_gm-close.gif) no-repeat center center;
  top:20px;
}
#header .block-topcart ol li .product-details {
}

#header .block-topcart .actions {
  clear:both;
}
```

Please refer to the code bundle included with this book for the full CSS.

Creating a stunning CSS3 3D flip animation

Now we are going to add a stunning effect to the hover status of the book.

Planning the hover animation

We plan to insert the following three pieces of information on hovering the box:

- The product title
- A short description of the product
- The **Book Details** button

The effect that we are going to create with CSS3 is the rotation of the book using the CSS3 property called **perspective**. In this way, when the users hover the cursor over the book, the front side will rotate with a 3D animation and display back of the book.

In the following screenshot, you can see the off status on the left and the hover status on the right:

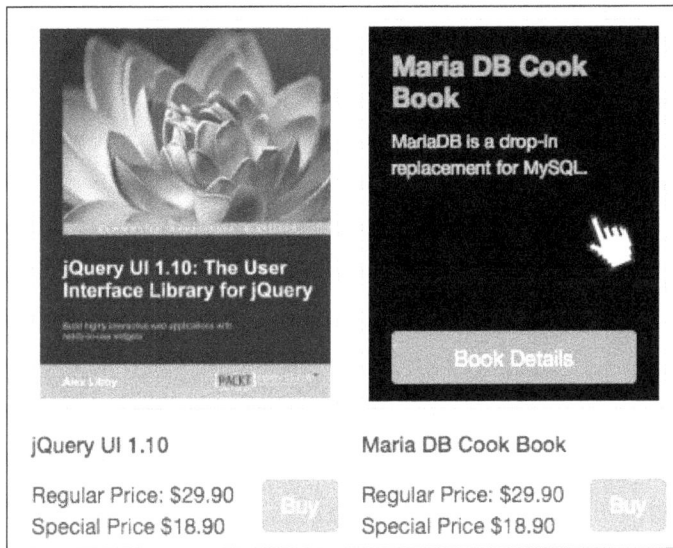

The HTML code of list-home.phtml

As we said in the previous section, we apply the rotating effect to the products list on the home page of our theme, but after going through this section, you can replicate the structure of the `list-home.phtml` file that we are going to edit to the `list.phtml` file. The basic structure that we are going to use is shown in the following code:

```
<div class="item-container">
  <div class="item-flipper">
    <div class="item-front"><img src="…"></div>
    <div class="item-back">Back informations…</div>
  </div>
</div>
```

The `item-container` attribute will contain `item-flipper`, which is the 3D container that will contain the 3D rotating animation of the front and back covers of our book.

In order to apply this structure to our file, we need to edit the structure of the item in the `list-home.phtml` file located in `app/design/frontend/bookstore/default/template/products/`.

Open the `list-home.phtml` file and find the following code that generates the image within the item block:

```
<a href="<?php echo $_product->getProductUrl() ?>" title="<?php
  echo $this->stripTags($this->getImageLabel($_product,
  'small_image'), null, true) ?>" class="product-image">
```

```
<img src="<?php echo $this->helper('catalog/image')-
  >init($_product, 'small_image')->resize(250,310); ?>" alt=
  "<?php echo $this->stripTags($this->getImageLabel($_product,
  'small_image'), null, true) ?>" class=
  "img-responsive img-thumbnail" />
</a>
```

Then, replace the preceding code with the following code:

```
<div class="item-container img-thumbnail">
  <div class="item-flipper">
    <div class="item-front">
      <!-- front content -->
      <a href="<?php echo $_product->getProductUrl() ?>"
        title="<?php echo $this->stripTags($this-
        >getImageLabel($_product, 'small_image'), null, true)
        ?>" class="product-image"><img src="<?php echo $this-
        >helper('catalog/image')->init($_product, 'small_image')-
        >resize(250,310); ?>" alt="<?php echo $this-
        >stripTags($this->getImageLabel($_product, 'small_image'),
        null, true) ?>" class="img-responsive" /></a>
    </div>

    <div class="item-back">
      <!-- back content -->
      <div class="book-info">
      <div class="h4"><a href="<?php echo $_product-
        >getProductUrl() ?>" title="<?php echo $this-
        >stripTags($_product->getName(), null, true) ?>"><?php
        echo $_helper->productAttribute($_product, $_product-
        >getName(), 'name') ?></a></div>

      <div class="short-description"><?php echo $_helper-
        >productAttribute($_product, $_product-
        >getShortDescription(), 'short_description') ?></div>
      </div>
      <p><a href="<?php echo $_product->getProductUrl() ?>"
        title="<?php echo $this->stripTags($_product->getName(),
        null, true) ?>" class="btn btn-block btn-success"><?php
        echo $this->__('Book Details')?></a></p>
    </div>
  </div>
</div>
```

This is the structure that includes an image on the front cover and the information on the back cover of the book.

Creating the CSS animation

Now we are going to see, step by step, the main CSS information that will make the book flip from the front cover to the back cover. We start by customizing the `item-container` attribute, which is the main container, with the following CSS code:

```css
.item-container {
  -webkit-perspective:300px;
  -moz-perspective:300px;
  perspective:300px;
  margin:0 auto;
  height:250px;
  margin-bottom:10px;
  width:100%;
}
```

We assign the perspective property that represents the perspective inclination from which an element is viewed, and that will affect the elements inside it.

Now, we assign the 3D rotation of 180 degree to the `item-flipper` element on the `item-container` hover status by using the CSS3 property transition `rotateY` in the following manner:

```css
.products-grid li .item-container:hover .item-flipper {
  -moz-transform:rotateY(180deg);
  -webkit-transform:rotateY(180deg);
  transform:rotateY(180deg);
}
```

Now we assign dimensions to our elements `item-front` and `item-back`, and customize the elements on the back cover, such as the title and the description.

We also need to set up the speed of the transition from the front cover to the back cover and declare whether we want to hide or show the faces while they are rotating, which we do with the `"backface-visibility: hidden"` property. Consider the following code:

```css
/* Hide the back on hover */
.products-grid li .item-front, .products-grid li .item-back {
  height:240px;
  width:100%;
  -webkit-backface-visibility:hidden;
  -moz-backface-visibility:hidden;
  backface-visibility:hidden;
  position:absolute;
  top:0;
```

```
    left:0;
    background:none;
}

/* Fix z-index for front block to place above the back */
.products-grid li .item-front {
    z-index:2;
}

/* back, initially hidden pane */
.products-grid li .item-back {
    -webkit-transform:rotateY(180deg);
    -moz-transform:rotateY(180deg);
    transform:rotateY(180deg);
    background:none repeat scroll 0 0 #000;
    color:#FFF;
    padding:15px;
}

.products-grid li .item-back .book-info {
    height:180px;
}

.products-grid li .item-back .book-info .h4 a {
    color:#FA9221;
    font-weight:700;
    margin-bottom:10px;
    display:block;
}

.products-grid li .item-back .book-info .short-description {
    font-size:12px;
    color:#ccc;
}
```

The code also includes the simple customization of the elements within the item.

> The .products-grid li .item-back element is initially hidden by a 180 degree rotation.

Now, in order to complete the animations, we specify that our flipper is the block where the 3D animation runs using the property `"preserve-3d"`. The following code will explain this better:

```
.products-grid li .item-flipper {
  -webkit-transition:.6s;
  -moz-transition:.6s;
  -ms-transition:.6s;
  transition:.6s;
  -moz-transform-style:preserve-3d;
  -webkit-transform-style:preserve-3d;
  transform-style:preserve-3d;
  position:relative;
}
```

And we are done! You can find the full CSS in the code bundle included with this book.

If you like 3D transformations and want to investigate them, you can read more about them at `http://24ways.org/2010/intro-to-css-3d-transforms/`, where you can read a useful article that explains the CSS 3D transformations better.

Creating a custom product images gallery

Magento's default zoom property to view the products is not at the top of its game. It is very old and, in fact, has been used since the first version of Magento released and the more views images (the additional product images) opens into a pop up.

One of the best practices and the most requested feature by clients is a Lightbox on the product view page that will not open new windows but will display the zoomed image in a better way on the same page.

I usually integrate **prettyPhoto** in my projects, and now we are going to learn how to integrate it in our theme, overriding the default zoom system. prettyPhoto is a totally free jQuery Lightbox clone plugin that you can integrate in your projects with some simple steps.

We will also learn how to create a switch image if there are multiple images.

Planning the work

Now we have to plan what we want to do.

Magento can manage multiple product pictures and display them on the product page. They are called *more views* and we plan to do the following process:

- Integrating prettyPhoto to create nice zoom effects for the the main image and thumbnails by clicking on them
- Creating a custom script that changes the main image while hovering over a thumbnail of the more views block

Integrating prettyPhoto into Magento

prettyPhoto is a jQuery Lightbox clone created by Stéphane Caron. It supports almost everything: images, videos, Flash, YouTube, iFrames, and Ajax. It is very simple to integrate and customize, and is also compatible with every major browser.

Downloading prettyPhoto

You can download prettyPhoto 3.1.5 from `http://www.no-margin-for-errors.com/projects/prettyphoto-jquery-lightbox-clone/`. The page that opens should look the same as that shown in the following screenshot:

Open the plugin page and follow the ensuing steps in order to download and integrate prettyPhoto:

1. Download the minified **Production Version v.3.1.5. Compressed**.

2. Unzip the files and copy the JS `jquery.prettyPhoto.js` to your JS skin folder `skin/frontend/bookstore/default/js/`.

3. Copy the CSS `prettyphoto.css` to your `css` folder.

4. Finally, copy the prettyPhoto images from the `/images/prettyphoto` folder. The `prettyPhoto` folder includes the images for all the themes that you can use.

Integrating prettyPhoto JS and CSS

Now open the `local.xml` file and add the JS and the CSS. In order to load
prettyPhoto only on the product view page, you can place `addItem` in the `action`
method to declare the JS and `addCss` to declare the CSS in the `<catalog_product_view>` handle as follows:

```
<catalog_product_view>

    <reference name="root">
      <action method="setTemplate">
        <template>page/1column.phtml</template></action>
    </reference>

    <reference name="head">
      <action method="addItem">
        <type>skin_js</type>
        <name>js/jquery.prettyPhoto.js</name>
      </action>
    <!-- Adding the prettyphoto.css -->
      <action method="addCss">
        <stylesheet>css/prettyPhoto.css</stylesheet>
      </action>
    </reference>

</catalog_product_view>
```

> If you want to use prettyPhoto for all the themes, simply add the CSS
> and the JS in the default handle.

Customizing the media.phtml code

The file that generates the product gallery into the product view page is
`media.phtml`.

As usual, you can copy this file from the base theme or create an empty one
in `app/design/frontend/bookstore/template/catalog/product/view/`.
Then follow these steps to customize the file:

1. First, we get the product information using the following code:
   ```php
   <?php
       $_product = $this->getProduct();
       $_helper = $this->helper('catalog/output');
   ?>
   ```

2. Then we create the block for the main image as shown in the following code:

```
<!-- This is the main product image ->
<p class="product-image img-thumbnail">
  <?php
        $_img = '<img id="product_main_img" src="'.$this-
            >helper('catalog/image')->init($_product,
            'image')->resize(500,600).'" alt="'.$this-
            >escapeHtml($this->getImageLabel()).'"
            title="'.$this->escapeHtml($this-
            >getImageLabel()).'" class="img-responsive" />';
        echo $_helper->productAttribute($_product, $_img,
'image');
    ?>
  <!-- this link will trigger the prettyPhoto zoom ->
  <a id="zoom" href="#" class="visible-md visible-lg">Zoom
    Images</a>
</p>
```

As you can see, we inserted the link `<a id="zoom" href="#"
class="visible-md visible-lg">Zoom Images</a>` after the main image,
which will trigger the prettyPhoto function.

> The scope of this link is to make the zoom function accessible
> only on large devices and not small devices. Note that the
> `visible-md visible-lg` Bootstrap classes will show the
> link only on medium and large devices.

3. Now, we create the `more-views` block, which includes all the additional
images of the product:

```
<!-- Display the additionals images of the product ->
<?php if (count($this->getGalleryImages()) > 0): ?>
<div class="more-views">
  <?php foreach ($this->getGalleryImages() as $_image): ?>
  <a href="#" title="<?php echo $this->escapeHtml($_image-
    >getLabel()) ?>" class="img-thumbnail"><img src="<?php
    echo $this->helper('catalog/image')->init($this-
    >getProduct(), 'thumbnail', $_image->getFile())-
    >resize(56); ?>" rel="<?php echo $this-
    >helper('catalog/image')->init($this->getProduct(),
    'thumbnail', $_image->getFile())->resize(500,600); ?>"
    width="56" height="56" alt="<?php echo $this-
    >escapeHtml($_image->getLabel()) ?>" /></a>

  <!-this is the hidden link for prettyphoto zoom ->
  <a style="display:none" href="<?php echo $this-
```

```
>helper('catalog/image')->init($this->getProduct(),
'thumbnail', $_image->getFile()); ?>"
rel="prettyPhoto[productGallery]"></a>
<?php endforeach; ?>
</div>
<?php endif; ?>
```

As you can see, the link that will launch the zoom property is not on the thumbnails but in external hidden links for the same reason described previously: to make the zoom property accessible only on medium and large devices.

In other words, the link with the ID `zoom` will launch the prettyPhoto gallery when it's clicked, which is represented by the hidden links inside the `more-views` block. If the link is hidden, users on mobile phones will not have the capability to launch the zoom.

> This is recommended because on a smartphone the user can see the main image that fits the device width and you may not need to zoom in. However, if you want to enable the zoom property for all devices, please remove the CSS class `visible-md visible-lg`.

The full code of the `media.phtml` file will look as follows:

```
<?php
    $_product = $this->getProduct();
    $_helper = $this->helper('catalog/output');
?>


<p class="product-image img-thumbnail">
  <?php
        $_img = '<img id="product_main_img" src="'.$this-
>helper('catalog/image')->init($_product, 'image')->resize(500,600).'"
alt="'.$this->escapeHtml($this->getImageLabel()).'" title="'.$this-
>escapeHtml($this->getImageLabel()).'" class="img-responsive" />';
            echo $_helper->productAttribute($_product, $_img, 'image');
    ?>
  <a id="zoom" href="#" class="visible-md visible-lg">Zoom Images</a>
</p>
<?php if (count($this->getGalleryImages()) > 0): ?>
<div class="more-views">
  <?php foreach ($this->getGalleryImages() as $_image): ?>
  <a href="#" title="<?php echo $this->escapeHtml($_image->getLabel())
?>" class="img-thumbnail"><img src="<?php echo $this->helper('catalog/
image')->init($this->getProduct(), 'thumbnail', $_image->getFile())-
>resize(56); ?>" rel="<?php echo $this->helper('catalog/image')-
>init($this->getProduct(), 'thumbnail', $_image->getFile())-
```

```
>resize(500,600); ?>" width="56" height="56" alt="<?php echo $this-
>escapeHtml($_image->getLabel()) ?>" /></a>

  <a style="display:none" href="<?php echo $this->helper('catalog/
image')->init($this->getProduct(), 'thumbnail', $_image->getFile());
?>" rel="prettyPhoto[productGallery]"></a>

  <?php endforeach; ?>
</div>
<?php endif; ?>
```

Initializing prettyPhoto

Now that the prettyPhoto plugin and the HTML structure are integrated, let's initialize the JS as follows:

```
jQuery("a[rel^='prettyPhoto']").prettyPhoto({
  theme: 'facebook',
  opacity: 0.50
});
```

prettyPhoto includes a lot of options. Take a look at the `theme` option. There are six themes to choose from; in this case, we are using the `facebook` theme with a custom opacity of `0.5` (the default is `0.8`).

To launch prettyPhoto, you usually have to click on the link that has the `rel="prettyphoto"` attribute, but we will launch it from the zoom link as described earlier. To do this, add the following code to your `jquery.scripts.js` file:

```
jQuery("#zoom").click(function() {
  jQuery("a[rel^='prettyPhoto']:first").click();
});
```

In other words, this code will simulate clicking on the first hidden link of the gallery by clicking on the `#zoom` button.

Creating a nice image swap effect for when you hover the cursor over a thumbnail

Now that we have integrated prettyPhoto, let's learn how to add a simple image-change effect for when you hover the cursor over the thumbnail. The aim is to show the preview image instantly magnified in the main image box, as shown in the following screenshot:

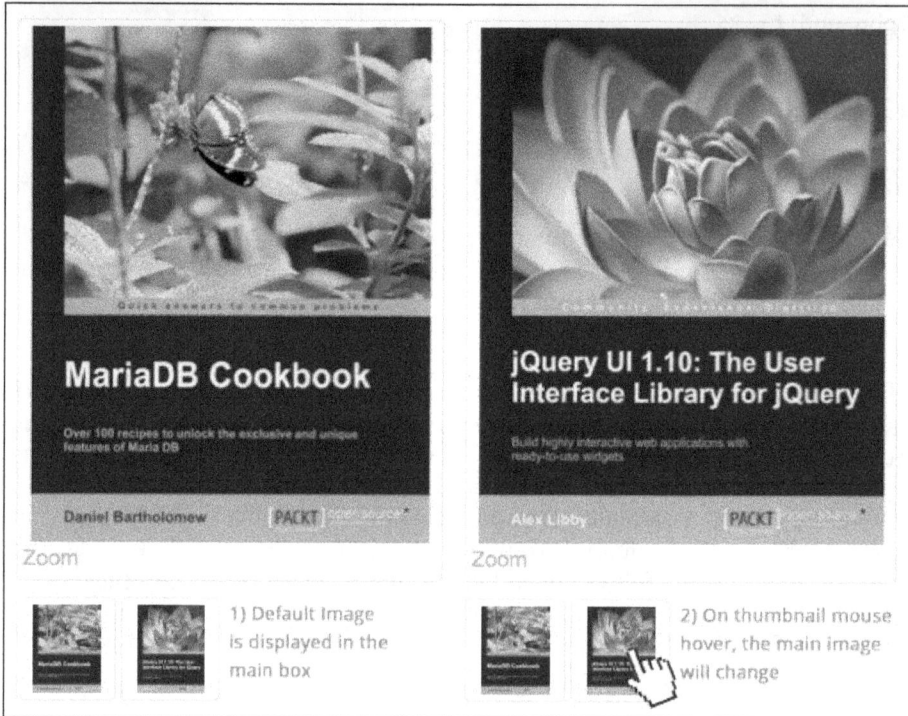

To get this effect, we create a variable called hoverImg, which contains the rel attribute of the image inside the <a> link that is hovered, and then we assign that link to the src attribute of the main product img as follows:

```
jQuery(".more-views a").hover( function() {
  var hoverImg = jQuery(this).find("img").attr("rel");
  jQuery("#product_main_img").attr("src", hoverImg);
});
```

The portion of code for the `media.phtml` file, which is where the effect will show, is as follows:

```
<a href="#" title="<?php echo $this->escapeHtml($_image->getLabel())
?>" class="img-thumbnail">

<img src="<?php echo $this->helper('catalog/image')->init($this-
>getProduct(), 'thumbnail', $_image->getFile())->resize(56);
?>" rel="<?php echo $this->helper('catalog/image')->init($this-
>getProduct(), 'thumbnail', $_image->getFile())->resize(500,600);
?>" width="56" height="56" alt="<?php echo $this->escapeHtml($_image-
>getLabel()) ?>" />

</a>
```

> The `rel` attribute of the image contains the link to an image with the same
> dimensions as the main product image generated by the following code:
> ```
> <?php echo $this->helper('catalog/image')->init($this-
>     >getProduct(), 'thumbnail', $_image->getFile())-
>     >resize(500,600); ?>"
> ```

Done! You now have a custom product page zoom and a gallery!

Adding a custom font to our theme

In recent years, the typography on the Web has always been very limited. In fact, it was only possible to use the so-called Web-safe font or the font system present on all computers, such as Arial, Verdana, and Georgia.

As you can understand, this was a very big limitation and did not allow the application of proper graphic styles for websites. Additionally, many times, images were used to include text and that caused weighting the web pages.

Now, though, it is possible to apply a font that is specific to the look and feel you want to achieve, and companies can now project their visual branding through typography.

This is possible with the new `@font-face` CSS rule that specifies the name of the font, its location, and the font weight. All the major modern browsers support `font-face`.

Soon, we will learn how to integrate a font in our theme.

Sources to find free and premium web-safe font

When browsing the Internet, you can find a lot of sites with high-quality, modern, and easy-to-use font. Let's see the most important sites for fonts:

- Google fonts (`https://www.google.com/fonts`)
- Font Squirrel (`http://www.fontsquirrel.com/`)
- Typekit by Adobe (`https://typekit.com/`)

Google fonts

Google fonts is the place where you can always go to find a lot of free, modern fonts to integrate in your site. Google's free font directory is one of the best directories to find free, high-quality Web fonts. At the moment, the Google directory has a lot of free fonts and the collection is growing continually.

In the following screenshot, you can see the Google font directory page:

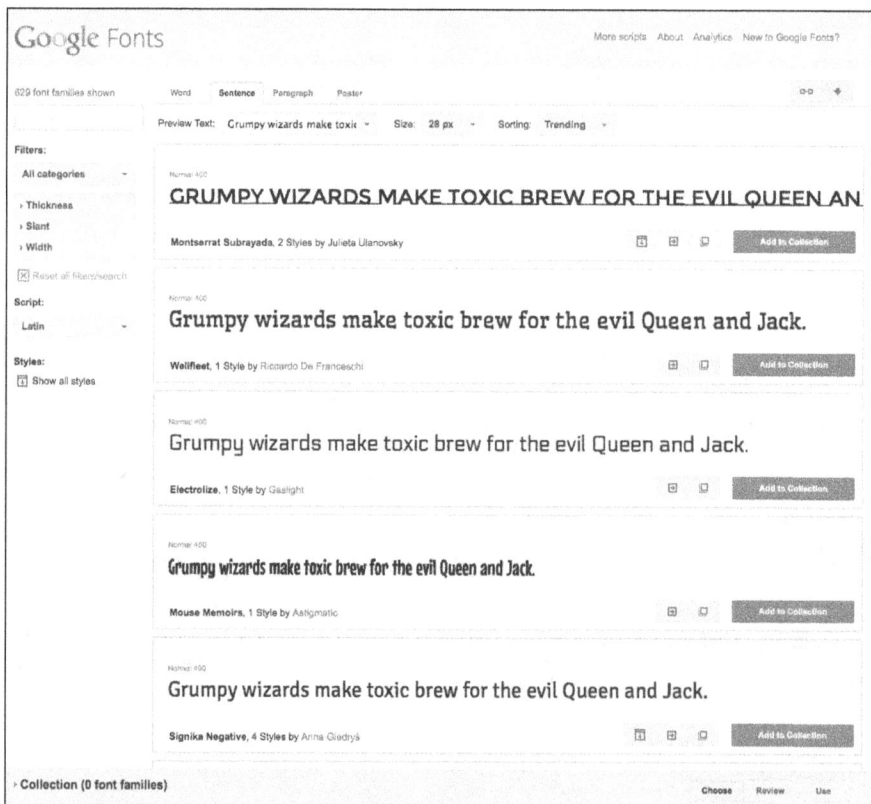

For more information, visit `http://www.google.com/fonts/`.

Font Squirrel

Font Squirrel is an another great site where you can find high-quality free fonts. All the fonts are free for personal as well as commercial use. So, if you are looking for a free font to use commercially, you'll know that any font you find here is a safe bet.

If you're going to use the font on a website, you can preview each font and see what it will look like on the Internet with the test-drive function.

The following screenshot shows the Font Squirrel website homepage:

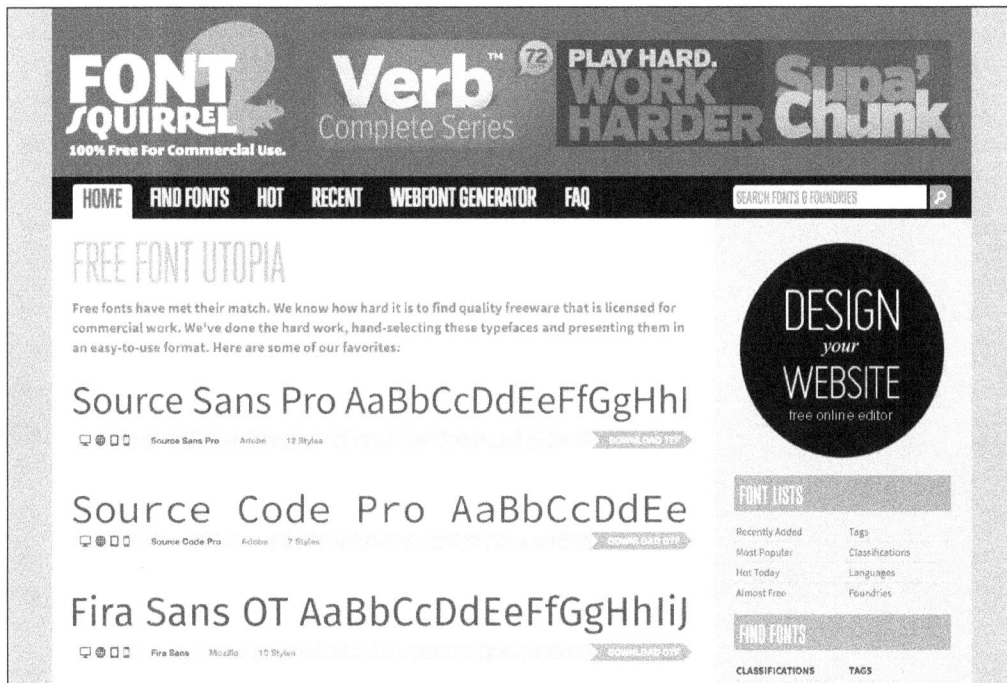

For more information, visit `http://www.fontsquirrel.com`.

Adobe TypeKit

Typekit is a free-font premium edition where you can use real fonts to integrate in any of your site by creating premium accounts. On Typekit, you can find quality fonts from the most important font foundries, which offer an astounding choice of beautiful commercial typefaces.

This is a premium service but if you need to integrate great fonts into your projects, you can try it for free for one project or choose a plan starting from $24.99/year.

You can see the Typekit website in the following screenshot:

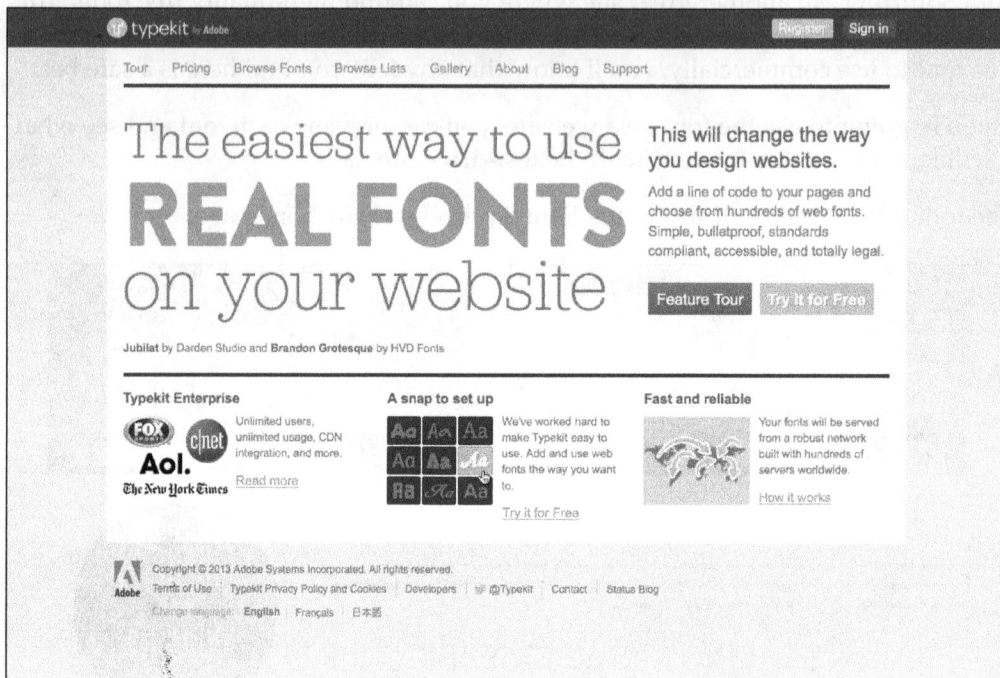

For more information, visit `https://typekit.com`.

Integrating a Google font in our theme

Now you know where you can find some great fonts for your project. Let's learn how to integrate a font face into the theme. We will integrate a Google font using the following steps:

1. First, select one or two fonts from the Google font directory. We are going to use a free Google font called **Crete Round** for the title headings.

2. Once you select the fonts, open the font details and follow the instructions.

3. Choose the styles you want. Some fonts include more styles (light, normal, bold, italics, and so on). If you choose only the styles that you need, you'll help prevent your webpage from loading slowly.

4. Choose the character sets you want and add the following code to your website. Open the `head.phtml` file located in `app/design/frontend/`

`bookstore/default/template/html/` and add the following code that will load the Google font you selected:

```
<link href=
   'http://fonts.googleapis.com/css?family=Crete+Round'
   rel='stylesheet' type='text/css'>
```

5. Define the font family in your CSS.

6. Now, simply assign the following property to the items in the site to which you want to assign this font. For example, if we want to set the font Crete Round only to the title headings, we can do so using the following code snippet:

```
h1, h2, h3, h4, h5, h6 {
    font-family: 'Crete Round', serif;
}
```

7. Now refresh the page and admire the beauty of the font you've integrated! As you can see in the following screenshot, the font was applied correctly for all the headings:

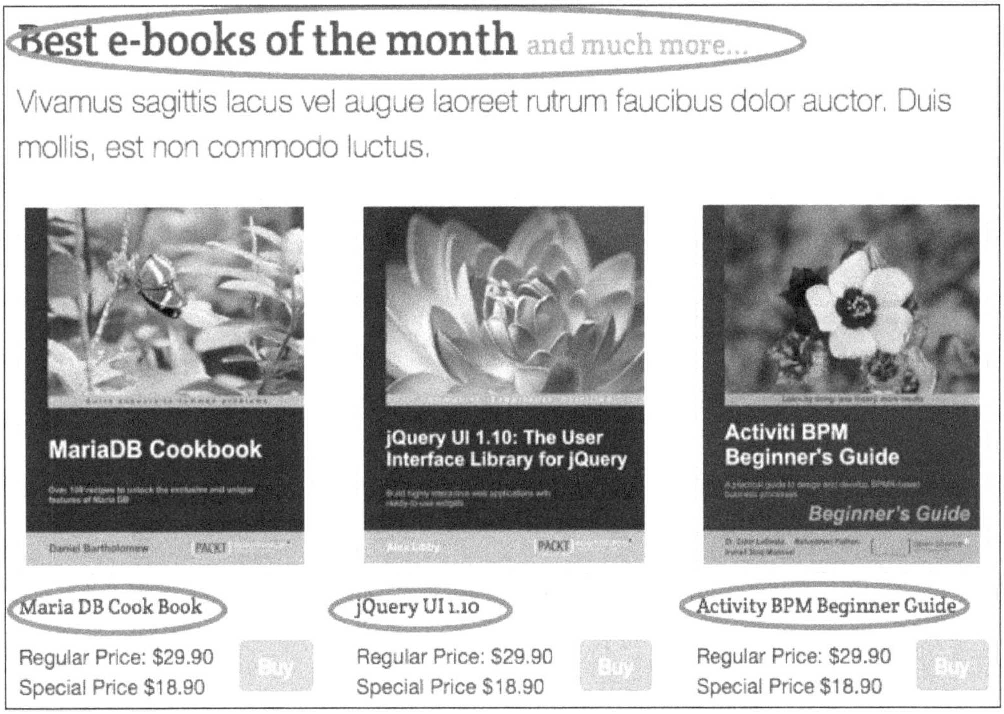

Adding a custom icon font to our theme

An icon font is one that includes special characters, usually icons, instead of normal characters. Bootstrap includes the **Glyphicon** icon font that we already integrated in our theme in *Chapter 2, Creating a Responsive Magento Theme with Bootstrap 3*.

Alternatively, we can integrate another great icon font that includes more than 300 icons that are ready to use. This awesome icon font is called **Font Awesome**! The following screenshot shows the **Font Awesome** website:

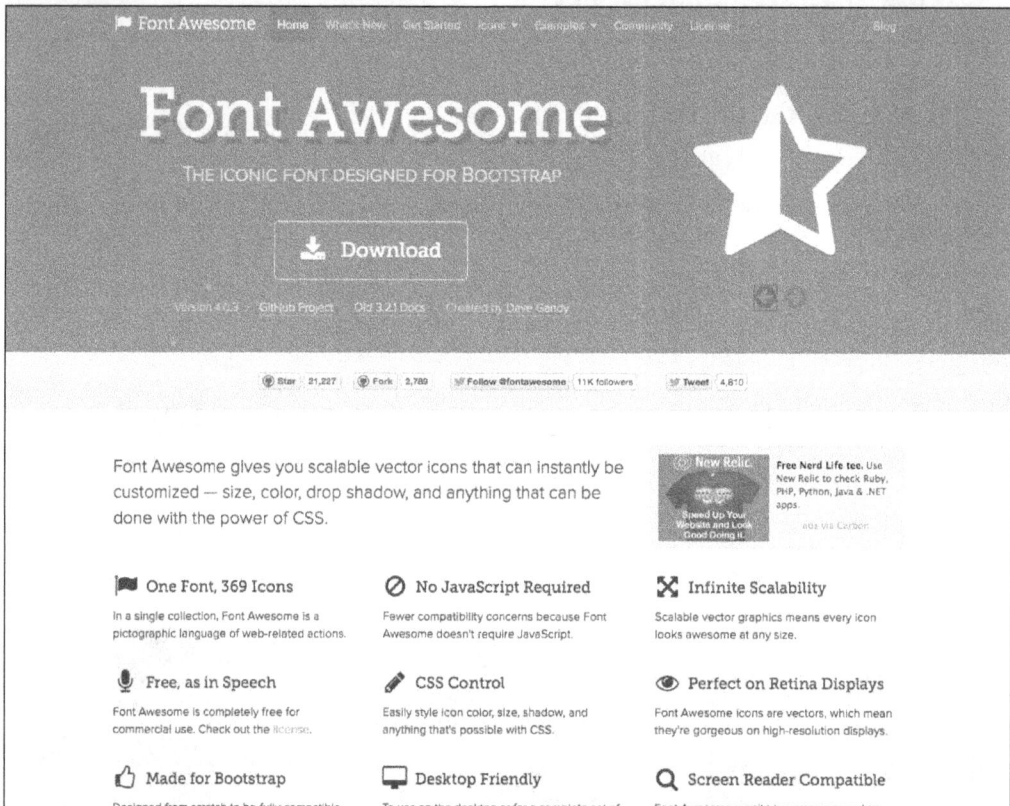

You can decide to use this icon font instead of the font released along with Bootstrap.

To integrate Font Awesome into your theme, follow the ensuing steps:

1. First, download the font from `http://fortawesome.github.io/Font-Awesome/`.

2. Then, unzip the file and within the folder, navigate to the `css` folder.

3. Now, link the CSS file from the `local.xml` file by including the following actions within the reference `name="head"`, which is placed within the default handle, as follows:

```
<!-- Adding FONT AWESOME Css -->
<action method="addCss">
<stylesheet>css/font-awesome.min.css</stylesheet>
</action>
```

4. Now that the font is integrated, let's perform a test.

It is very simple to insert a symbol into the theme. Let's suppose that you want to add a book icon. Search for one at the Font Awesome website and click on it as shown in the next screenshot:

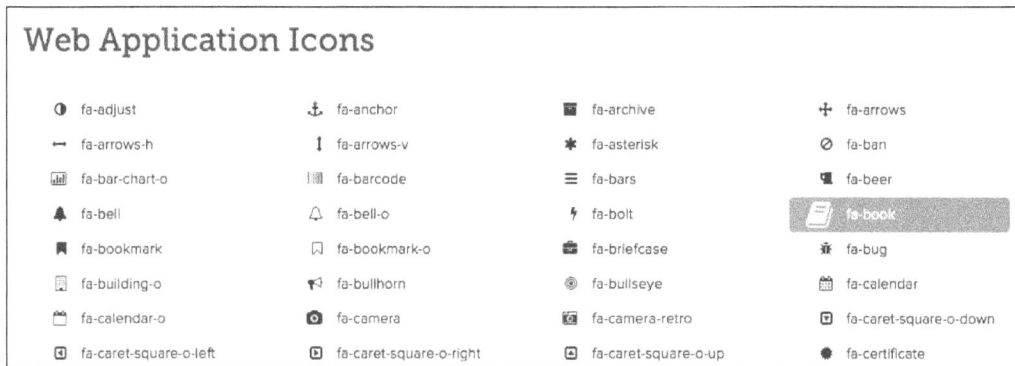

Once you click on the book icon, a new page will open as shown in the following screenshot:

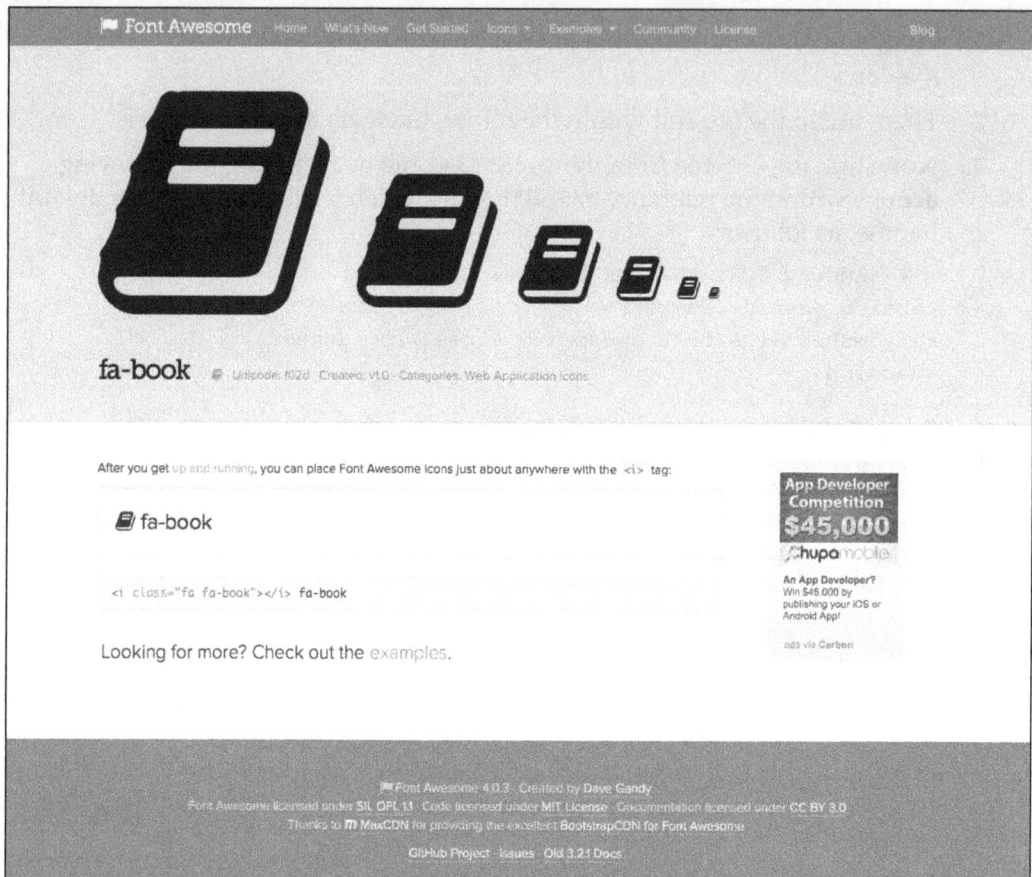

On this page, you can see the different size in which the icon is available for use and the following code to generate them:

```
<i class="fa fa-book"></i>
```

To insert icon into the theme, simply copy and paste the code, and the icon will show up.

You can target that specific icon with its own CSS class `fa-book`. So, if you want to make it big and orange, you can execute the following code in your CSS file `style.css`:

```css
.fa-book {
  font-size:30px;
  color: #F89223;
}
```

> The icon font is a font such as Helvetica, Arial, Times, and so on. This means that you can apply all the CSS properties that you can add to a font.

Summary

In this chapter, we learned how to play with modern CSS3 transitions and how to customize the look and feel of the theme by adding animations and using custom fonts. Try to customize your theme with other effects and change the default font to one that fits better within the graphic style of your theme.

In the next chapter, we will make the theme fully responsive by adding specific Bootstrap classes and testing it for mobile and tablet devices along with discussing some tips and great free tools.

5
Making the Theme Fully Responsive

Bootstrap is a framework that helps you to create responsive websites. It may happen that while developing websites, including the basis of a framework responsive-frontend, such as Bootstrap, can present problems for some display resolutions and devices. So, it's very important to optimize the UI for all the devices. The responsive element is particularly essential for an e-commerce website to increase the possibility of purchases by users. In fact, when users navigate through a website with a layout that is optimized and intuitive, they can buy products quickly and easily.

The mobile e-commerce has developed greatly in recent years, and the statistics of the growth are impressive. The following are some numbers of the analysis carried out for mobile e-commerce:

- 10 percent of all e-commerce sales are made via mobile or tablet
- 96 percent of smartphone users research a product on their phone
- 62 percent of smartphone shoppers make purchases on their mobile phone at least once a month

The source of these statistics is OuterBox design. You can read more about this at `http://www.outerboxdesign.com/web-design-articles/mobile-ecommerce-statistics`, and you can also find neat information on graphics to understand better the importance of a responsive design for e-commerce websites.

In this chapter, we are going to learn how to solve the most common issues and make our theme usable with any device, using media queries and Bootstrap classes.

The following topics will be covered in the chapter:

- Our goal
- Using specific CSS3 media queries
- Optimizing the theme for multiple devices
- Tips and tools for responsive optimization

Our goal

By the end of this chapter, you will be able to optimize your theme for all the devices with simple techniques. Our goal is to have a fully responsive website, as you can see in the following mockup:

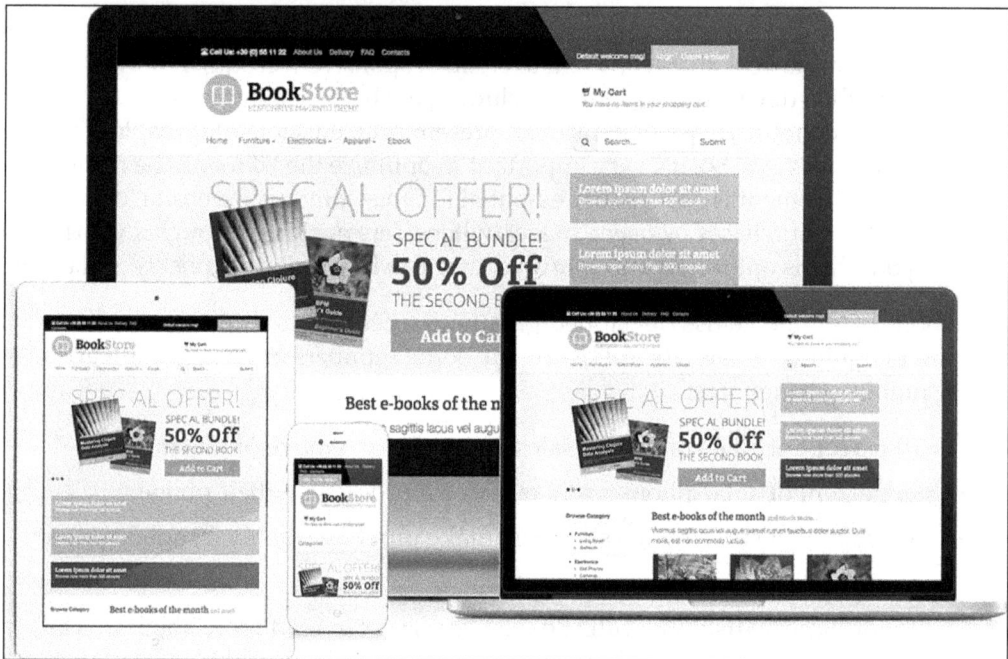

This responsive website is optimized for smartphones, tablets, laptops, and large desktops. It is recommended that you prepare a mockup for every responsive view in order to not waste time designing it on the browser.

Using specific CSS3 media queries

In order to set different styles for each resolution, you can use the CSS3 media queries.

Media queries can be defined directly in the CSS or into an external CSS file. We will discuss the first method, that is, inserting the code inside our `style.css` located into `skin/css`.

The following code snippet is an example of a media query, also known as breakpoint:

```
@media screen and (max-width: 980px)
  div {
    width: 95%;
  }
}
```

In this example, all the `div` elements will have a width of `95%` for all the resolutions under 980 pixels, defined by the CSS property `max-width`. This is a very simple example, but keep in mind that you can play with media queries to have a different design for each resolution and customize your theme as you want.

As we said before, we have four main scenarios; for each of them, we can use a media query, and write inside them the code that we need to customize the theme.

Now, let's discuss the main media queries that we are going to use into the theme for the most used devices' resolutions:

- Large devices
- Medium or standard devices
- Tablet devices
- Smartphone devices

Large devices (.container width – 1170 px)

The width of 1170 px is the default width that Bootstrap assigns to the `div` container. So, we don't need a media query for this resolution. This resolution is used for large devices such as desktop computers and large laptops, as shown in the following figure:

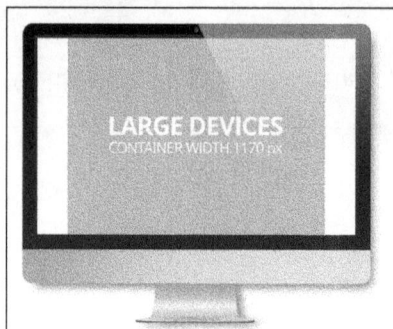

If you take a look at Bootstrap CSS, you can see that the container has the width set with the following media query:

```
@media only screen and (min-width: 1200px) {
/* styles for browsers larger than 1200px */
.container {
  width: 1170px;
}
}
```

Medium devices (.container width – 970 px)

This is the resolution for small laptops and medium screens (or browser windows) with a maximum width of 1200 px. This is the most used resolution and it is shown in the following figure:

If the viewport is narrower than 992px, we can make all the changes to the CSS for small desktops with the following media query that Bootstrap uses to set the container width:

```
@media only screen and (max-width: 992px) {

/* styles for browsers smaller than 992px; */
.container {
  width: 970px;
}

}
```

Tablet devices (.container width – 750 px)

A tabled viewport is a little smaller than the desktop and it sometimes needs advanced optimization. To make the theme compatible with the most used tablet viewports, we can use a container width of 750 px as shown in the following figure:

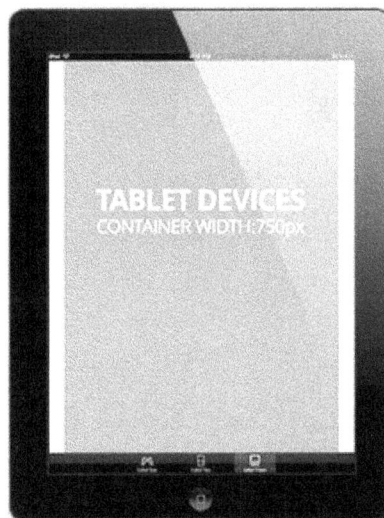

If the viewport is narrower than 768px, we can make all the changes to the CSS for tablets with the following media query that Bootstrap uses to set the container width:

```
@media only screen and (max-width: 768px) {

  /* styles for browsers smaller than 768px */
  .container {
    width: 750px;
  }
}
```

Smartphones

For smartphones, we will not use a fixed width. For a viewport, the layout will remain fluid for a maximum width of 320 px, to allow all smartphone resolutions to adapt correctly as shown in the following figure:

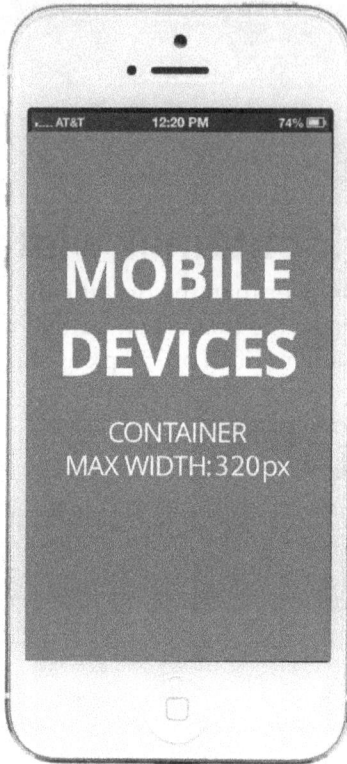

You can insert your custom styles for small devices with the following media query:

```
@media only screen and (max-width: 320px) {

/* styles for browsers smaller than 320px */
.container {
   width: 300px;
  }
}
```

> Note that the container width is already set in the Bootstrap CSS; you only need to copy the media query in the CSS and write modifications in it.

Optimizing the theme for multiple devices

Now that you understood how media queries work, let's apply some fix to our theme. In this topic, we will mostly use the default Bootstrap classes to fix minor bugs.

Testing the responsiveness of a website

First, we need a tool to test the responsiveness. There are many tools to test the responsiveness of a website. You can simply resize the browser window or you can test directly on the devices. Alternatively, you can use a great tool called **Viewport Resizer**.

Viewport Resizer is a responsive design bookmark script created by Malte Wassermann. This script generates a very useful toolbar in your page that allows you to select the device to test and automatically resizes the page you are viewing into an iFrame with the required width.

You can download and save this useful bookmark from the author's website at `http://lab.maltewassermann.com/viewport-resizer`. It only takes 2 seconds! Simply click on the big button **CLICK OR BOOKMARK** to save the bookmark as shown in the following screenshot:

Once you save the bookmark, open your theme page and click on the Resizer bookmark. Now the toolbar will appear with a neat dropdown effect, as shown in the following screenshot:

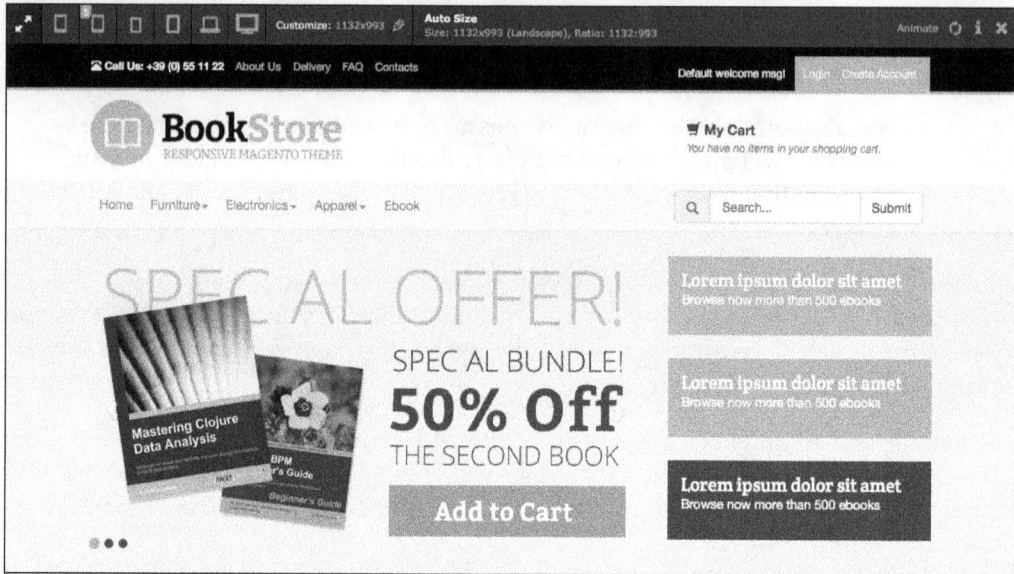

In the following screenshot, on the left you can see buttons that will resize the page to the width of common devices such as iPad, iPhone, and iPad mini. You can also set your own size to test by clicking on **Customize**:

Optimizing the top bar of the header

Now that we've got this great tool in our browser, let's begin to optimize the theme for tablets and smartphones, beginning from the top of the screen view.

If you try to resize the theme to different resolutions, you will see that the design is not so good and the elements are not aligned; however, with some simple tricks we will fix all the problems.

If you click on the **Tablet** button, you can see that it almost looks fine. This is because Bootstrap is already responsive and the classes we added to the columns are good.

But as you can see in the following screenshot, some things need to be fixed. In fact, the user links that should be placed on the right are on the left and other elements too look misaligned.

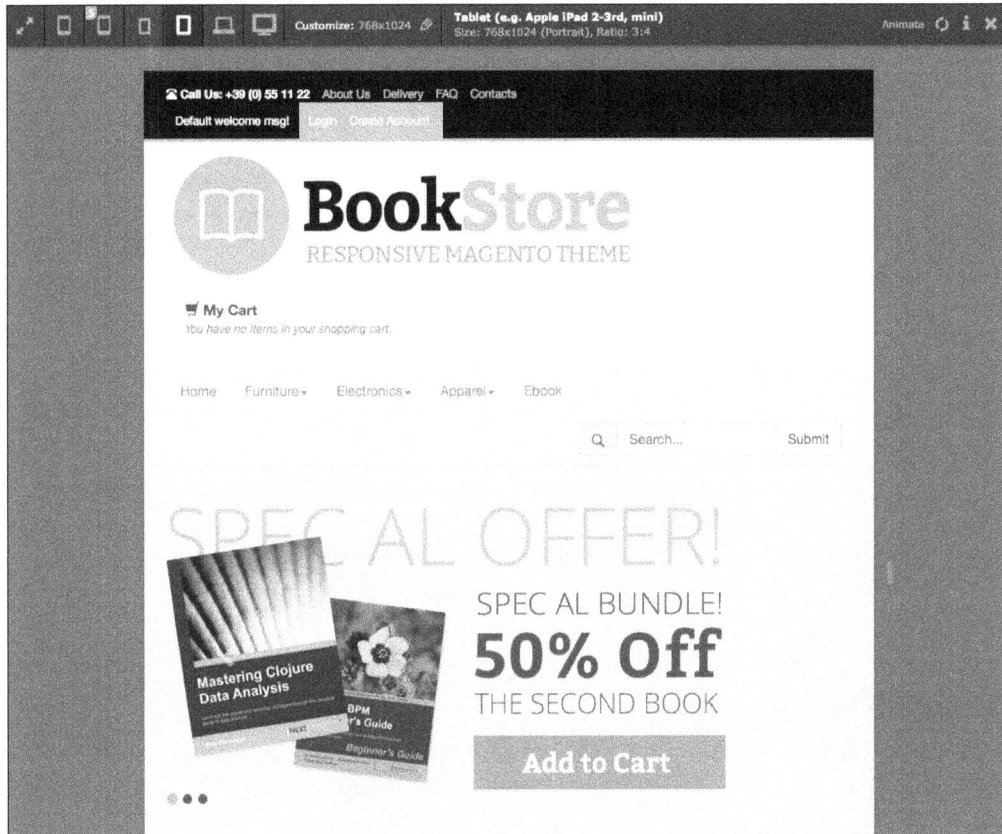

We need to put the customer area on the right of the large screen. To do this, we only need to add the `col-sm-7` class to the left of `div` that already has the `col-md-8` class. In this way, we are telling the theme to have `div` of seven columns on tablet devices.

> The `col-md-X` class is used for the columns of desktop devices, and `col-sm-X` is used for tablet devices. For small devices, you can use `col-xs`. For more information, you can read the Bootstrap documentation at `http://getbootstrap.com/css/#grid-example-basic`.

To do the modifications, find the following code snippet in the `header.phtml` file:

```
<div class="col-md-8">
    <?php echo $this->getChildHtml('topbar_cmslinks') ?>
</div>
```

Replace this with the following code snippet:

```
<div class="col-md-8 col-sm-7">
    <?php echo $this->getChildHtml('topbar_cmslinks') ?>
</div>
```

Also, change the user block on the right from `<div class="user-links col-md-4">` to `<div class="user-links col-md-4 col-sm-5">`.

As you can see in the following screenshot, we fixed this problem for a tablet:

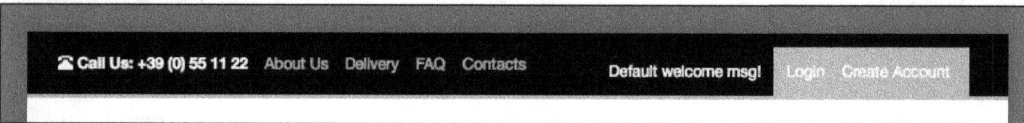

To see how the theme looks on a mobile phone, click on the button with an iPhone icon. To optimize it, you can use the same principle with the class prefix `col-xs-` instead of `col-sm-`.

Fixing the logo row

The logo and the cart are now too big. We can simply fix this in the same manner: add the `col-sm-5` class to the logo, changing `<div class="logo col-md-4">` to `<div class="logo col-md-4 col-sm-5">`.

Then, add the `col-sm` class to the cart and the empty `div` blocks as well:

```
<div class="logo col-md-4 col-sm-5">

<div class="col-md-4 col-sm-2">

<div class="col-md-4 col-sm-5">
```

In this way, we changed the width of the columns for small devices, changing the columns of the first logo box from 4 to 5, the second box from 4 to 2, and the last from 4 to 5. In this way, we are making the main `div` blocks (the logo and cart boxes) larger because they are very important.

> Remember that the grid is made up of 12 columns.

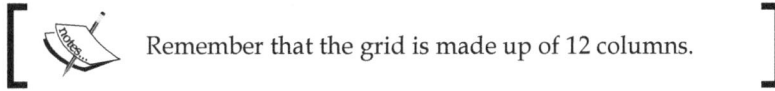

Fixing the menu bar

For tablets, the menu only needs to change the padding within the links.
So, add the following CSS code into your CSS file `style.css` that will overwrite the Bootstrap CSS:

```
@media(min-width:768px) {

  .navbar-nav > li > a {

    padding: 15px 10px;

  }
}
```

For smartphone devices, we need to make some other modifications, giving the links a full width of the device and moving the dropdown arrow to the right, as follows:

```
@media(max-width:767px) {
  .navbar-nav > li {
    border-bottom: 1px solid #DDDDDD;
    display: block;
  }
  .nav .caret {
    display: block;
    float: right;
    margin-top: 10px;
  }
}
```

In the following screenshot, you can check out the final result on tablet:

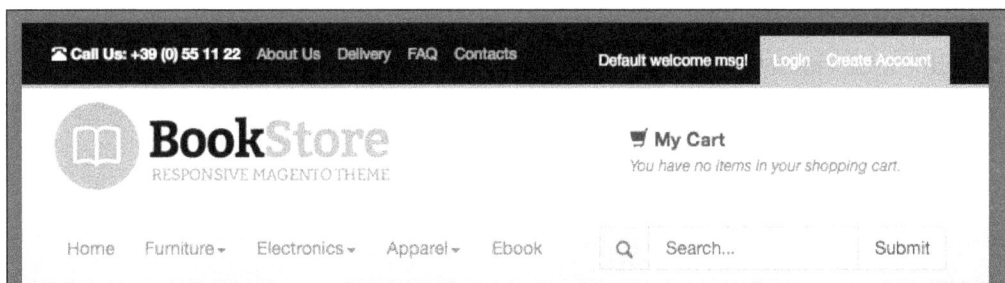

In the following screenshot, you can see the final result on the smartphone with the expanded menu:

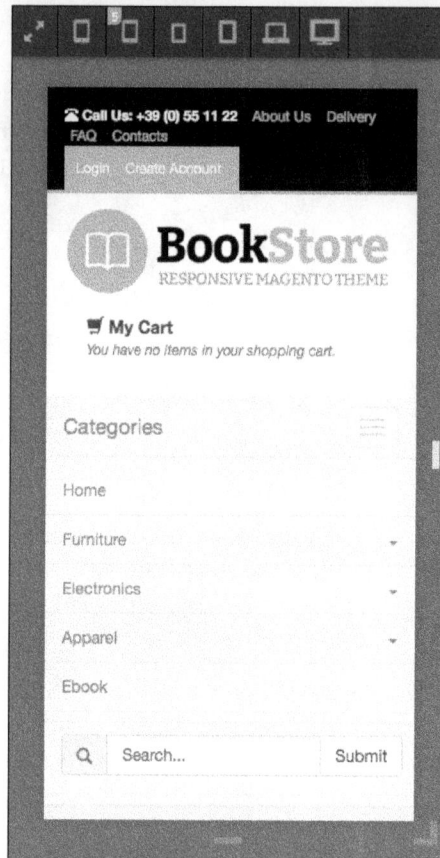

Fixing the main content column

Scrolling down the screen, the slider and banners will seem ok, so we can leave them like this. However, we need to fix the main content area that contains the sidebar and the products grid.

To fix this area, open the 2columns-lef.phtml file located in app/design/ frontend/bookstore/default/template/page/ and add the col-sm-3 class to the sidebar div of <aside> as follows:

```
<aside class="col-left sidebar col-md-3 col-sm-3">
```

Also, add the col-sm-9 class to the col-main element of the div tag as follows:

```
<div class="col-main col-md-9 col-sm-9">
```

Fixing the products grid

The products grid looks good on smaller and medium resolutions. Now we only need to fix a small issue for a mini tablet by adding a new class `col-xs`, used for resolutions between smartphones and tablets.

The only modification that we are going to do now is adding the `col-xs-6` class to the product item generated inside the `<?php foreach . . . ?>` statement with the following code:

```
<li class="item<?php if(($i-1)%$_columnCount==0): ?> first<?php
   elseif($i%$_columnCount==0): ?> last<?php endif; ?> col-md-4
   col-sm-4 col-xs-6">
```

The file of products grid in the home page is `list-home.phtml` located in `app/design/frontend/bookstore/default/template/products/`.

Adjusting the footer

The footer needs some modifications. Let's begin from the `block footer-cmslinks` static and modify the footer by performing the following steps:

1. Replace the code of the `footer.phtml` file present in `app/design/frontend/bookstore/default/template/page/html` with the following to fix the responsiveness of the columns for the tablet:

    ```
    <div class="row">
    <div class="col-sm-3">
    <h4>About Us</h4>
    <ul>
      . . .
    </ul>
    </div>

    <div class="col-sm-3">
    <h4>Customer Service</h4>
    <ul>
      . . .
    </ul>
    </div>

    <div class="col-sm-3">
    <h4>Customer Services</h4>
    <ul>
      . . .
    </ul>
    ```

```
  </div>

  <div class="col-sm-3">
  <h4>User Area</h4>
  <ul>
    . . .
  </ul>
  </div>
  </div>
```

As you can see, all the `col-md-3` classes are replaced with `col-sm-3`.

2. Now, open the `footer.phtml` file and change the class of the newsletter container and the class of the social box container from `col-md-6` to `col-sm-6`. The footer on tablets will look like what is shown in the following screenshot:

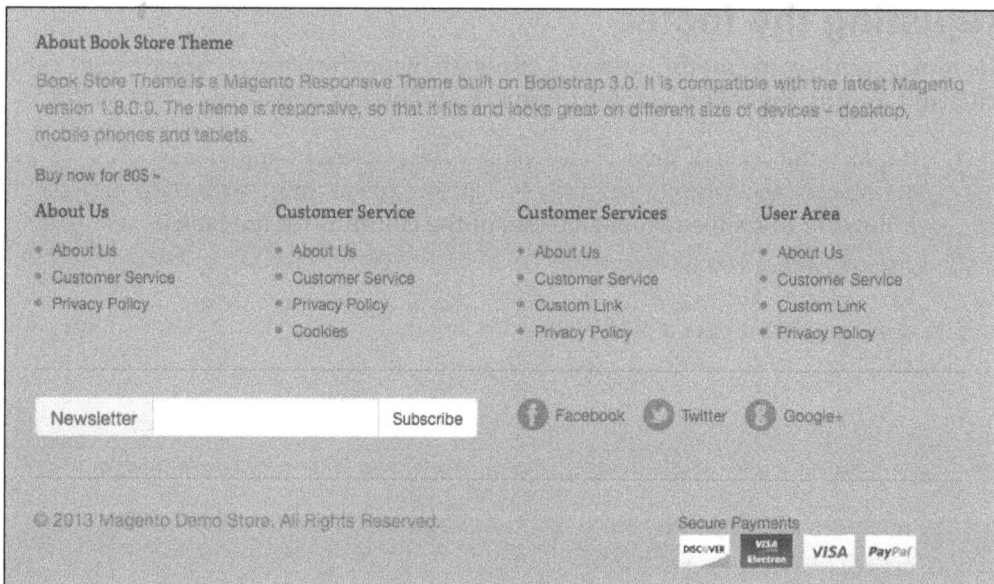

For smartphone resolutions, we don't need to do the modifications because every box will take the full width of the device.

Tips and tools for responsive coding

The responsive design is the base of Bootstrap. By reading the official documentation, you will find a lot of useful tips and information to create fully responsive elements.

Now we are going to discuss the most important classes to integrate into our theme, to have the control while optimizing it for all the devices.

Hiding the unnecessary blocks for lower resolutions

With media queries, we can hide content on screens with smaller resolutions, show content on screens with a higher resolution, or vice versa. The easiest way to hide images or unnecessary blocks of content on mobile devices is by using some Bootstrap classes that would suit this purpose.

The following table taken from Bootstrap documentation shows all the classes that you can use to show or hide elements:

	Extra small devices Phones (<768px)	Small devices Tablets (≥768px)	Medium devices Desktops (≥992px)	Large devices Desktops (≥1200px)
.visible-xs	Visible	Hidden	Hidden	Hidden
.visible-sm	Hidden	Visible	Hidden	Hidden
.visible-md	Hidden	Hidden	Visible	Hidden
.visible-lg	Hidden	Hidden	Hidden	Visible
.hidden-xs	Hidden	Visible	Visible	Visible
.hidden-sm	Visible	Hidden	Visible	Visible
.hidden-md	Visible	Visible	Hidden	Visible
.hidden-lg	Visible	Visible	Visible	Hidden

To learn more from Bootstrap, you can refer to its documentation by accessing the website (`http://getbootstrap.com/css/#responsive-utilities`) and navigating to **CSS | Responsive utilities**.

Flexible images

Another important task to do is to make all the images flexible. To make the images flexible, simply add the `img-thumbnail` class to the `<img>` elements.

The following simple example helps you understand better what the CSS class `img-thumbnail` can do.

As you can see in the following screenshot, the image with a width of 500 px inside `div` with the CSS class `col-md-4` is bigger than the container, and hence, it overflows:

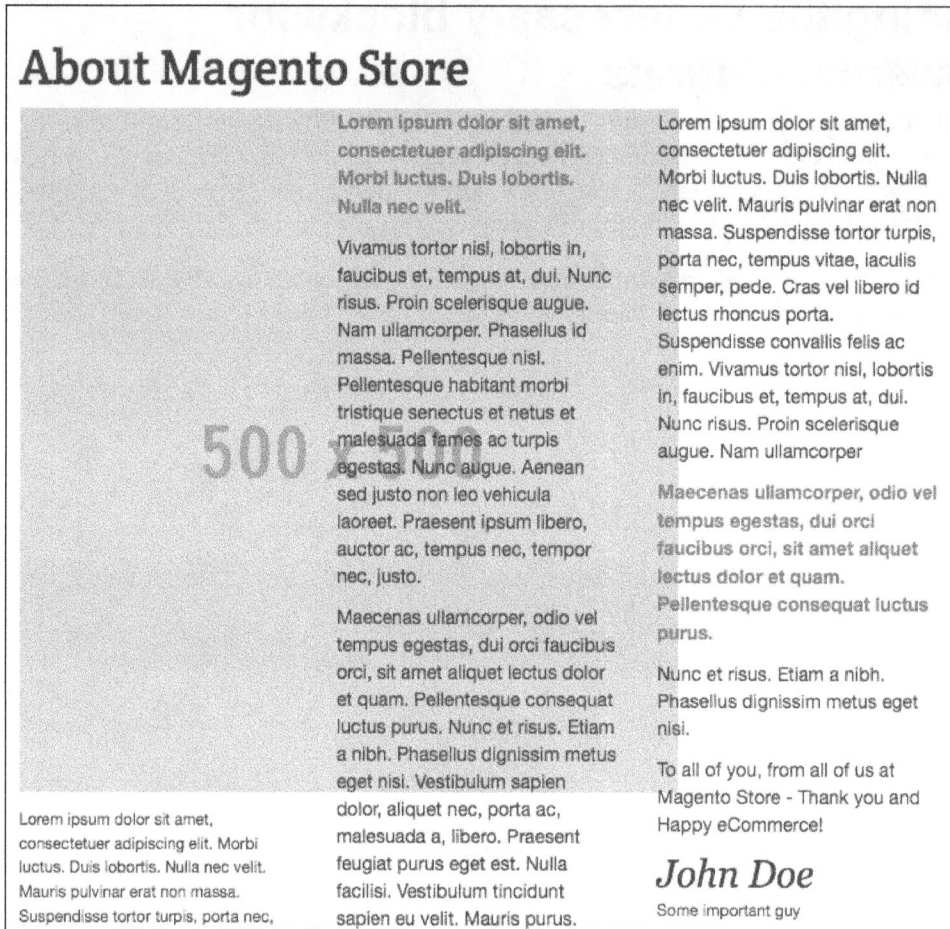

The test is conducted in the CMS page with the ID `about-magento-demo-store`, with the following code:

```
<div class="page-title">
<h1>About Magento Store</h1>
</div>

<div class="row">
  <div class="col-md-4">
    <a href="http://www.varien.com/">
    <img src="http://placehold.it/500x500" title="Varien"
```

```
        alt="Varien" class="img-responsive" />
    </a>
  </div>

  <div class="col-md-4">
  . . .
  </div>

  <div class="col-md-4">
  . . .
  </div>
</div>
```

To avoid the problem, add the `img-responsive` class to the image in the following way:

```
<img src="http://placehold.it/500x500" title="Varien" alt="Varien"
    class="img-thumbnail" />
```

The `img-responsive` class will adapt the width to the container, as you can see in the following screenshot:

Initial scale meta tag (iPhone)

On an iPhone, Safari shrinks HTML pages to fit into the iPhone screen. To avoid this, we can add a simple meta tag that tells the browser to use the width of the device as the width of the viewport and disable the initial scale, as follows:

```
<meta name="viewport" content="width=device-width; initial-
   scale=1.0">
```

If not already inserted, open the `head.phtml` file of your theme placed in `app/design/frontend/bookstore/default/template/page/html/` and insert the meta tag.

Adding mobile icons

Did you know that you can add custom home screen icons for iPhone, iPad, and other tablets or smartphones for your website?

If you have an iPhone, for example, you know that it has the possibility to save a site bookmark into the phone, which will be displayed as an app.

Now, we will learn how to create a custom icon and how to integrate it into the theme.

First, we need to know that there are several icon sizes that can be created, and the following are the most-used icon sizes:

- iPhone/iPod icon size: 60 x 60 px
- iPhone/iPod retina icon size: 120 x 10 px
- iPad icon size: 76 x 76 px
- iPad retina icon size: 152 x 152 px

You can see all the dimensions on the Apple Developer site at `https://developer.apple.com/library/ios/documentation/userexperience/conceptual/mobilehig/IconMatrix.html#//apple_ref/doc/uid/TP40006556-CH27-SW1`.

To create your custom icon, perform the following steps:

1. Download a free icon from `http://ios.robs.im/`. The mockup that comes in the PSD Photoshop version has been created by Rom Sim. So, open the site that you can see in the following screenshot:

2. Once you have downloaded a free icon, open it and look for the advanced object in the level. If you don't see the level window, navigate to **Window | Levels**.

3. Then, double click on the advanced object level called **Edit and Save**, as shown in the following screenshot:

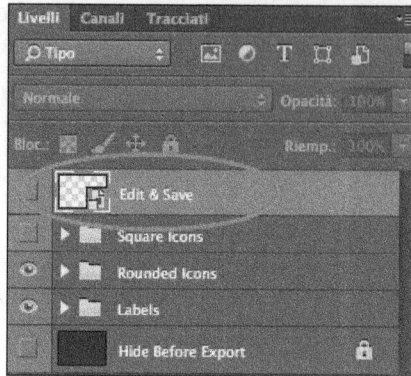

4. In the new page that opens, if you navigate through the levels, you can see some neat gradients that you can use. Now, insert your custom icon here, as you can see in the following screenshot:

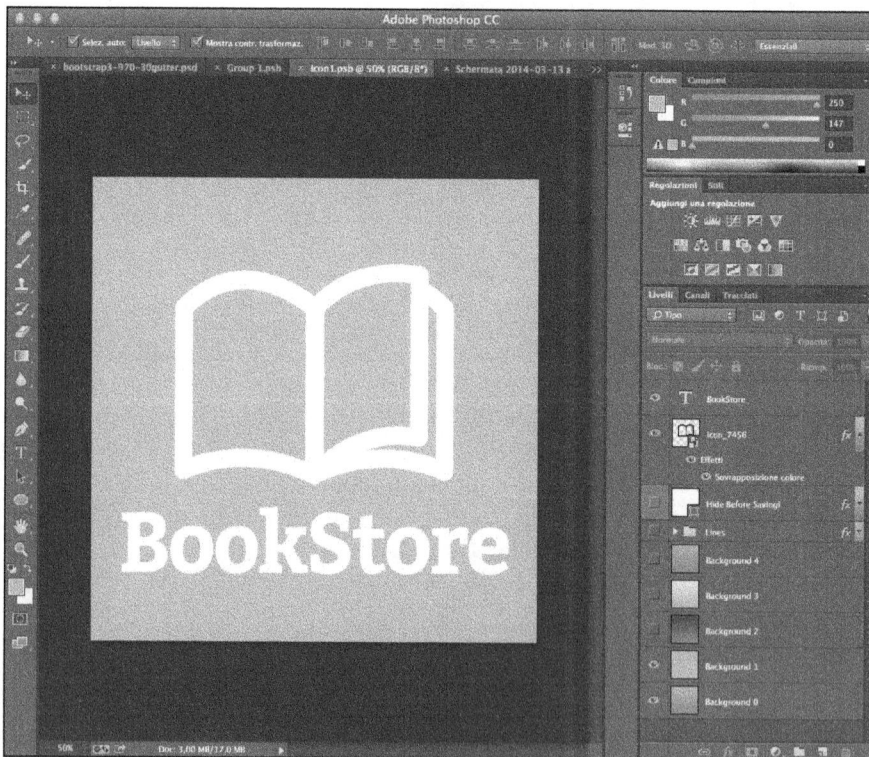

This is an example of what the screen in this program looks like.

5. Save and close the page.

6. Now, return to the full mockup, where you can see the icon in all the different sizes, as shown in the following screenshot:

7. Now, it's time to export the icons. Go to **File** | **Save** for Web and then hit **Save**. The document is set to export every icon automatically inside a folder called `App Icon`.

8. Once all the icons are saved, copy them into your theme `skin` folder in `skin/frontend/bookstore/default/images/app-icon/`.

9. Next, just add the following code in the `head.phtml` file, so the devices can find your icons' images. This file is located in `app/design/frontend/bookstore/default/template/page/html`:

```
<link href="<?php echo $this->getSkinUrl() ?>/images/app-
  icon/iPhone.png" rel="apple-touch-icon" />

<link href="<?php echo $this->getSkinUrl() ?>/images/app-
  icon/iPhone@2x.png" rel="apple-touch-icon"
  sizes="76x76" />

<link href="<?php echo $this->getSkinUrl() ?>/images/app-
  icon/apple-touch-icon-120x120.png" rel="apple-touch-icon"
  sizes="120x120" />
```

```
<link href="<?php echo $this->getSkinUrl() ?>/images/app-
   icon/iPad@2x.png" rel="apple-touch-icon" sizes=
   "152x152" />
```

10. Now, let's conduct a test. Open the site with your iPhone browser, Safari.

11. Then click on the icon highlighted in the following screenshot:

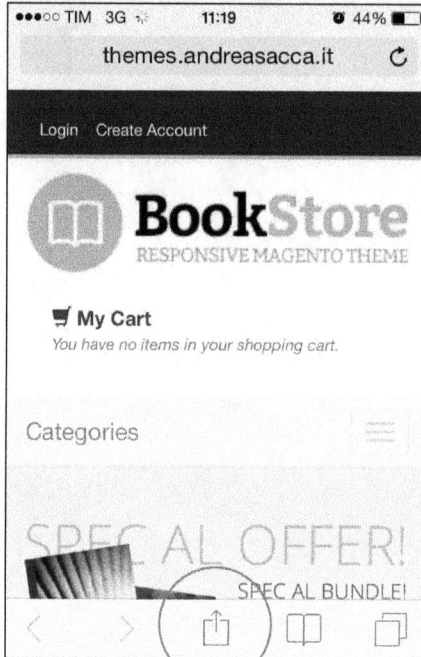

12. The panel shown in the following screenshot appears; click on the **Add to Home** button:

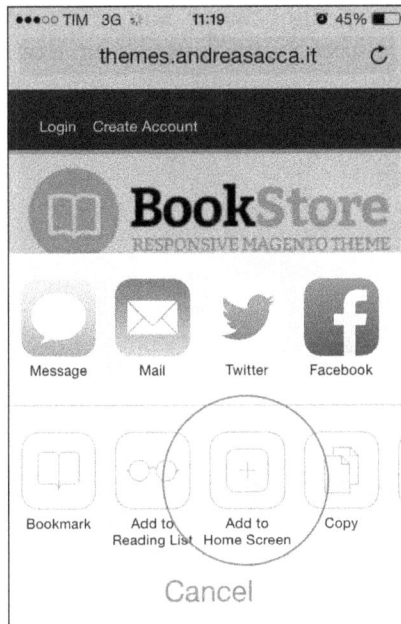

13. Now, if everything is working and the iPhone loads the icon correctly, you should see it in the next screen, as shown in the following screenshot. Here, you can also add a custom text.

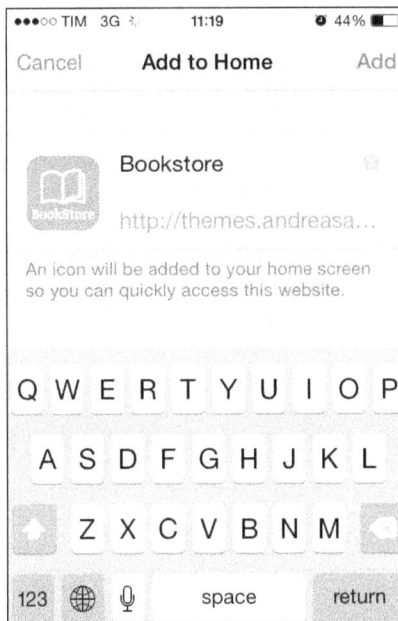

14. Click on **Add** on the top-right corner, and your site has now been added to your iPhone home screen with your custom icon, as shown in the following screenshot:

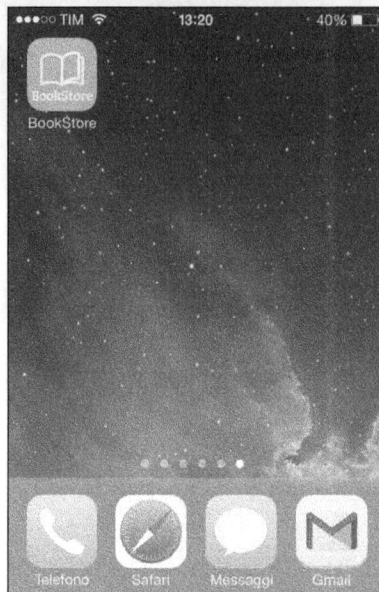

Summary

We have learned how to use media queries and the most important Bootstrap classes to optimize the theme to be fully responsive.

Using all these little tricks, the user experience will be better and optimized on every device used, such as smartphones, tablets, or desktops.

In the next chapter, we will see how to integrate social widgets into the theme and make it ready to share the products on the most important social networks such as Facebook, Twitter, Google+, and Pinterest.

6
Making the Theme Socially Ready

With the proliferation of social networks in recent years, all websites integrate buttons that allow users to share pages, images, and contents. This happens simply through social buttons such as the classic "Like", "Tweet", "Pin", and so on.

For an e-commerce site, this feature is very important because it allows you to create a network of connections that measures the site and the product's popularity on the Web.

In this chapter, we are going to learn how to integrate these buttons and how to insert social boxes, such as the classic Facebook Like box, into our theme.

The following is the list of topics that will be covered in the chapter:

- Introduction
- Integrating AddThis social sharing buttons
- Embedding the Facebook Like box

Getting started with social media integration

For our theme, we need to think carefully about where to place the blocks, because the position is important in order to create the right connections.

In our case, we need to focus attention on two positions:

- Social sharing for the whole website
- Social sharing and publicizing for the product

For the website, we can place the social buttons on the top header or on the footer, either with a link that links various social networks with the respective icons, or with the share link.

For the product, we have to add the feature of sharing, which will increase its possibility of purchase.

Integrating the social plugin in the product page

It is very important to integrate social media buttons into the product page; in fact, it is from this page that the user can share the product with his or her friends, increasing the possibility of purchase of the product.

To do this, we will use the excellent free service, AddThis. AddThis is a great ready-to-use plugin that allows you to add links to the social networks. You can either utilize the service for free, or you can register and create an account that will allow you access to advanced statistics.

Now we will perform the following steps to integrate the version without an account:

1. Open the **AddThis** site, scroll down and open the social sharing link, or click on the orange **Get the Code** button on the top-right corner and select **Share Buttons**, as shown in the following screenshot:

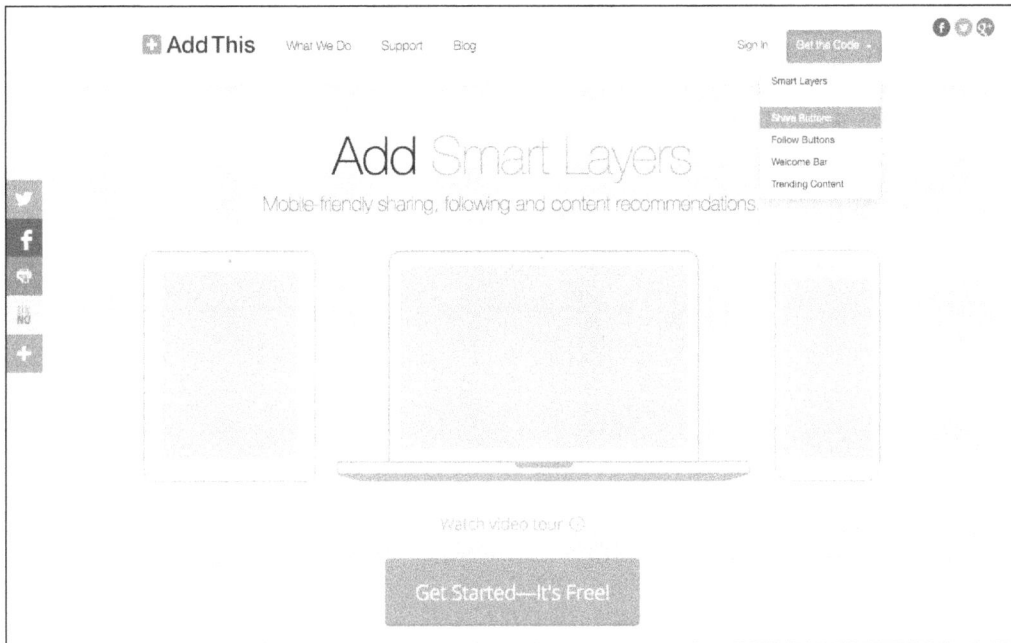

You can integrate **Add This** manually, or you can use one of the premade extensions.

It is easy to install the extension because you can install a simple Magento module; however, we will learn how to integrate it manually, so you can distribute it with your theme without additional extensions. In fact, sometimes you cannot distribute the theme with third-party extensions because of license terms.

2. On the next page, select **A Website** on the left-hand side, and then select the style of the buttons that you want to add to your site. As you can see in the following screenshot, you can select some options to customize the appearance of the widget:

Share Buttons

Increase traffic and engagement with the world's most popular sharing buttons for sites, blogs, and even newsletters. Available for WordPress, Tumblr, and more.

Get the Code   Features   API

Options

Get sharing buttons for

- ◉ 🌐 A Website
- ○ Ⓦ WordPress
- ○ 📄 Blogger
- ○ ✉ Email Newsletter

More options...

Select style

- ◉ 👍 Like 🐦 Tweet 📌 Pin it ⊕ Share 1.7M
- ○ 📘📘📘📘📘 832
- ○ 📘📘📘📘📘 832
- ○ ⊂ SHARE 📘📘📘
- ○ 👍 3K ○ 📘 ○ 📘
      👍 Like   📘   📘
      316   📘   📘

Preview

👍 Like 84k 🐦 Tweet 10.2K ✕ ⊕ Share 2.2M

AddThis boosts sharing by automatically showing the right buttons to each user based on their location and activity across the web. Dismiss and select your own buttons.

Add to your site

Copy and paste the code below into your page between the <body> and </body> tags. The buttons will appear wherever you place them. Want to customize? Use our API.

| Sign In | Create Account |

Choose the second option, the one with the large icons, under the **Select style** section, as you can see in the following screenshot:

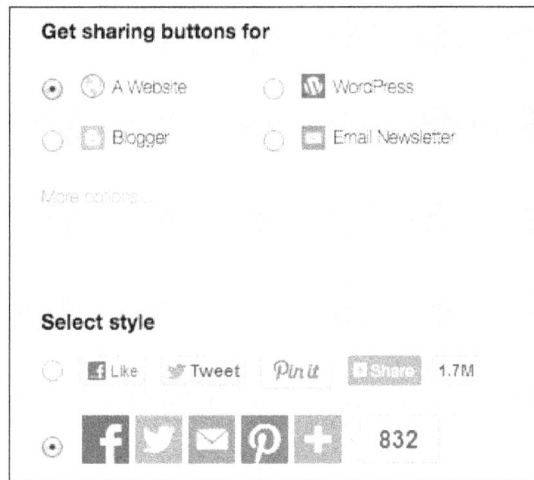

3. Now, towards the right-hand side of the screen, check the live preview of the buttons. You can leave it as it is, or you can choose different buttons for your plugin. To select the social buttons, click on the **Disable and select your own buttons** link, as shown in the following screenshot:

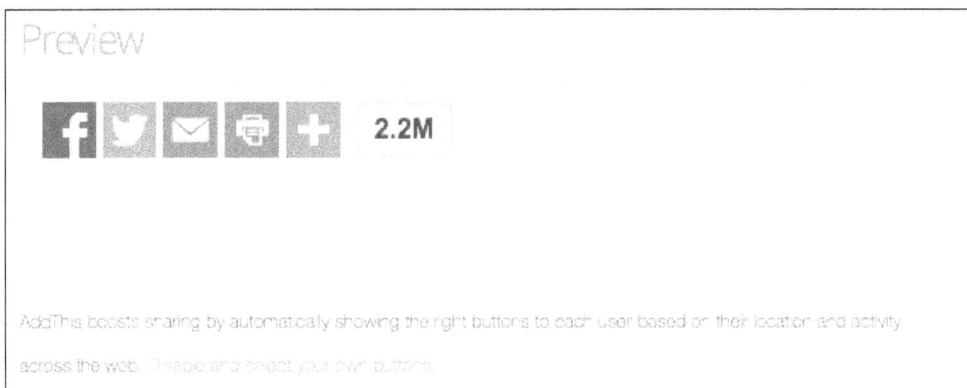

4. As you can see, a new box appears to give you the option to choose a custom selection of buttons. In this case, choose Facebook, Twitter, Pinterest, and Google+ buttons, as shown in the following screenshot:

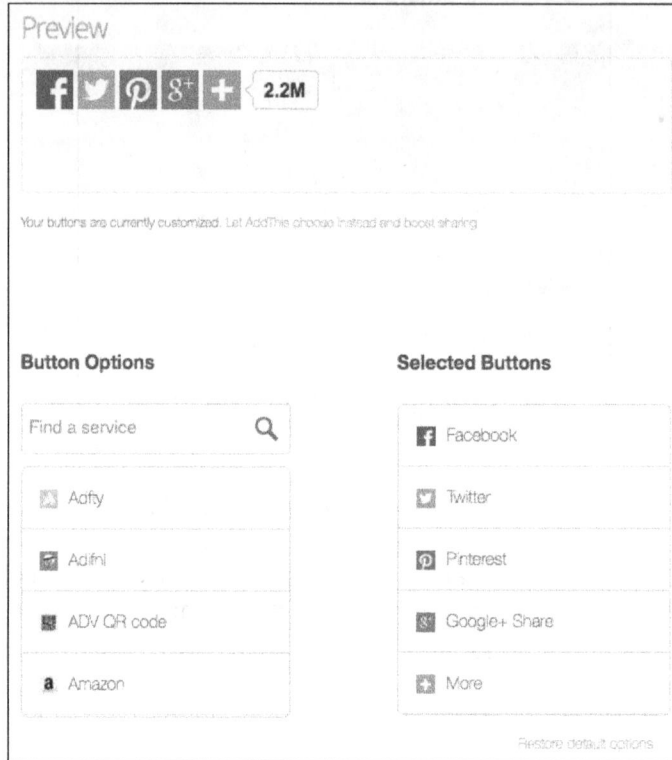

Preview

f 🐦 🅿 8+ ➕ ‹ 2.2M

Your buttons are currently customized. Let AddThis choose instead and boost sharing.

Button Options

Find a service 🔍

🖼 Aofy

🖼 Adifni

▦ ADV QR code

a Amazon

Selected Buttons

f Facebook

🐦 Twitter

🅿 Pinterest

8+ Google+ Share

➕ More

Restore default options

5. Now, it's time to code. Sign in, then copy and paste the code that appears in the box into your page. You can use the code inside a CMS page or copy it into a template file of your theme, just where you want to make it appear. As you can see in the following screenshot, the code to grab is inside a yellow box:

```
Add to your site

Copy and paste the code below into your page between the <body> and </body>
tags. The buttons will appear wherever you place them. Want to customize? Use
our API.

<!-- AddThis Button BEGIN -->
<div class="addthis_toolbox addthis_default_style addthis_32x32_style">
<a class="addthis_button_facebook"></a>
<a class="addthis_button_twitter"></a>
<a class="addthis_button_pinterest_share"></a>
<a class="addthis_button_google_plusone_share"></a>
<a class="addthis_button_compact"></a><a class="addthis_counter addthis_b
</div>
<script type="text/javascript">var addthis_config = {"data_track_addressb
<script type="text/javascript" src="//s7.addthis.com/js/300/addthis_widge
<!-- AddThis Button END -->
```

Grab It   By publishing this code, you are accepting our Terms of Service.

6. Now copy the code created by the site:

```html
<div class="social-sharing">

  <!-- AddThis Button BEGIN -->
  <div class="addthis_toolbox addthis_default_style
    addthis_32x32_style">
    <a class="addthis_button_facebook"></a>
    <a class="addthis_button_twitter"></a>
    <a class="addthis_button_pinterest_share"></a>
    <a class="addthis_button_google_plusone_share"></a>
    <a class="addthis_button_compact"></a>
      <a class="addthis_counter addthis_bubble_style"></a>
  </div>
  <script type="text/javascript">var addthis_config =
    {"data_track_addressbar":true};</script>
  <script type="text/javascript"
    src="//s7.addthis.com/js/300/addthis_widget.js#pubid=ra-
    5023e72a4129d9cf"></script>
  <!-- AddThis Button END -->
</div>
```

Integrating the code in the product page

Let's suppose that we want to add the code only in the product page. To do this, perform the following steps:

1. Go to your theme folders and create a file called `addthis.phtml` in `app/design/frontend/bookstore/default/template/social`.

2. Paste the copied code, as mentioned in the previous section, in the file and save it.

3. Now, we need to open the `local.xml` file and find the `<catalog_product_view>` product view handle (for your reference, this handle is defined first inside the `catalog.xml` file of the base theme in `app/design/frontend/base/default/layout`) and inside it, in `<reference name="content">`, add the following code that will declare a `core/template` block to be displayed on the product page:

   ```
   <reference name="content">
   <block type="core/template" name="socialsharing"
     template="social/addthis.phtml" before="-" />
   </reference>
   ```

   Now, open the file of the product page, `view.phtml`, located in `app/design/frontend/bookstore/default/template/catalog/product/view.phtml`.

4. If you don't have the `view.phtml` file already in the folder, you can create it, or to test all the features of the product page, copy it from the base theme in `app/design/frontend/base/default/template/catalog/product`.

5. Place the following `php` statement that will generate the code of the `addthis.html` file just inside the `div` tag with the `product-img-box` CSS class:

   ```
   <?php echo $this->getChildHtml('socialsharing') ?>
   ```

6. To position the block in the breadcrumbs line, add styles with the following code:

   ```
   .container { position: relative; }
   .social-sharing { position:absolute; top:10px; right: 15px; }
   ```

7. Now you are done! Open the product page and you will see the social sharing buttons where you have placed them, on the right-hand side area, as shown in the following screenshot:

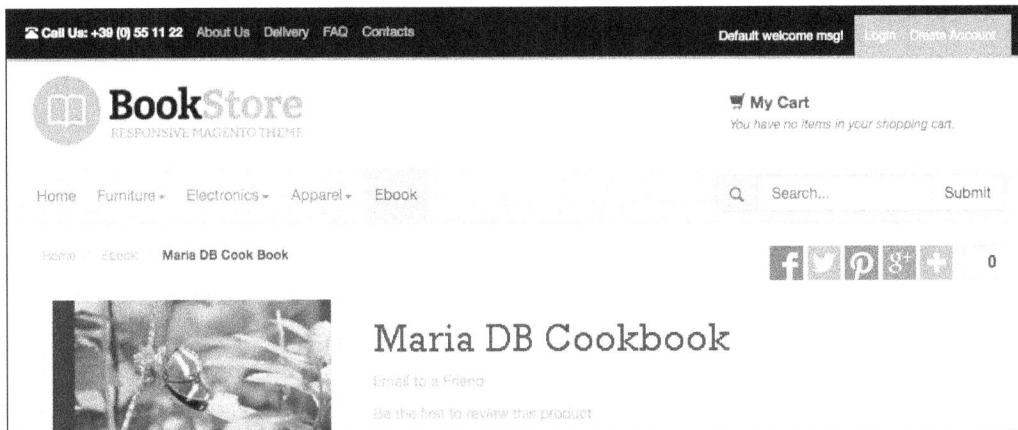

As you can see the social sharing buttons are positioned on the right of the window, after the search box.

Now let's test all the buttons.

Facebook's Like button

After clicking on the Facebook icon, a pop up will appear. The user can add some extra information in the pop up before posting the product on the page. Consider the following screenshot:

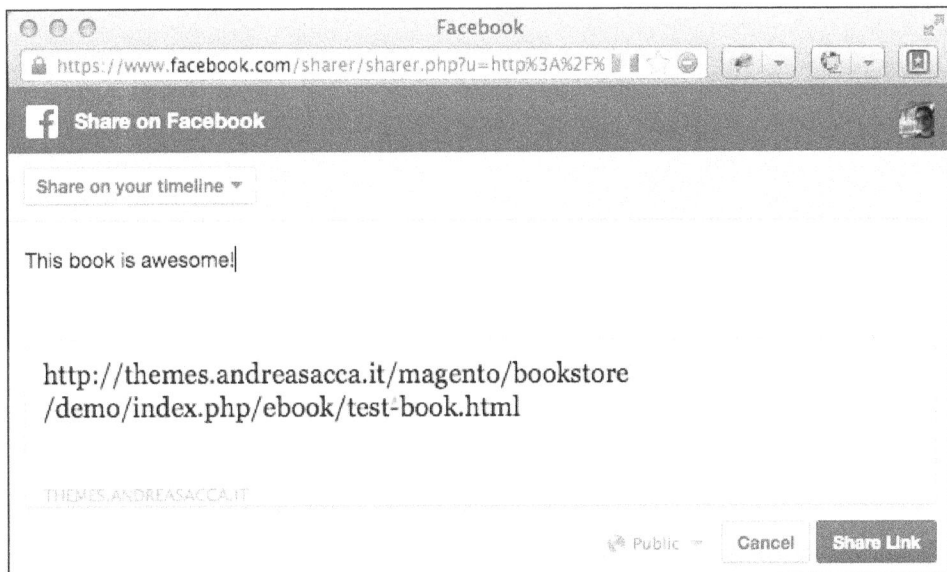

Twitter's Tweet button

After clicking on the Twitter icon, a pop up will appear. Through the pop up, you can write your own hashtag and tweet before sending the link, as shown in the following screenshot:

Pinterest's Pin button

Now if you click on the Pinterest button, you can see that the pop up will appear as a Lightbox, and here you will have the option to select the image to pin on the social networking site, as shown in the following screenshot:

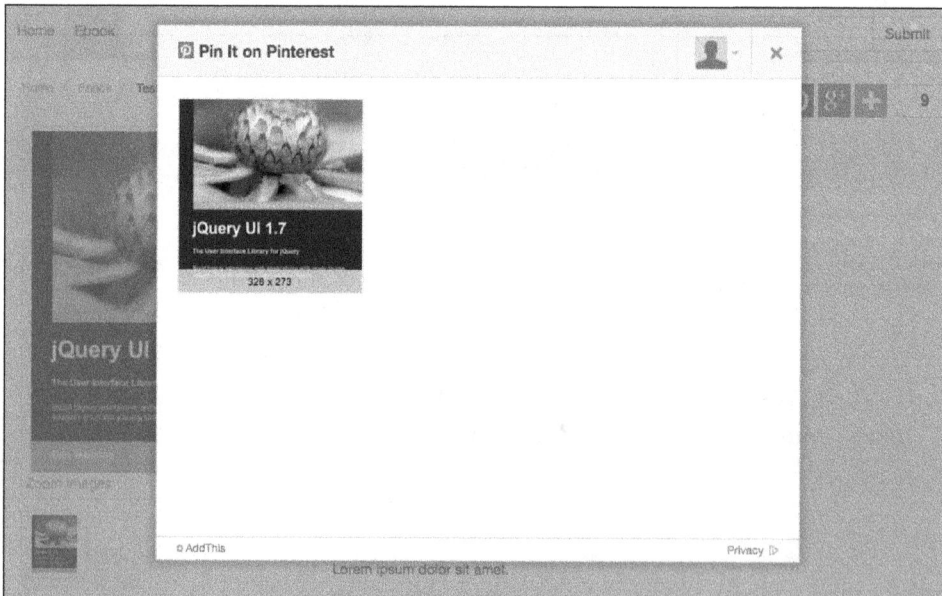

The Google+ button

After clicking on the Google+ button, a pop up will appear, just like when the Facebook and Twitter buttons were clicked on, as shown in the following screenshot:

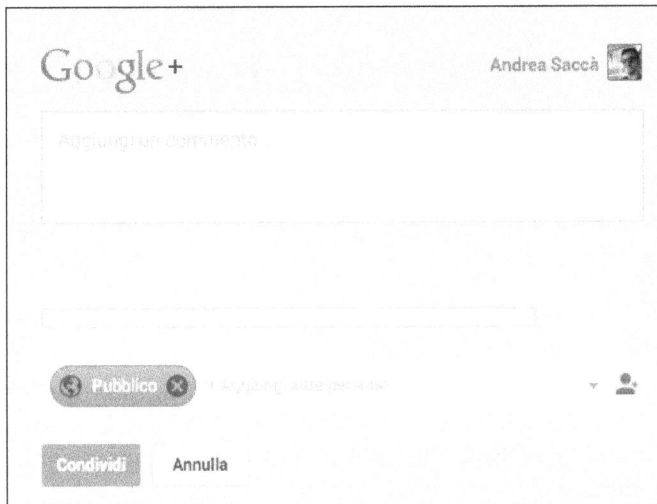

The + button

At the end of the list, you can see the icon with a + sign, which indicates that you can share the page through other services, as shown in the following screenshot:

> If you explore the **AddThis** social website, you will find a lot of neat social sharing add-ons that will help you integrate code in your site or theme.

Adding the Facebook Like box to the left sidebar

You have surely seen Facebook with the Like button and the classic box with smileys on a fan page. Now we are going to insert them in our theme in the left sidebar by performing the following steps:

1. First, you need to go to `https://developers.facebook.com/docs/plugins/like-box-for-pages/`.

2. Then, set all the parameters to customize your Like box. Set **Width**, **Height**, and the other options. In the **Facebook Page URL** option, you can add your Facebook page link. The following screenshot shows the plugin configuration page:

Like Box

The Like Box is a special version of the Like Button designed only for Facebook Pages. It allows admins to promote their Pages and embed a simple feed of content from a Page into other sites.

Facebook Page URL

http://www.facebook.com/FacebookDevelopers

Width

232

Height

250

Color Scheme

light

☑ Show Friends' Faces

☐ Show Posts

☐ Show Header

☐ Show Border

Facebook Developers
☑ Mi piace Ti piace.

Facebook Developers piace a te e altre
2.756.584 persone.

Plug-in sociale di Facebook

Get Code

After you have inserted all the fields, click on the blue button to get the code. In the pop up that appears, as shown in the following screenshot, select **HTML5**:

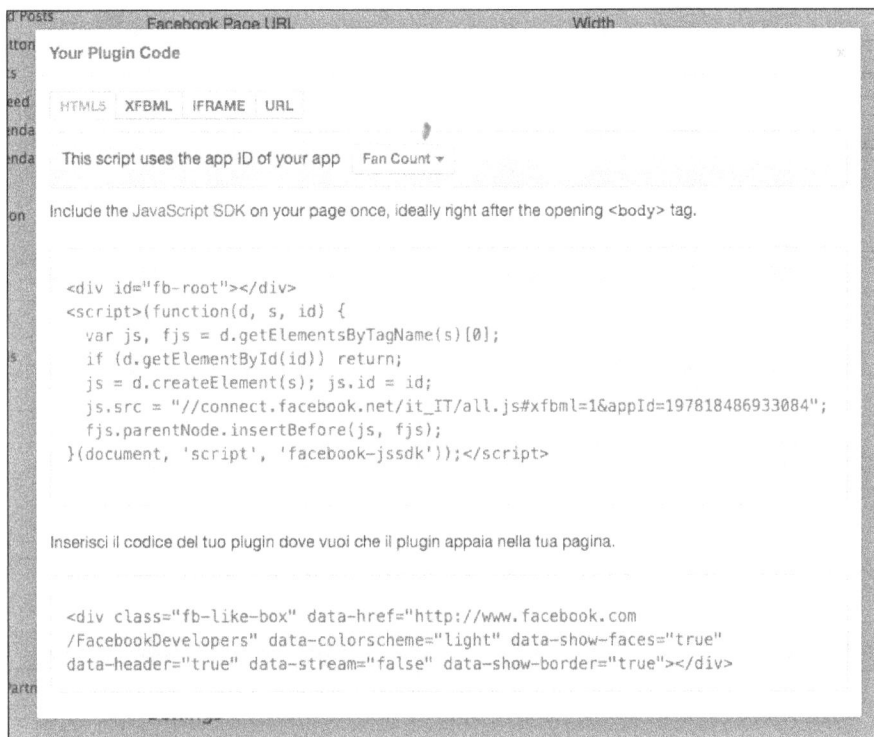

3. To enable the Lightbox script, you need an API key. You can get this at `http://www.facebook.com/developers/apps.php`, and create a new Facebook application.

4. Once you create your app, select the application from the drop-down list, and your code is ready to use.

Installing the Like box on your site

Now we have to insert the code in the theme's left sidebar. To do this, perform the following steps:

1. Copy the following code generated in the Facebook Like box page:

```
<div class="social-facebooklikebox">
  <div id="fb-root"></div>
  <script>(function(d, s, id) {
```

```
   var js, fjs = d.getElementsByTagName(s)[0];
   if (d.getElementById(id)) return;
   js = d.createElement(s); js.id = id;
   js.src =
      "//connect.facebook.net/it_IT/all.js#xfbml=1&appId=
      XXXXXXXXXXXXXX";
   fjs.parentNode.insertBefore(js, fjs);
 }(document, 'script', 'facebook-jssdk'));</script>

<div class="fb-like-box" data-
   href="http://www.facebook.com/YourFanPageUrl" data-
   colorscheme="light" data-show-faces="true" data-
   header="true" data-stream="false" data-show-
   border="true"></div>
</div>
```

> XXXXXXXXXXXXXX is your API key and `YourFanPageUrl` is the
> URL of your Facebook fan page.

2. Now, go to your theme folders and create a file called `facebooklikebox.phtml` in `app/design/frontend/bookstore/default/template/social/`.

3. Paste the copied code of step 1 in the file and save it.

4. Now, to declare a `core/template` block to be displayed in the left sidebar, open the `local.xml` file, find the `<default>` default handle, and in the reference name, place the following code:

```
<block type="core/template" name="socialsharing" template="social/
facebooklikebox.phtml" after="-" />
```

5. Now you are done. Open the product page and you will see the social sharing buttons where you placed them!

As you can see in the following screenshot, the Like box will appear on the left sidebar column.

Summary

You know that the social media sharing option is a must for an e-commerce website and, in this chapter, we have learned how to integrate this interesting and always popular feature into the theme with custom PHTML files and blocks in an XML file.

Using AddThis, you can choose the best social sharing solution for the theme or for your customer and following the same block of steps, integrate other kinds of dynamic or static content into the theme.

In the next chapter, we will learn how to create a Magento widget to allow store managers and business users with no technical knowledge to add the same social sharing icon buttons in a CMS page or static blocks.

Creating a Magento Widget

7

The Magento Community Edition Version 1.4 introduces a new concept of customizable widgets that provides more control over the user experience.

In this chapter, we will learn how to create two simple widgets that will include the social sharing functionality. In this way, the store manager will be able to insert the social share buttons in every CMS page from the admin panel in just a few seconds.

The following topics will be covered in this chapter:

- Getting started with the Magento widget
- Developing a widget
- Creating a widget with options
- Adding a widget in the admin panel

Getting started with Magento widgets

Magento widgets allow the administrator of the store with no technical knowledge to easily add dynamic content (for example, including product data) to the pages in Magento stores.

The following screenshot represents the Magento widget logo:

In this way, you can add the following dynamic content into the website through the administrator panel:

- Dynamic product data and information in CMS pages
- Promotional images to position in different CMS blocks
- External elements and action blocks such as subscription forms or videos
- Social media sharing links

We have already learned how to integrate social media buttons into our theme in the product page in *Chapter 6, Making the Theme Socially Ready*. Now we are going to create a simple widget that inserts the social sharing icons into CMS pages within a few seconds, without having programming knowledge.

Developing a widget

The method of developing a widget does not differ much from that of developing a regular Magento module. In a few words, a Magento widget is a Magento module that generates admin add-ons, which you can easily insert into CMS pages or CMS blocks with simple actions.

We will start by creating a sample module that provides one simple widget.

The widget called **Social Widget Icons** outputs a block that includes the **AddThis** social sharing icons, the same sharing icons that we added in *Chapter 6, Making the Theme Socially Ready*.

The final frontend result is shown by the following screenshot:

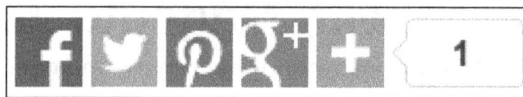

Creating an empty module

Let's start by creating the module's directory structure and the main files. The module `folder` must be located into `app/code`.

Here, you have to decide in which code pool you want to create the module. Usually, you can create your module under the local code pool.

> Never create a module inside the core folder of Magento and never edit the files inside the core. It can compromise the full store.

The following screenshot will show you the folder and the files that you need to create this widget:

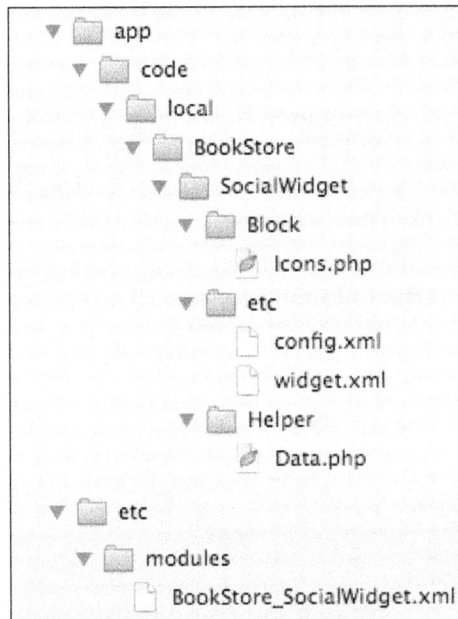

```
▼ 📁 app
    ▼ 📁 code
        ▼ 📁 local
            ▼ 📁 BookStore
                ▼ 📁 SocialWidget
                    ▼ 📁 Block
                            📄 Icons.php
                    ▼ 📁 etc
                            📄 config.xml
                            📄 widget.xml
                    ▼ 📁 Helper
                            📄 Data.php
    ▼ 📁 etc
        ▼ 📁 modules
                📄 BookStore_SocialWidget.xml
```

You can create all the folders and the files that you can see in the preceding screenshot, and then perform the following steps to create each file of the module:

1. Now that we created the module, open the `BookStore_SocialWidget.xml` file located in the `etc` folder, and create the file that will enable the module with the following code:

```xml
<?xml version="1.0"?>
<config>
  <modules>
    <BookStore_SocialWidget>
      <active>true</active>
      <codePool>local</codePool>
      <depends>
        <Mage_Cms/>
      </depends>
    </BookStore_SocialWidget>
  </modules>
</config>
```

> By changing `<active>true</active>` to `<active>false</active>`, you can enable or disable the module. This file is the same for each module; so, if you want to enable or disable some module, you can do so in this way.

2. Now, let's create the default module `Helper`. The default helper should be defined to make the translation subsystem work properly. You need not write any code here; you only need to define a class that extends the core helper, `Mage_Core_Helper_Abstract`.

   Open the `Data.php` file in app/code/local/BookStore/SocialWidget/Helper/ and insert the following code:

   ```php
   <?php
   /**
    * BookStore Social Widget
    */
   class BookStore_SocialWidget_Helper_Data extends Mage_Core_Helper_
     Abstract
   {
   }
   ```

> If you don't create this file with the preceding code, the system will generate an error.

3. Now to set up the module configuration, we need to create the configuration file called `config.xml`. Every module has this file and it contains a lot of information such as the module version and the default configurations. It is also used to define the helper and blocks' base class names.

   So, let's create the `config.xml` file in app/code/local/BookStore/SocialWidget/etc/ with the following code:

   ```xml
   <?xml version="1.0"?>
   <config>
     <modules>
       <BookStore_SocialWidget>
         <version>0.0.1</version>
       </BookStore_SocialWidget>
     </modules>
     <global>
       <helpers>
         <socialwidget>
           <class>BookStore_SocialWidget_Helper</class>
   ```

```
    </socialwidget>
  </helpers>
  <blocks>
    <socialwidget>
      <class>BookStore_SocialWidget_Block</class>
    </socialwidget>
  </blocks>
  </global>
</config>
```

4. Then, we need to declare the widgets. All the widgets provided by the module must be declared in the `widget.xml` file that is located inside the `etc` folder with the the `config.xml` file. In the `widget.xml` file you created, insert the following code that defines a single widget:

```xml
<?xml version="1.0"?>
<widgets>
    <socialwidget_icons type="socialwidget/icons">
        <name>Social Sharing Type: Icons</name>
        <description type="desc">Adds social sharing with
          Icons</description>
    </socialwidget_icons>
</widgets>
```

Of course you can define multiple widgets in the same file, for example:

```xml
<?xml version="1.0"?>
<widgets>
    <socialwidget_icons type="socialwidget/icons">
        <name>Social Sharing Type: Icons</name>
        <description type="desc">Adds social sharing with
          Icons</description>
    </socialwidget_icons>
    <socialwidget_buttons type="socialwidget/buttons">
        <name>Social Sharing Type: Buttons</name>
        <description type="desc">Adds social sharing with
          classics Buttons</description>
    </socialwidget_buttons>
</widgets>
```

Now we will work with a single widget definition as the first example. As you can see from the preceding code, the widget instance must contain the following information:

- A unique name node used in the system (in our case, `socialwidget_icons`)
- The widget `name`
- The `type="..."` attribute
- A short description of the widget

5. We will now create the frontend blocks for our widgets.

We will create the code that will return an output of the widget in the frontend. To do this, open the `Icons.php` file you created in `app/code/local/BookStore/SocialWidget/Block/Icons.php` and add the following code:

```php
<?php
class BookStore_SocialWidget_Block_Buttons extends
  Mage_Core_Block_Abstract implements
  Mage_Widget_Block_Interface
{

    protected function _toHtml()
    {
      $html = ' . . .';   // code to be displayed in the
        frontend
      return $html;
    }
}
```

We have just created a class that implements an interface, but we don't have all the methods of that interface because they are already implemented in the ancestors of the `method toHtml()` class, which is implemented in `Mage_Core_Block_Abstract`.

6. Now that we have created the frontend block, we need to insert the expected output into HTML. As planned, we want to add the `addthis` code in the `Icons.php` file inside the `$html` variable. The following code is the same code used in *Chapter 6, Making the Theme Socially Ready*:

```html
<!-- AddThis Button BEGIN -->
<div class="addthis_toolbox addthis_default_style
  addthis_32x32_style">
<a class="addthis_button_facebook"></a>
<a class="addthis_button_twitter"></a>
```

```
<a class="addthis_button_pinterest_share"></a>
<a class="addthis_button_google_plusone_share"></a>
<a class="addthis_button_compact"></a><a class="addthis_counter
addthis_bubble_style"></a>
</div>
<script type="text/javascript" src="//s7.addthis.com/js/300/
addthis_widget.js#pubid=xa-
   52cae78918520295"></script>
<!-- AddThis Button END -->
```

7. Simply copy the code, insert it into the $html variable, and save the Icons. php file, which should look like the following code:

```php
<?php
class BookStore_SocialWidget_Block_Icons extends
  Mage_Core_Block_Abstract implements
  Mage_Widget_Block_Interface
{

protected function _toHtml() {

$html ='<!-- AddThis Button BEGIN -->
<div class="addthis_toolbox addthis_default_style
  addthis_32x32_style">
<a class="addthis_button_facebook"></a>
<a class="addthis_button_twitter"></a>
<a class="addthis_button_pinterest_share"></a>
<a class="addthis_button_google_plusone_share"></a>
<a class="addthis_button_compact"></a><a
  class="addthis_counter addthis_bubble_style"></a>
</div>
<script type="text/javascript" src=
  "//s7.addthis.com/js/300/addthis_widget.js#pubid=xa-
  52cae78918520295"></script>
<!-- AddThis Button END -->';

return $html;

 }
}
```

Adding the widget to the CMS page

Now our first widget is completed, and we are done with programming. Let's go to the admin panel and check if our brand new widget is available to be added to either a CMS page or a static block. To do this, follow these steps:

1. Let's go to **CMS** | **Pages** in the admin panel and add the widget instance on the **About Us** page. Open it from the list of CMS pages, and click on the **Content** tab on the left.

   If you have the **WYSIWYG** editor enabled to insert the widget, click on the second button on the left, the one with the Magento logo icon, as shown in the following screenshot:

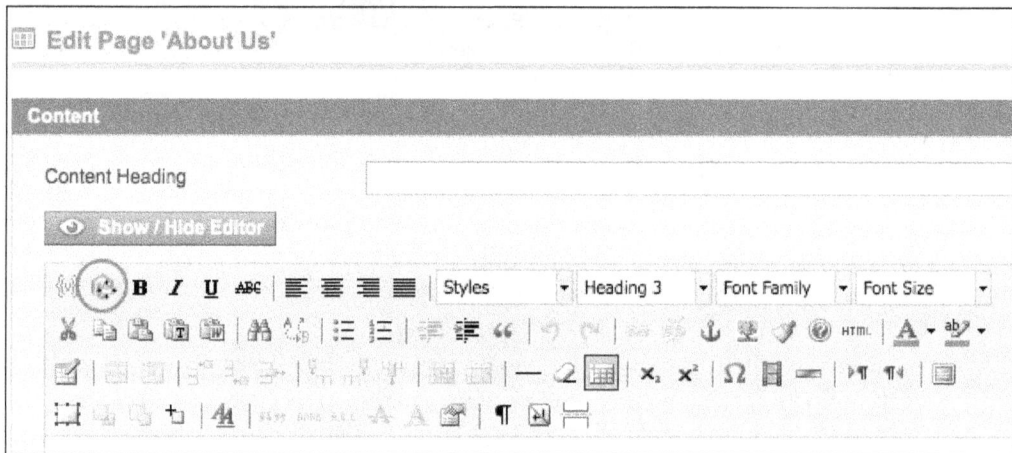

   Otherwise, click on the **Insert Widget** button with the editor disabled, as shown in the following screenshot:

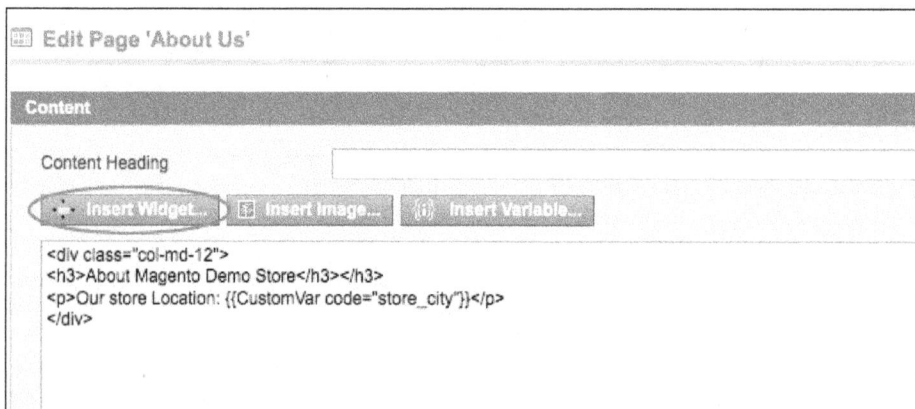

A widget selection and configuration pop-up opens with the options of all the available widgets.

2. Select the new widget **Social Sharing Type: Icons** and click on the **Insert Widget** button.

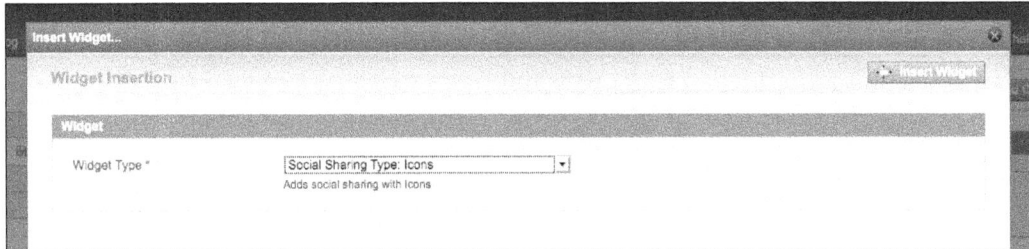

As you can see in the CMS page content, the result is a short piece of code that calls the widget:

```
{{widget type="socialwidget/icons"}}
```

With the editor enabled, you will see an icon that indicates the presence of a widget, as shown in the following screenshot:

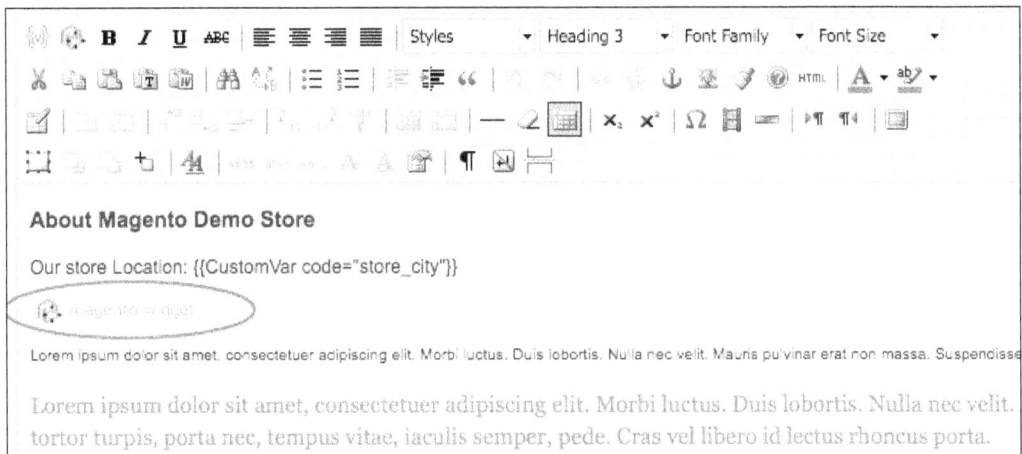

3. Open the page at the frontend and you will see the social sharing icons where you placed the widget.

We are done! We've just created our first Magento widget.

Creating a widget with options

If you select one of the existing widgets, you can see that some of them come with configurations options. The widget we created is very basic and now we are going to see how to add some simple options that will allow the store manager to customize the frontend block. The plan is to allow the user to choose which services to display on the frontend.

The options we are going to insert are as follows:

- One checkbox option that shows or hides the shares count bubble
- One input textbox that allows you to insert a block title

Adding options to our widget.xml

To add some options to our widget, you need to edit the `widget.xml` file by adding the following parameters:

- `required`: This is used to define if an option is required or not
- `visible`: This is used to set the visibility of an option
- `label`: This is used to set the option title
- `type`: This is used to set the type of the option (checkbox, text, and so on)

To start adding options to the widget, return to the `widget.xml` file and inside the first widget, insert the following highlighted code just after the `</description>` tag:

```
<socialwidget_share type="socialwidget/share" translate="name
  description" module="socialwidget">
<name>Social Sharing Widget (with options)</name>
<description type="desc">Adds social sharing
  services</description>

<parameters>

    <block_title translate="Block Title">
      <required>1</required>
      <visible>1</visible>
      <label>Block Title</label>
      <type>text</type>
    </block_title>

    <show_count>
      <required>0</required>
      <visible>1</visible>
```

```
        <label>Show Share Count Bubble</label>
        <type>checkbox</type>
        <value>true</value>
    </show_count>

  </parameters>

</socialwidget_share>
```

As you can see, the `<parameters>` block contains the two options.

Our final `widget.xml` file should now contain the following code:

```
<?xml version="1.0"?>
<widgets>

  <socialwidget_icons type="socialwidget/icons">
    <name>Social Sharing Type: Icons</name>
    <description type="desc">Adds social sharing with
      Icons</description>
  </socialwidget_icons>

  <socialwidget_share type="socialwidget/share" translate="name
    description" module="socialwidget">
  <name>Social Sharing Widget (with options)</name>
  <description type="desc">Adds social sharing
    services</description>

    <parameters>

      <block_title translate="Block Title">
        <required>1</required>
        <visible>1</visible>
        <label>Block Title</label>
        <type>text</type>
      </block_title>

      <show_count>
        <visible>1</visible>
        <label>Show Share Count Bubble</label>
        <type>checkbox</type>
        <value>true</value>
      </show_count>

    </parameters>
```

```
    </socialwidget_share>

  </widgets>
```

Creating the frontend widget block

As we have seen previously, we need to create a block that generates the code in the frontend. In this case, we insert some conditions to display the user choice. To create the block, perform the following steps:

1. Open or create the `Share.php` file in `app/code/local/BookStore/SocialWidget/Block` and insert the following code:

```php
<?php
class BookStore_SocialWidget_Block_Share extends
  Mage_Core_Block_Abstract implements
  Mage_Widget_Block_Interface
{

protected function _toHtml() {

}
}
```

2. Then, inside the `_toHtml` function, we first retrieve the data from the options we created in the XML file, in the following way:

```php
$block_title = $this->getData('block_title');
$show_count = $this->getData('show_count');
```

3. Then, we create a condition to check the checkbox value to enable or disable the social count bubble:

```php
$bubblecode = "";
if($show_count=='true')$bubblecode = "<a
  class='addthis_counter addthis_bubble_style'></a>";
```

4. Finally, we generate the output in HTML with the following variables:

```php
$html = '<div class="social-share">
<div class="block-title"><strong>'. $block_title
  .'</strong></div>';

$html .='
<div class="addthis_toolbox addthis_default_style
  addthis_32x32_style">
<a class="addthis_button_facebook"></a>
```

```
    <a class="addthis_button_twitter"></a>
    <a class="addthis_button_pinterest_share"></a>
    <a class="addthis_button_google_plusone_share"></a>
    <a class="addthis_button_compact"></a>'.$bubblecode.'
    </div>
    <script type="text/javascript" src="//s7.addthis.com/js/300/
    addthis_widget.js#pubid=xa-
      52cae78918520295"></script>

    </div>';

    return $html;
```

We are done! We have created our widget with options! The full code of the Share.
php file is as follows:

```php
<?php
class BookStore_SocialWidget_Block_Share extends
  Mage_Core_Block_Abstract implements Mage_Widget_Block_Interface
{

protected function _toHtml() {

// Get Widget Data
$block_title = $this->getData('block_title');
$show_count = $this->getData('show_count');

// Variable that contains the bubble count code
$bubblecode = "";
if($show_count=='true')$bubblecode = "<a class='addthis_counter
  addthis_bubble_style'></a>";

$html = '<div class="social-share">
<div class="block-title"><strong>'. $block_title
  .'</strong></div>';

$html .='
<div class="addthis_toolbox addthis_default_style
  addthis_32x32_style">
<a class="addthis_button_facebook"></a>
<a class="addthis_button_twitter"></a>
<a class="addthis_button_pinterest_share"></a>
<a class="addthis_button_google_plusone_share"></a>
<a class="addthis_button_compact"></a>'.$bubblecode.'
</div>
```

```
<script type="text/javascript" src=
  "//s7.addthis.com/js/300/addthis_widget.js#pubid=xa-
  52cae78918520295"></script>

</div>';

return $html;
  }
}
```

Adding the widget in the admin panel

Now that the widget has been created, let's perform the following steps to add it in the admin panel:

1. Let's go to **CMS** | **Pages** in the admin panel and add a widget instance to the **About Us** page in a WYSIWYG editor or plain text mode, and select the new widget **Social Sharing Widget (with options)**. Once loaded, you can see the options as shown in the following screenshot:

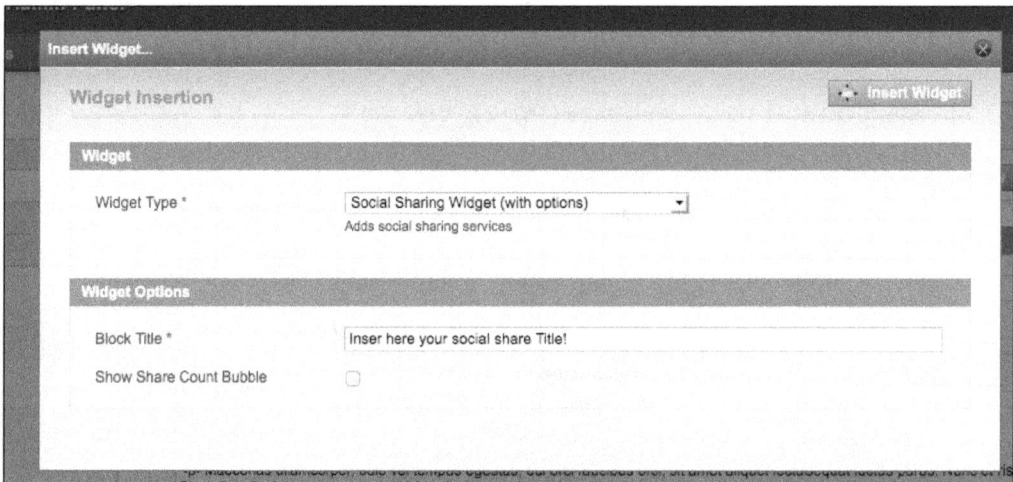

2. Insert the title that you prefer into the block.
3. Then, leave **Show Share Count Bubble** unchecked.
4. Click the **Insert Widget** button, and the following code will be added into the page code:

    ```
    {{widget type="socialwidget/share" block_title=
      "Inser here your social share Title!"}}
    ```

5. Now, save the page and go to the frontend. You will see the social sharing options with the custom title and the social share count bubble disabled, as shown in the following screenshot:

Summary

As you can see, it is not so hard to create a Magento widget. The Magento widgets allow you to insert neat add-ons that will add value to your theme.

This is a very simple example of what you can do with widgets. You can try to create a more advanced and complex one that includes more options and customizable fields!

In the next chapter, we will learn how to create a theme admin panel with the same module structure, which allows a store manager to customize some important theme parts. The powerful admin theme will include options in a dedicated section in the Magento system configuration section in the backend.

8
Creating a Theme Admin Panel

Now that we have a full working theme, we are going to create a powerful admin theme options panel. Through this awesome panel, the store manager will have the option of configuring some settings of the theme without having programming knowledge.

To create the admin theme options panel, we need to develop a custom Magento module that will have the scope of creating options in the backend, which will make changes in the frontend.

The following are the topics that will be covered in this chapter:

- Creating the theme options module
- Overviewing the `System.xml` fields
- Creating the advanced admin options panel
- Interfacing the admin panel with the theme
- Advanced options features
- Creating a visual color picker in admin
- Defining default values for options fields
- A quick theme option panel recap

Creating the theme options module

As we said in the previous chapter, to start a new Magento module, you have to create a module code folder under an appropriate code pool. We are going to use the local code pool for our module here.

We can use the same namespace used for the `Widget` module, `BookStore`, and create the module inside that folder. We are going to name it `ThemeOptions`.

Let's start creating the basic module. The following is the folder structure:

```
app
- code
  - local
    - BookStore
      - ThemeOptions
        - etc
        - Helper
        - Model
- etc
```

Activating the module

To activate the module, we need to do the following three simple operations:

1. Create the `BookStore_ThemeOptions.xml` file in `app/etc/modules/` with the following code to activate the module:

```xml
<?xml version="1.0"?>
<config>
  <modules>
    <BookStore_ThemeOptions>
      <active>true</active>
      <codePool>local</codePool>
      <depends>
        <Mage_Cms/>
      </depends>
    </BookStore_ThemeOptions>
  </modules>
</config>
```

2. Then, **Disable** or **Refresh** the cache. To do this, go to admin and open **System | Cache Management**. Remember that once you create a theme, a module, and so on with Magento and you find some visualization issues or 404 errors, first check if the cache is disabled; if so, refresh and delete all the cache.

3. Then, in the admin panel, go to the **System | Configuration | Advanced** tab on the left-hand side and check if the module is present and enabled as shown in the following screenshot:

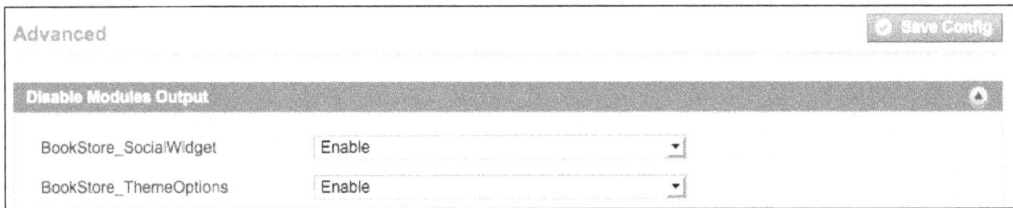

Creating the module helper

To make the module work correctly, you need to create the module helper file. This file is needed to make the system of translations work correctly. In fact, if you don't create this file, you will get an error on the screen. So, let's create the `Data.php` file in `app/code/local/BookStore/ThemeOptions/Helper/` with the following code:

```php
<?php
/**
 * BookStore Theme Options
 */
class BookStore_Themeoptions_Helper_Data extends Mage_Core_Helper_
  Abstract
{

}
```

Creating the configuration file config.xml

The configuration file is very important for a Magento module, and in our case, it will show the tab in **System | Configuration**. In order to use Magento's configuration section, you need to define models' and helpers' locations by performing the following steps:

1. Let's create the `config.xml` file in `app/code/local/BookStore/ThemeOptions/etc/` with the following basic code structure:

    ```xml
    <?xml version="1.0" encoding="UTF-8"?>

    <config>

    </config>
    ```

2. Then, inside `<config>`, you need to define models and helpers locations as follows:

```
<global>
  <models>
    <themeoptions>
      <class>BookStore_ThemeOptions_Model</class>
    </themeoptions>
  </models>
  <helpers>
    <themeoptions>
      <class>BookStore_ThemeOptions_Helper</class>
    </themeoptions>
  </helpers>
</global>
```

3. Finally, in order to avoid the "permission denied" problem, you need to always add the following code inside the `<config>`and `</config>` tags:

```
<adminhtml>
  <acl>
    <resources>
      <all>
        <title>Allow Everything</title>
      </all>
      <admin>
        <children>
          <system>
            <children>
              <config>
                <children>
                  <bookstore>
                    <title>Bookstore - All</title>
                  </bookstore>
                </children>
              </config>
            </children>
          </system>
        </children>
      </admin>
    </resources>
  </acl>
</adminhtml>
```

The following is the full code of the `config.xml` file:

```xml
<?xml version="1.0" encoding="UTF-8"?>
<config>

  <modules>
    <BookStore_ThemeOptions>
      <version>0.0.1</version>
    </BookStore_ThemeOptions>
  </modules>

  <!-- define models and helpers -->
  <global>
    <models>
      <themeoptions>
        <class>BookStore_ThemeOptions_Model</class>
      </themeoptions>
    </models>
    <helpers>
      <themeoptions>
        <class>BookStore_ThemeOptions_Helper</class>
      </themeoptions>
    </helpers>
  </global>


  <!--  in order to avoid "404 and Permission Denied -->
  <adminhtml>
    <acl>
      <resources>
        <all>
          <title>Allow Everything</title>
        </all>
        <admin>
          <children>
            <system>
              <children>
                <config>
                  <children>
                    <bookstore>
                      <title>Bookstore - All</title>
                    </bookstore>
                  </children>
                </config>
```

```
            </children>
          </system>
        </children>
      </admin>
    </resources>
  </acl>
</adminhtml>

</config>
```

Creating the options file system.xml

Now we need to create a file that will manage all the options of our theme by performing the following steps:

1. Create the file `system.xml` in `app/code/local/BookStore/ThemeOptions/etc/` with the following basic code:

```
<config>
  <tabs>

    . . .

  </tabs>
  <sections>

    . . .

  </sections>
</config>
```

2. Inside the `<tabs></tabs>` tags, you need to define the tab that will be displayed on the left in system configuration. In our case, we create the **Bookstore** tab and place it at the very top of the left sidebar with `<sort_order>000</sort_order>` as follows:

```
<bookstore translate="label">
  <label>BookStore Theme</label>
  <sort_order>000</sort_order>
</bookstore>
```

3. And now the fun part! Let's create the options. Inside the `<sections></section>` tags, insert the following code that will define the section of our module's tab:

```
<bookstore translate="label">
  <label>Theme Options</label>
  <tab>bookstore</tab>
```

```
<frontend_type>text</frontend_type>
<sort_order>1000</sort_order>
<show_in_default>1</show_in_default>
<show_in_website>1</show_in_website>
<show_in_store>1</show_in_store>
<groups>
   . . .
</groups>
</bookstore>
```

4. Now, to make the module appear in the admin, we need to insert at least one option. All the options are located inside the `<groups></groups>` tags that we defined in the previous step. Here, all the options must be organized in subgroups that you can name as you prefer. In this case, we are going to create a test field inside the group `general` with the following code:

```
<general translate="label" module="themeoptions">
  <label>Test Group</label>
  <frontend_type>text</frontend_type>
  <sort_order>01</sort_order>
  <show_in_default>1</show_in_default>
  <show_in_website>1</show_in_website>
  <show_in_store>1</show_in_store>
  <fields>
    <text_field translate="label">
    <label>Input Text Field</label>
    <frontend_type>text</frontend_type>
    <sort_order>00</sort_order>
    <show_in_default>1</show_in_default>
    <show_in_website>1</show_in_website>
    <show_in_store>1</show_in_store>
    </text_field>
  </fields>
</general>
```

5. Now, go to **System | Configuration** in admin, and you should see the new **BOOKSTORE THEME** tab in the left-hand side column, as shown in the following screenshot:

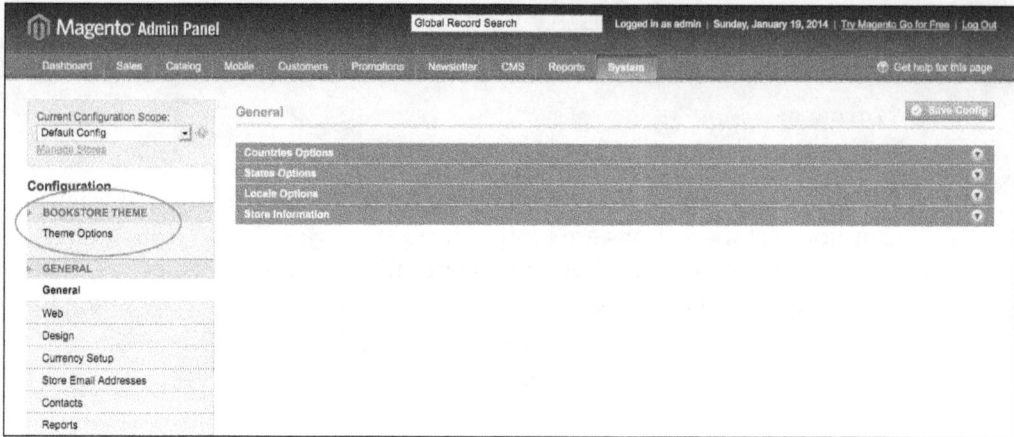

As you can see, we chose the `bookstore` tab to instruct Magento to place this section inside the brand new tab defined in the previous step.

If you want to add the section inside one of the present tabs, you need to indicate the tab inside the `<tab></tab>` tag.

Let's suppose that you want to add a section **Theme Options** inside the **General** settings tab. To display the new section there, you need to define the `general` tab in the following way:

```
<tab>general</tab>
```

The output will be like what is shown in the following screenshot:

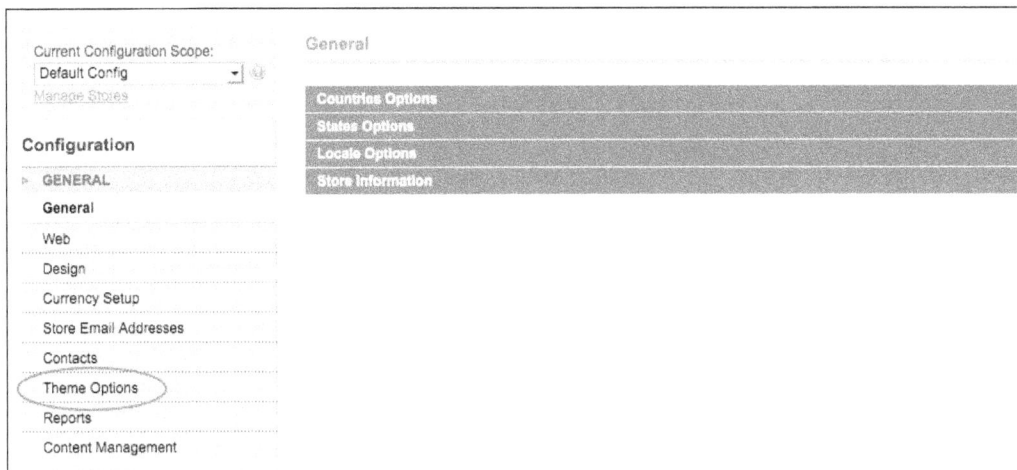

Only for your reference, the following is the full code of the `system.xml` file that we have created:

```
<config>
  <tabs>
    <bookstore translate="label">
      <label>BookStore Theme</label>
      <sort_order>000</sort_order>
    </bookstore>
  </tabs>
  <sections>
    <bookstore translate="label">
      <label>Theme Options</label>
      <tab>bookstore</tab>
      <frontend_type>text</frontend_type>
      <sort_order>1000</sort_order>
      <show_in_default>1</show_in_default>
      <show_in_website>1</show_in_website>
      <show_in_store>1</show_in_store>
      <groups>
        <general translate="label" module="themeoptions">
          <label>Test Group</label>
          <frontend_type>text</frontend_type>
          <sort_order>01</sort_order>
          <show_in_default>1</show_in_default>
          <show_in_website>1</show_in_website>
          <show_in_store>1</show_in_store>
          <fields>
```

```
            <text_field translate="label">
              <label>Input Text Field</label>
              <frontend_type>text</frontend_type>
              <sort_order>00</sort_order>
              <show_in_default>1</show_in_default>
              <show_in_website>1</show_in_website>
              <show_in_store>1</show_in_store>
            </text_field>
          </fields>
        </general>
      </groups>
    </bookstore>
  </sections>
</config>
```

Getting started with options fields

Now that we created the left tab, the section button, and the default group with a test option field, we are going to explore how to create a custom options panel with groups and options.

Before starting, let's take a look at the following screenshot that shows you the module we created with **Tabs**, **Sections**, **Groups**, and **Fields**:

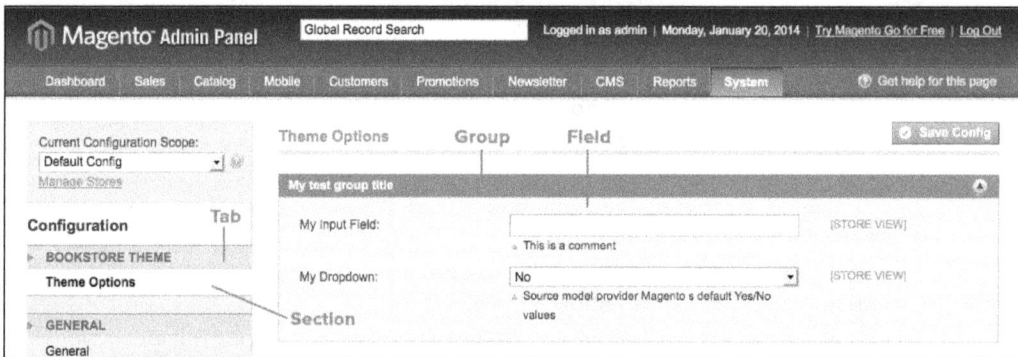

As we have seen, we need to set the groups and fields inside the `<groups></groups>` tags, and also set the real options of the module / theme options panel.

A group can contain several fields, as you can see in the example shown in the following code, where we create two fields, an `input field`, and a drop-down select `Yes/No` field:

```
<groups>
  <mygroup translate="label" module="themeoptions">
    <label>My test group title</label>
    <frontend_type>text</frontend_type>
    <sort_order>01</sort_order>
    <show_in_default>1</show_in_default>
    <show_in_website>1</show_in_website>
    <show_in_store>1</show_in_store>
    <fields>
      <my_input_field translate="label">
        <label>My Input Field: </label>
        <comment>This is a comment</comment>
        <frontend_type>text</frontend_type>
        <sort_order>20</sort_order>
        <show_in_default>1</show_in_default>
        <show_in_website>1</show_in_website>
        <show_in_store>1</show_in_store>
      </my_input_field>
      <my_select_field translate="label">
        <label>My Dropdown: </label>
        <comment>Source model provider Magento's default Yes/No
          values</comment>
        <frontend_type>select</frontend_type>
        <sort_order>90</sort_order>
        <show_in_default>1</show_in_default>
        <show_in_website>1</show_in_website>
        <show_in_store>1</show_in_store>
        <source_model>adminhtml/
          system_config_source_yesno</source_model>
      </my_select_field>
    </fields>
  </mygroup>
</groups>
```

The result of this new group with two fields is the following:

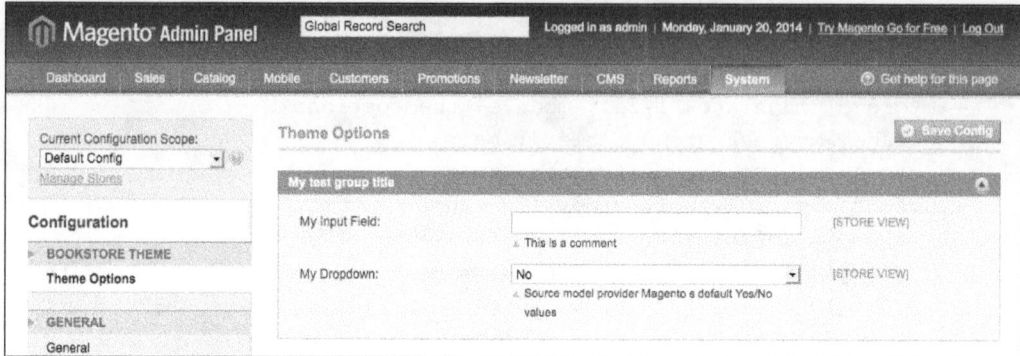

Sometimes, if you are already logged in and you click on the **Theme Options** tab, the **404 Error** can appear as shown in the following screenshot. This happens as a result of caching problems. To solve this, simply log out and log in again, and then refresh the cache.

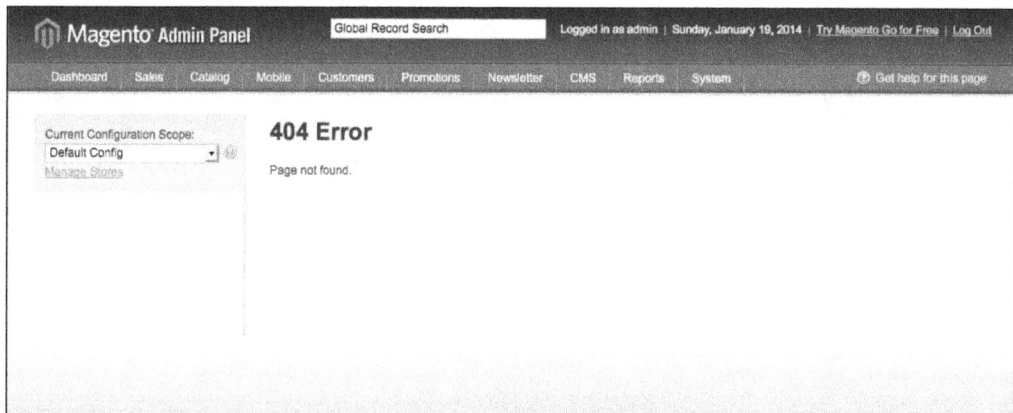

Overviewing the System.xml fields

If you take a look at the code created previously, you can see that the fields are grouped inside the `<fields></fields>` tags, and each field includes many parts; let's explain them.

The following code is an example of single input field:

```
<input_field translate="label">
  <label>My Input Field: </label>
  <comment>This is a comment</comment>
```

```
    <frontend_type>text</frontend_type>
    <sort_order>20</sort_order>
    <show_in_default>1</show_in_default>
    <show_in_website>1</show_in_website>
    <show_in_store>1</show_in_store>
</input_field>
```

The elements used in the code are explained as follows:

- `<input_field>`: This is the unique node name of the option
- `<Label>`: This is the title of the field, displayed on the left
- `<Comment>`: This is useful to provide extra descriptions or information for the store manager
- `<frontend_type>`: This is the type of the option (you can see more details about this in the following lines)
- `<sort_order>`: This is used to order the fields inside the group
- `<show_in...>`: This is used to enable the option to make the field editable for each store/website scope

As said before, `frontend_type` is the type of the options that you can use; for example, an input text, a text area, and a drop-down list. All of them are defined in `/lib/Varien/Data/Form/Element/` directory.

The following are the most used options:

- Input text field
- Textarea
- Dropdown with Yes/No values
- Dropdown with Enable/Disable values
- Dropdown with custom values
- Multiselect
- File upload
- Time
- Editable items
- Heading

As you can see, we have many types of fields, and this allows us to create a custom admin panel with all the options that you need. The more options you insert in your theme, the more possibilities you give the store manager to customize the theme without editing the code.

Now, we will discuss the most used fields in detail.

Creating an input text

You can use an input text for short text values, for example, a telephone number or a link. Consider the following screenshot:

Input Text Field

To create an input text option, you can use the following code:

```
<text_field translate="label">
  <label>Text Field</label>
  <frontend_type>text</frontend_type>
  <sort_order>10</sort_order>
  <show_in_default>1</show_in_default>
  <show_in_website>1</show_in_website>
  <show_in_store>1</show_in_store>
</text_field>
```

Creating textarea

You can use the **Textarea** for larger text values, such as a paragraph in which a company is talked about. Consider the following screenshot:

Textarea

To create a textarea option, you can use the following code:

```
<textarea_field translate="label">
  <label>Textarea</label>
  <frontend_type>textarea</frontend_type>
  <sort_order>20</sort_order>
  <show_in_default>1</show_in_default>
  <show_in_website>1</show_in_website>
  <show_in_store>1</show_in_store>
</textarea_field>
```

Creating a dropdown with Yes/No values

You can use the dropdown to enable or disable something. Consider the following screenshot:

To create a **Yes**/**No** option, you can use the following code:

```
<yes_no_field translate="label">
  <label>Dropdown Yes No</label>
  <frontend_type>select</frontend_type>
  <source_model>adminhtml/
    system_config_source_yesno</source_model>
  <sort_order>1</sort_order>
  <show_in_default>1</show_in_default>
  <show_in_website>1</show_in_website>
  <show_in_store>1</show_in_store>
</yes_no_field>
```

Creating a dropdown with Enable/Disable values

Almost the same as the previous one, but instead of **Yes** and **No**, you will get **Enable** and **Disable**:

To create an **Enable/Disable** option, you can use the following code:

```
<enable_disable_field translate="label">
    <label>Dropdown Enable/Disable</label>
    <frontend_type>select</frontend_type>
    <sort_order>40</sort_order>
    <source_model>adminhtml/system_config_source_enabledisable
        </source_model>
    <show_in_default>1</show_in_default>
    <show_in_website>1</show_in_website>
    <show_in_store>1</show_in_store>
</enable_disable_field>
```

Creating a dropdown with custom values

The following is a custom dropdown with custom set of values generated by the source model:

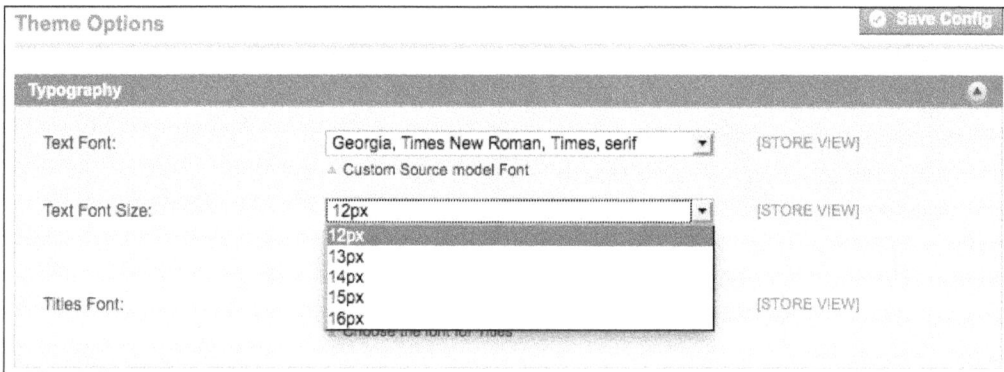

The creation of a custom dropdown value is more complex than a **Yes/No** dropdown. But don't worry, we will discuss this in the next topic.

Creating a File Upload option field

The **File Upload** option field allows us to choose a file to upload. You can set the destination folder too; in this example, the file will be saved in the `[root]/media/bookstore` directory:

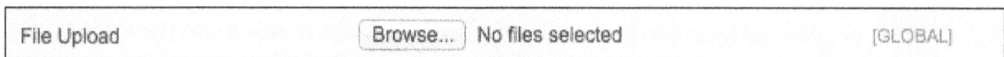

To create the **File Upload** option, you can use the following code:

```
<file translate="label comment">
    <label>File</label>
    <frontend_type>file</frontend_type>
    <backend_model>adminhtml/system_config_backend_file</
      backend_model>
    <upload_dir>media/bookstore</upload_dir>
    <sort_order>70</sort_order>
    <show_in_default>1</show_in_default>
    <show_in_website>1</show_in_website>
    <show_in_store>1</show_in_store>
</file>
```

We can use this field to create, for example, a logo upload field in our theme options inside the header group.

Creating the advanced admin options panel

Now that you got all the basics for options, let's see how to organize and create powerful and custom admin panel options for your theme.

Before starting, let's organize the groups that you want to create. This is an important phase of the process that will help you to organize the module and the project workflow better.

In this case, we are going to create the following groups of options:

- Typography settings
- Header settings
- Footer settings

Feel free to organize the code as you like! You can see the result of what we are going to create. The following screenshot shows you how the groups appear in the admin once you create it:

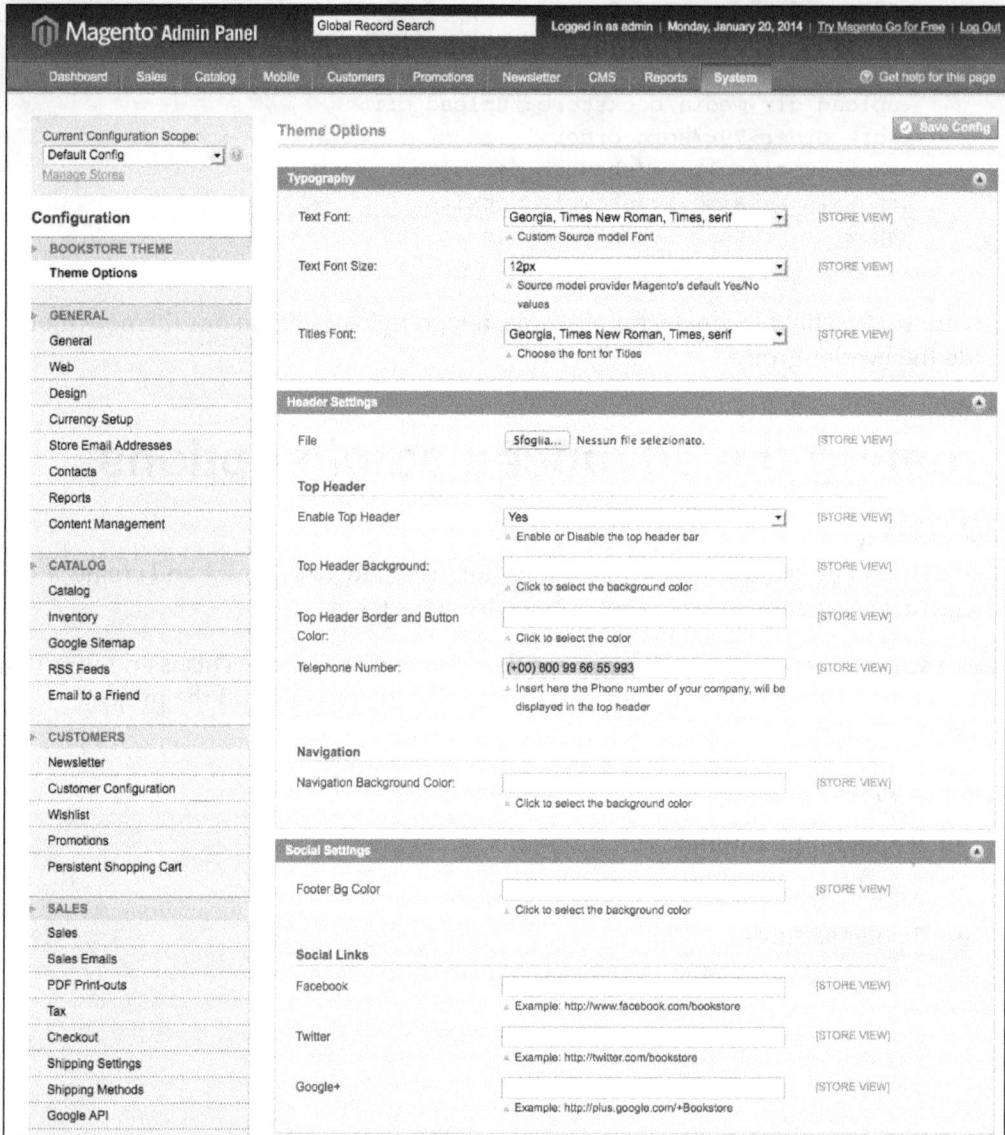

To create the main structure of the options group, let's start by creating all the groups inside the `<bookstore>` sections in the `<groups>` tags, which is always in the `system.xml` file. Perform the following steps:

1. Create the group for the **TYPOGRAPHY** options as follows:

```
<!-- TYPOGRAPHY GROUP -->

<typography translate="label" module="themeoptions">
  <label>Typography</label>
  <frontend_type>text</frontend_type>
  <sort_order>01</sort_order>
  <show_in_default>1</show_in_default>
  <show_in_website>1</show_in_website>
  <show_in_store>1</show_in_store>
  <fields>

  <!-- insert the option fields here -->


  </fields>
</typography>
```

2. Then, create the group for the **HEADER** options as follows:

```
<!-- HEADER GROUP -->

<header translate="label" module="themeoptions">
  <label>Header Settings</label>
  <frontend_type>text</frontend_type>
  <sort_order>02</sort_order>
  <show_in_default>1</show_in_default>
  <show_in_website>1</show_in_website>
  <show_in_store>1</show_in_store>
  <fields>

  <!-- insert the option fields here -->


  </fields>
</header>
```

3. Finally, create the group for the **FOOTER** options as follows:

```
<!-- FOOTER GROUP -->

<footer translate="label" module="themeoptions">
  <label>Social Settings</label>
  <frontend_type>text</frontend_type>
  <sort_order>03</sort_order>
  <show_in_default>1</show_in_default>
```

```
            <show_in_website>1</show_in_website>
            <show_in_store>1</show_in_store>
            <fields>

            <!-- insert the option fields here -->

            </fields>
        </footer>
```

The first group of options called **Typography** contains only custom drop-down options and, as I promised previously, I will now show you how to create these useful options.

Creating a custom dropdown field

To create a custom dropdown options field, such as the selection of a family font or the font size, we need to perform the following steps:

1. Create a new field defining the source model from your module as follows:

```
<font_text translate="label">
  <label>Text Font: </label>
  <comment>Custom Source model Font</comment>
  <frontend_type>select</frontend_type>
  <sort_order>1</sort_order>
  <show_in_default>1</show_in_default>
   <show_in_website>1</show_in_website>
  <show_in_store>1</show_in_store>
  <source_model>themeoptions/source_font</source_model>
</font_text>
```

2. Now, we need to create our custom model where we will insert all the dropdown options. So, navigate into the module in app/code/local/ BookStore/ThemeOptions/Model and create the Source folder. Inside the Source folder, create the Font.php file with the following code:

```
<?php
class BookStore_ThemeOptions_Model_Source_Font
{
  public function toOptionArray()
  {
    return array(
      array('value' => 'serif', 'label' =>
        Mage::helper('themeoptions')->__('Georgia,
        Times New Roman, Times, serif')),
      array('value' => 'sansserif', 'label' =>
```

```
            Mage::helper('themeoptions')->__('Arial, Helvetica,
            sans-serif')),
        array('value' => 'monospace', 'label' =>
            Mage::helper('themeoptions')->__('"Courier New",
            Courier, monospace'))
        );
    }
}
```

The result in the admin will be the following dropdown selection of **Text Font**:

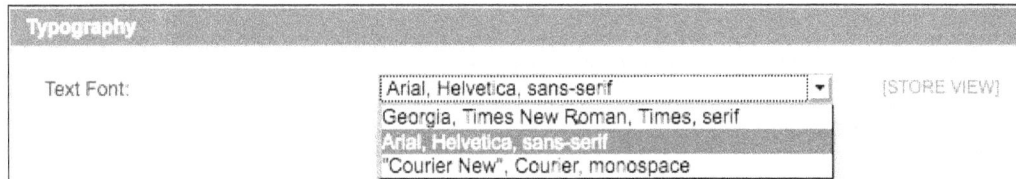

Done! Now we will also create a font size selection with the same method by creating a new field in `system.xml` with a custom source model, as follows:

```
<font_text_size translate="label">
        <label>Text Font Size: </label>
        <comment>Custom Source Model Fontsize</comment>
        <frontend_type>select</frontend_type>
        <sort_order>2</sort_order>
        <show_in_default>1</show_in_default>
        <show_in_website>1</show_in_website>
        <show_in_store>1</show_in_store>
            <source_model>themeoptions/source_fontsize</source_
model>
        </font_text_size>
```

Create a new source model file called `Fontsize.php` in the `Source` folder with the following code:

```
<?php
class BookStore_ThemeOptions_Model_Source_Fontsize
{
  public function toOptionArray()
  {
    return array(
      array('value' => '12px', 'label' =>
        Mage::helper('themeoptions')->__('12px')),
      array('value' => '13px', 'label' =>
        Mage::helper('themeoptions')->__('13px')),
```

```
      array('value' => '14px', 'label' =>
        Mage::helper('themeoptions')->__('14px')),
      array('value' => '15px', 'label' =>
        Mage::helper('themeoptions')->__('15px')),
      array('value' => '16px', 'label' =>
        Mage::helper('themeoptions')->__('16px'))
  );
  }
}
```

The result is a dropdown with font size selection as shown in the following screenshot:

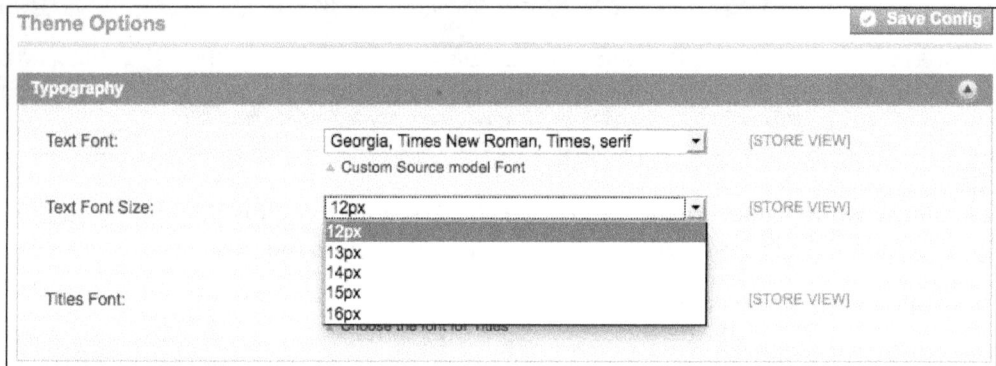

If you understand the power and the flexibility of the fields, you can create a custom admin panel with a lot of configurations.

Interfacing the admin panel with the theme

Now that we have a full working theme admin panel, and you know how to create any type of option, we need to show the values in the frontend.

Retrieving the data saved in your configuration is quite easy. You can use the following code:

```
<?php echo Mage::
  getStoreConfig(bookstore/general/options,Mage::app()-
  >getStore());
?php>
```

In the preceding code, bookstore is the sections, general is the fields group, and option is the options field.

Customizing the frontend

Now it is very easy to customize the frontend, because you need to change the stuff in the frontend with the options you created and some conditions. Let's start with a basic example: let's set the telephone number in the header from the admin panel.

Getting the value of an input text field

To get the value of the input text field, we will perform the following steps:

1. Open the `header.phtml` file in `app/design/frontend/bookstore/default/template/html` and find the following lines of code:

   ```
   <div class="col-md-8 col-sm-7">
       <?php echo $this->getChildHtml('topbar_cmslinks') ?>
   </div>
   ```

   Now the block is managed by a CMS static block, so to place the configuration field, change to:

   ```
   <div class="col-md-8 col-sm-7">
   <?php echo Mage::getStoreConfig('bookstore/header/
   telephone',Mage::app()->getStore()); ?>
   </div>
   ```

   Just to remind you, the piece of code that generates the field in the admin panel is in the `system.xml` file, as follows:

   ```
   <telephone translate="label">
               <label>Telephone Number: </label>
               <comment>Insert here the Phone number of your
                 company, will be displayed in the top
                 header</comment>
               <frontend_type>text</frontend_type>
               <sort_order>04</sort_order>
               <show_in_default>1</show_in_default>
               <show_in_website>1</show_in_website>
               <show_in_store>1</show_in_store>
               <depends>
                 <topheader_enable>1</topheader_enable>
               </depends>
           </telephone>
   ```

   This part of code is present in the `header` group inside the `bookstore` section.

2. Now, go in the backend and insert a custom phone number in the field:

Header Settings

Telephone Number:	(+00) 800 99 66 55 993
	⚠ Insert here the Phone number of your company, will be displayed in the top header

3. Then, save the configuration. Go to the frontend and the telephone number **(+00) 800 99 66 55 993** that you inserted should appear in the top bar, as shown in the following screenshot:

(+00) 800 99 66 55 993

Conditional options

Let's suppose that you want to show content if the options are filled and other options in case of the opposite. To do this, add a simple condition in the frontend as follows:

```php
<?php if(Mage::getStoreConfig('bookstore/header/
telephone',Mage::app()->getStore())):
echo Mage::getStoreConfig('bookstore/header/telephone',Mage::app()-
>getStore());
else:
echo 'You need to fill in the options in the System Config';
endif;
?>
```

Done! In this way, the user who installs the theme will be alerted in the frontend that he or she needs to edit some parts.

Accessing a Yes/No dropdown

Let's see another example that will explain better with a Yes/No field. Let's suppose that we want to enable or disable the top bar (the black bar in the header).

We already created the option in the `system.xml` file as follows:

```
<topheader_enable translate="label">
            <label>Enable Top Header</label>
            <comment>Enable or Disable the top header bar</comment>
            <frontend_type>select</frontend_type>
            <sort_order>01</sort_order>
            <show_in_default>1</show_in_default>
            <show_in_website>1</show_in_website>
            <show_in_store>1</show_in_store>
            <source_model>adminhtml/system_config_source_yesno</
source_model>
        </topheader_enable>
```

Go to admin and select **No** and save the configuration.

Now, reopen the `header.phtml` file and wrap the top header `div` inside the
following code, to enable or disable the top header, depending on the options:

```
<?php if(Mage::
   getStoreConfig('bookstore/header/topheader_enable',Mage::
   app()->getStore())==1): ?>
. . .
<?php endif ?>
```

> The **Yes**/**No** option returns 1 for **Yes** and 0 for **No**.

Getting the uploaded image file

To get an uploaded image file, the process is the same. Now we are going to see
a live example with the `logo` field we created.

In `system.xml`, the `logo` field is defined in the following way:

```
<logo translate="label" module="themeoptions">
  <comment></comment>
  <label>Logo</label>
  <frontend_type>file</frontend_type>
  <backend_model>adminhtml/system_config_backend_file</
    backend_model>
  <upload_dir>media/bookstore</upload_dir>
  <sort_order>00</sort_order>
  <show_in_default>1</show_in_default>
  <show_in_website>1</show_in_website>
  <show_in_store>1</show_in_store>
</logo>
```

Now, open the `header.phtml` file located in `app/design/frontend/bookstore/default/template/html`.

Here we have the default logo URL. What we are going to do is use the uploaded logo from our theme options if present; if not, we will use the default Magento logo, which is always defined in the admin in **System Configuration | Design**.

But the uploader is always a better solution for customers, and if they find all the options to customize the theme in one place, it is better!

So now that you have opened the `header.phtml` file, find the line where the logo is declared in the following code:

```
<div class="logo col-md-4 col-sm-5">
  <a href="<?php echo $this->getUrl('') ?>" title="<?php echo
    $this->getLogoAlt() ?>">
  <img src="<?php echo $this->getLogoSrc() ?>" alt="<?php echo
    $this->getLogoAlt() ?>" class="img-responsive" /></a>
</div>
```

Replace the preceding code with the following code:

```
<div class="logo col-md-4 col-sm-5">
  <a href="<?php echo $this->getUrl('') ?>" title="<?php echo
    $this->getLogoAlt() ?>">
  <?php if(Mage::
    getStoreConfig('bookstore/header/logo',Mage::
    app()->getStore())): $logourl = $media . 'media/bookstore/
    ' . Mage::getStoreConfig('bookstore/header/logo',Mage::
    app()->getStore());
else:
$logourl = $this->getLogoSrc();
endif;
?>
<img src="<?php echo $logourl  ?>" alt="<?php echo $this->getLogoAlt()
?>" class="img-responsive" />
</a>
</div>
```

What we've done here is a simple condition that displays the uploaded logo if present. Try to upload a custom logo now, and you will see that it appears in the site header, as shown in the following screenshot:

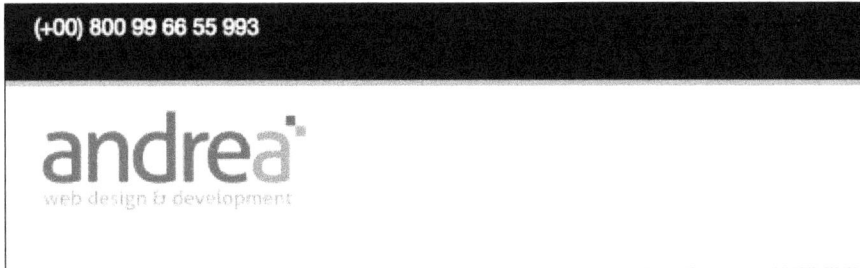

To remove the uploaded logo, return to the admin theme options and select the **Delete File** checkbox and save the configuration, as shown in the following screenshot:

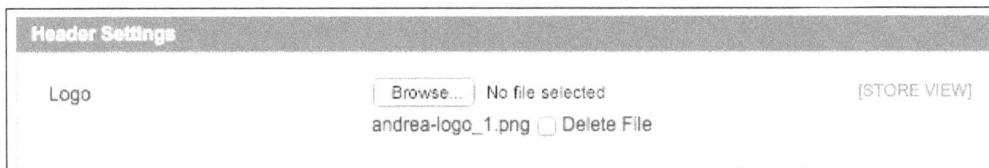

Advanced options features

There are some features that you can add to the options to create a very modular and advanced configuration panel, such as the dependent field and the option to add JavaScripts inside the comment tag. Let's analyze these features.

A dependent field

One of the advanced features is the `<depends>` tag to create dependent fields. When navigating the configuration of Magento, you may have noticed that sometimes when you you switch from **Yes** to **No**, some options disappear and if you select **Yes**, they reappear.

This is illustrated in the following screenshot:

Header Settings			⌃
Top Header			
Enable Top Header	Yes ▾	[STORE VIEW]	
	⌄ Enable or Disable the top header bar		
Top Header Background:		[STORE VIEW]	
	⌄ Click to select the background color		
Top Header Border and Button Color:		[STORE VIEW]	
	⌄ Click to select the color		
Telephone Number:	(+00) 33 00 66 77 99	[STORE VIEW]	
	⌄ Insert here the Phone number of your company, will be displayed in the top header		
Navigation			
Test Field		[STORE VIEW]	
	⌄ Click to select the background color		
Navigation Background Color:		[STORE VIEW]	
	⌄ Click to select the background color		

In the preceding screenshot, you can see some options after the first one, and in the following screenshot, you can see that by selecting **No**, some options below it disappear:

Header Settings			⌃
Top Header			
Enable Top Header	No ▾	[STORE VIEW]	
	⌄ Enable or Disable the top header bar		
Navigation			
Test Field		[STORE VIEW]	
	⌄ Click to select the background color		
Navigation Background Color:		[STORE VIEW]	
	⌄ Click to select the background color		

The options disappear because that field depends on the first one. Any field can depend on another one.

To create a dependent file, you simply need to add the following code to one of the fields that you want to make visible or not:

```
<depends>
  <field>1</field>
</depends>
```

Inside the `depends` tag, you have to define the field on which it must depend and its value. For example, let's take the `<topheader_enable>` field which is a **Yes/No** option field as shown in the following code:

```
<topheader_enable translate="label">
  <label>Enable Top Header</label>
  <comment>Enable or Disable the top header bar</comment>
  <frontend_type>select</frontend_type>
  <sort_order>01</sort_order>
  <show_in_default>1</show_in_default>
  <show_in_website>1</show_in_website>
  <show_in_store>1</show_in_store>
  <source_model>adminhtml/system_config_source_yesno
    </source_model>
  </topheader_enable>
```

Then you have another field called `topheader_color`, which you want to show only if the `topheader_enable` option is set to **Yes**. Simply define the field and add the `depends` tag at the bottom of the code, with the value as given in the following code:

```
<topheader_color1 translate="label">
<label>Top Header Background: </label>
  <comment>Comment...</comment>
  <frontend_type>text</frontend_type>
  <validate>color</validate>
  <sort_order>02</sort_order>
  <show_in_default>1</show_in_default>
  <show_in_website>1</show_in_website>
  <show_in_store>1</show_in_store>
  <depends>
    <topheader_enable>1</topheader_enable>
  </depends>
</topheader_color1>
```

As you can see in the highlighted portion of the preceding code, the `<depends>` tag includes the name of the field on which it depends. In other words, if the value of `<topheader_enable>` is `1` (**Yes**), the field will be displayed.

Please note that any field can depend on another. The main purpose of this one is to hide/show the field, depending on the state of some other field.

Adding JavaScripts inside the comment tag

There is also one interesting cheat. You can use JavaScript inside the <comment> tag. To do this, simply wrap JavaScript in a CDATA tag; as shown in the following code:

```
<topheader_enable translate="label">
            <label>Enable Top Header</label>
        <comment>
            <![CDATA[
                <script type="text/javascript">
                    Event.observe('bookstore_header_
topheader_enable', 'change', function() {
                        alert('Warning! This will hide the
top bar!');
                    })
                </script>
            ]]>
        </comment>
        <frontend_type>select</frontend_type>
        <sort_order>01</sort_order>
        <show_in_default>1</show_in_default>
        <show_in_website>1</show_in_website>
        <show_in_store>1</show_in_store>
        <source_model>adminhtml/system_config_source_yesno</
source_model>
</topheader_enable>
```

In this case, if you change the **Enable Top Header** field, an alert message will pop up as shown in the following screenshot:

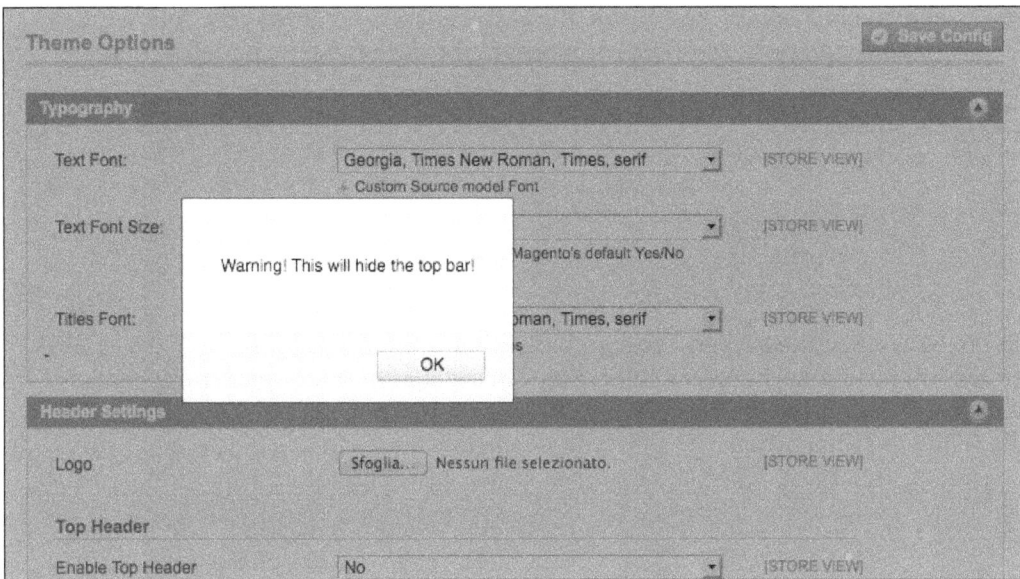

Creating a visual color picker in admin

Sometimes you may want to add color picker in the admin configuration page of
your Magento module or extension. In our case, this is a must-have option for a
theme configuration module. To do this, you don't have to download or add new
JavaScripts into the module, because Magento includes the `jscolor` picker by
default. Perform the following steps:

1. Create the `bookstore_themeoptions.xml` file in `app/design/adminhtml/`
   `default/default/layout` with the following code:

```xml
<?xml version="1.0"?>
<layout version="0.1.1">
  <adminhtml_system_config_edit>
    <reference name="head">
      <action method="addJs">
        <file>jscolor/jscolor.js</file>
      </action>
    </reference>
  </adminhtml_system_config_edit>
</layout>
```

2. Open `config.xml` and inside the `<adminhtml>` tag, insert the following layout update to the `jscolor` script in the admin theme panel section:

```
<layout>
  <updates>
      <themeoptions>
          <file>bookstore_themeoptions.xml</file>
      </themeoptions>
    </updates>
  </layout>
```

Done! Now open the backend and go to the theme admin panel section; if you click on the top header background color, you can see that the color picker appears and you are allowed to select the color by clicking on it! Cool, isn't it? You can see this in the following screenshot:

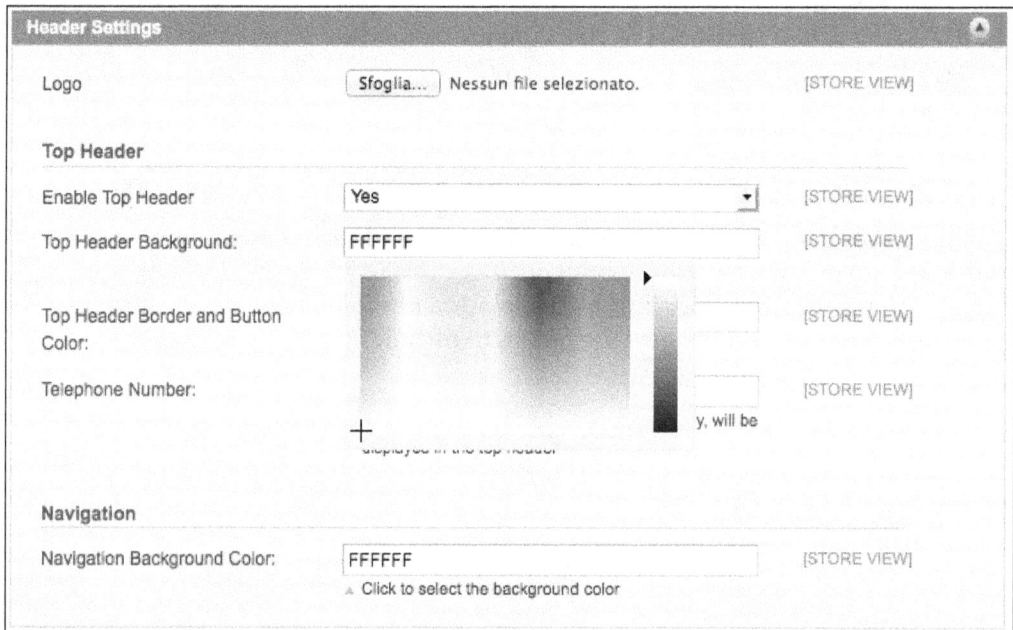

However, to make this happen, you need to pay attention to the field, which includes another tag: the `<validate>` `</validate>` tag. Take a look at one of the fields with the `<validate>color</validate>` tag, for example, see the following code:

```
<topheader_color1 translate="label">
<label>Top Header Background: </label>
<comment>Click to select the background color</comment>
<frontend_type>text</frontend_type>
<validate>color</validate>
```

```
<sort_order>02</sort_order>
<show_in_default>1</show_in_default>
<show_in_website>1</show_in_website>
<show_in_store>1</show_in_store>
<depends>
<topheader_enable>1</topheader_enable>
</depends>
</topheader_color1>
```

The preceding code allows the field to display the color picker. Now, you can retrieve the data in the frontend in the same way you did before.

In this case, the value is a CSS value, so to integrate the options in your theme, you can use the inline CSS injection, for example, use the following code:

```
<div id="topbar" <?php if(Mage::
    getStoreConfig('bookstore/header/topheader_color1',Mage::app()-
    >getStore())):
echo 'style="background-color:#'. Mage::
    getStoreConfig('bookstore/header/topheader_color1',Mage::app()-
    >getStore()) .'"'; endif; ?>>
```

In this case, when a user changes the top header background color from the backend, the style will be applied as you can see in the following screenshot:

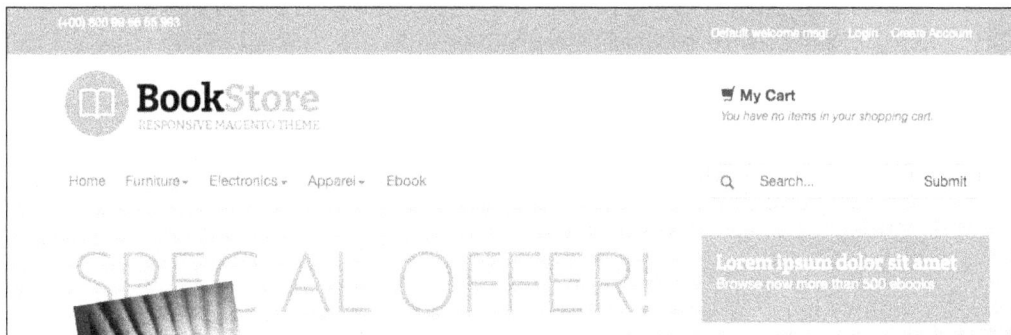

As you can see in the preceding screenshot, the background color of the top header switched from black to cyan.

Validate options

You can use the `<validate>` tag to make sure that the user inserts the right value into the option field based on the type of option. This tag generates a script that makes a particular type of validation based on the type of validation you want.

The validation starts when you try to save configuration from the orange action button on the admin theme option panel.

The following are the several types of validation:

- `validate-alpha`: This checks if the value inserted is text.
- `validate-alphanum`: This checks if the value inserted is alphanumeric.
- `validate-email`: This checks if the value inserted is a valid e-mail address.
- `validate-greater-than-zero`: This checks if the value inserted is a number greater than zero.
- `validate-not-negative-number`: This checks if the value inserted is a non-negative number.
- `validate-number`: This checks if the value inserted is a number.
- `validate-password`: This checks if the value inserted has at least six characters.
- `color`: This particular validation is the one we inserted now in the module. It enables the color picker.

Let's create an example with a validation for a number. If we want to validate the field for a telephone, just add the following code inside the `<telephone></telephone>` tags:

```
<validate>validate-password</validate>
```

Once you save, go to admin and try to insert the word `Hello` inside the input text for **Telephone Number**. Try to save, and you will get an alert message prompt under the input as you can see in the following screenshot:

Defining default values for options fields

Another cool task that you can do with the module is set default options for the module. Doing this is very simple. Open the `config.xml` file and within the `<config></config>` node, insert the `<default></default>` tag and inside it, all the options you created with the default values that you want to set. For example, consider the following code:

```
<!-- set default configurations -->
  <default>
    <themeoptions>
      <header>
        <menu_bg>CCCCCC</menu_bg>
      </header>
    </themeoptions>
  </default>
```

In this case, the default value of the `menu_bg` field will be `CCCCCC`.

> If you set default options after you save the module configuration page at least once, you will no longer see the default value set because the system will store the empty value field (if you save an empty value field).

A quick recap of the theme's option panel

Here we are! Our awesome theme admin panel is ready, and you can start customizing with tons of options, as you wish!

Let's go through a quick recap of the directory and the files used for this chapter:

```
app
- design
  - adminhtml
    - default
      - default
        - layout
          - bookstore_themeoptions.xml

- code
  - local
    - BookStore
      - ThemeAdmin
        - etc
          - config.xml
          - system.xml
        - Helper
      - Data.php
        - Model
      - Source
        - Font.php
        - Fontsize.php
- etc
  - modules
    BookStore_ThemeOptions.xml
```

Summary

In this chapter, we have seen how to create a custom and powerful theme options panel. With this great tool you created, the theme can be easily used by everyone, including the store manager who doesn't have programming knowledge.

Let's create your own admin panel with all the options you have in mind and render your theme unique and powerful!

In the next chapter, we will have a quick recap of all the files and how to collect them in a single ZIP file, and selling it in famous marketplaces such as ThemeForest.

Customizing the Backend of Magento

Now that we have created our custom Magento theme, we are going to learn how to customize the Magento admin panel. The default backend theme of Magento is pretty ugly; in this chapter, we are going to see how to create a custom skin for it.

The following is a list of topics that will be covered in this chapter:

- An overview of the admin design
- Changing the default admin panel
- Creating a custom Magento admin theme
- Creating a custom login page
- Installing the Magento Go admin theme

An overview of the admin design

The skin of the admin section is structured almost like the frontend area.

Since the birth of Magento, the admin panel has not undergone many changes; therefore, the graphics and the current design may seem to be in an "old style", as you can see in the following screenshot:

This is an example of what the screen in this program looks like

An old-fashioned admin panel can often give end users the impression that Magento is an older platform that has fewer capabilities and fewer updates than it actually does. Plus, having a custom Magento admin theme really sets the designer apart and gives the end user a feeling of quality and thoroughness with their custom theme.

Sometimes, you have the need to adapt the admin color scheme and logo to customer requests.

In this chapter, we will see how to transform the admin skin in order to adapt the design to the customer brand. In this case, we are going to customize it with the colors of the logo that we created in the last chapter: black, white, grey, and orange. The final result is shown in the following screenshot:

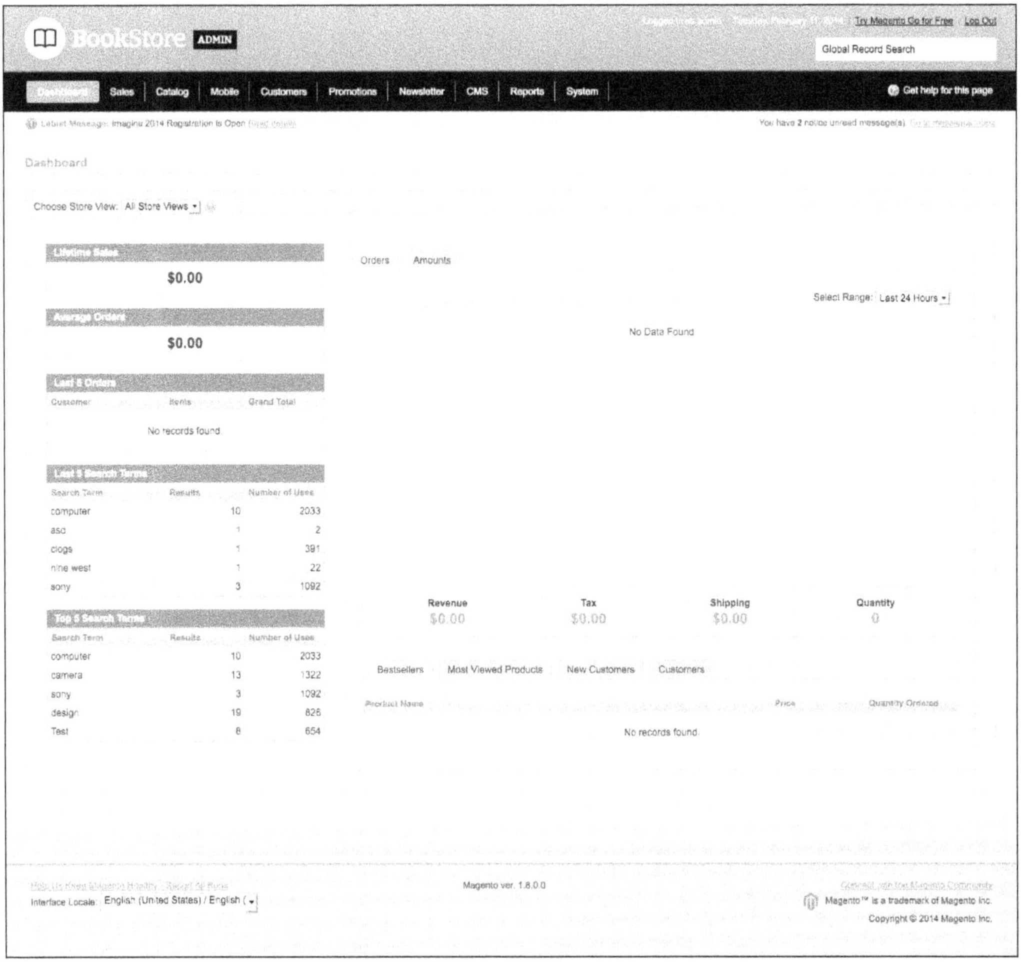

This is an example of what the screen in this program looks like.

The following are screenshots of the admin panel before and after applying the admin skin:

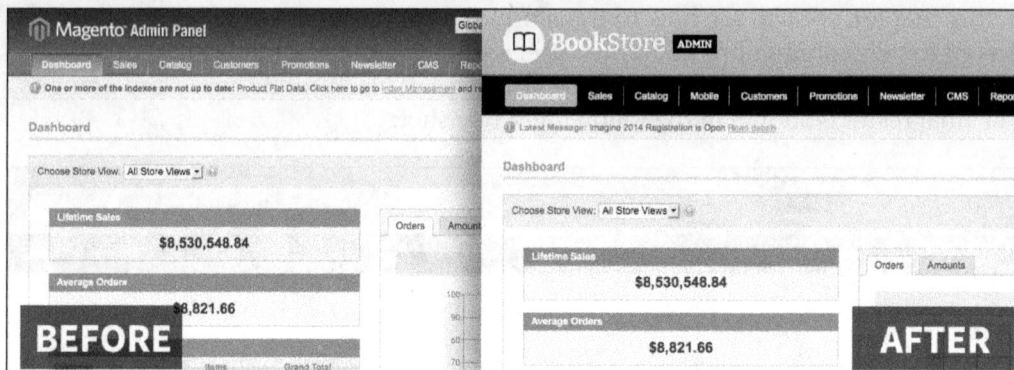

This is an example of what the screen in this program looks like.

Changing the default admin panel

To customize the admin, we need the **AdminTheme** module provided by Inchoo, one of the most popular companies that provides great Magento tutorials and services.

The module simply gives you the possibility to define the theme folder of the admin skin in the admin configuration.

Installing the module to change the folder path

You can download the module from `http://inchoo.net/ecommerce/magento/custom-admin-theme-in-magento/`. The following screenshot shows the module page on the Inchoo website, where you can download the module:

Read the article that opens on the website, and there you will find the link to download the module. After downloading it, use the following steps to install it and to create the admin theme folder:

1. Extract the folder and copy all the files into your Magento [root]/ folder.

2. Refresh the cache unless you had disabled the cache entirely during development.

3. Now, create your admin theme folder, for example, bookstore in the app/design/adminhtml/default/bookstore folder.

4. Also, create the skin admin folder under skin/adminhtml/default/ bookstore.

5. If you have already logged in the admin, log out and log in again in the admin to avoid the 404 error in the theme module page. You can experience this error even if the cache is disabled.

6. Now go to the admin and navigate to **System | Configuration | General | Design** (Default Config scope). As you can see, a new tab named **Admin Theme** appears on the right with a new input text field.

7. That field will allow you to define the admin theme folder, similar to the frontend package. So insert the name of your theme folder, bookstore, inside the field as shown in the following screenshot:

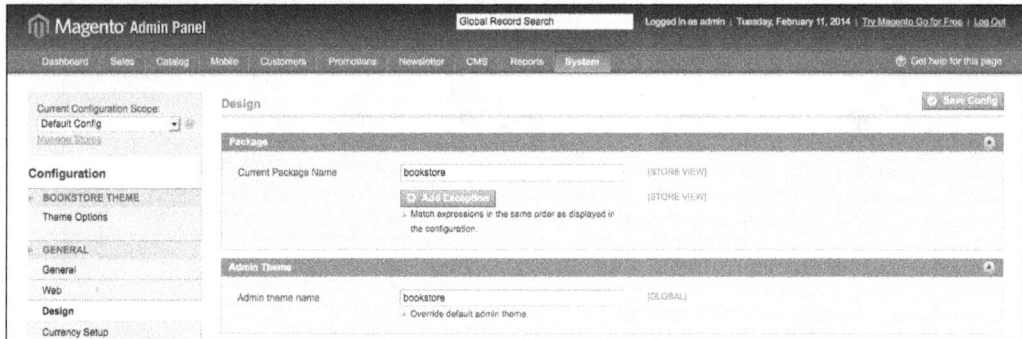

This is an example of what the screen in this program looks like.

8. Save the configuration.

Done. Now the admin theme will take the files from the bookstore folder.

If you refresh the page, you will not notice any change, because the fallback system will always take the files from the default admin theme.

Thus, it doesn't need to download all the base theme files to customize the admin skin, but just the files you need to edit.

Creating a custom Magento admin theme

Now that the module is installed and the folders of the new admin theme are ready, let's start creating the files that will overwrite the design.

Creating the custom.css file

We will begin by copying the `custom.css` file under `skin/adminhtml/default/` `default/` into the new theme folder, `bookstore`, under `skin/adminhtml/default/` `bookstore/`. In fact, if you take a look at the `main.xml` file located under `app/` `design/adminhtml/default/default/layout/`, you can see that there are some CSS files declared, and one of those is `custom.css`. The content of the `custom.css` file is as follows:

```
<action method="addCss">

<name>custom.css</name>

</action>
```

Checking the CSS overriding

Now, to run a quick test and check whether the module is working and if the fallback loads our file correctly, insert the following code inside `custom.css` to color the header background in black:

```
.header { background: #000; }
```

Now save the file. If everything is working, you will see the header color switching to black, as shown in the following screenshot:

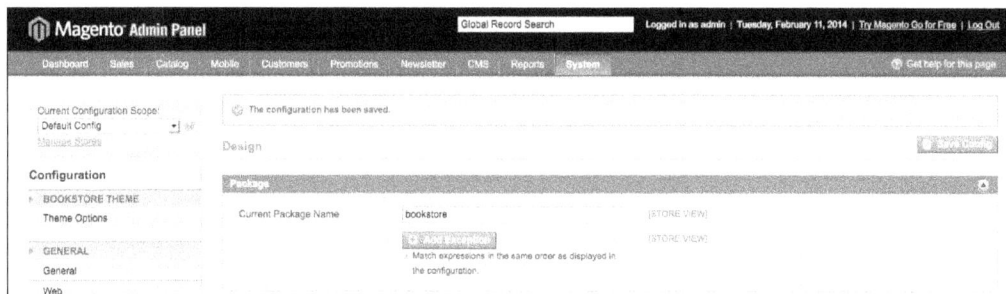

This is an example of what the screen in this program looks like.

Now that we've defined the location of our custom admin panel theme, we're ready to customize the look of the admin panel!

Changing the logo

The first thing that we are going to customize is the header. We start by changing the logo using the following steps:

1. To change the logo, simply save your logo in `.gif` format under `skin/adminhtml/bookstore/images/`.

2. Now open the `custom.css` file and add the following to overwrite the default logo header set into the default theme:

   ```
   .logo {


       height: auto;

   }
   ```

3. Then refresh the page to see your logo in the header of the admin panel, as shown in the following screenshot:

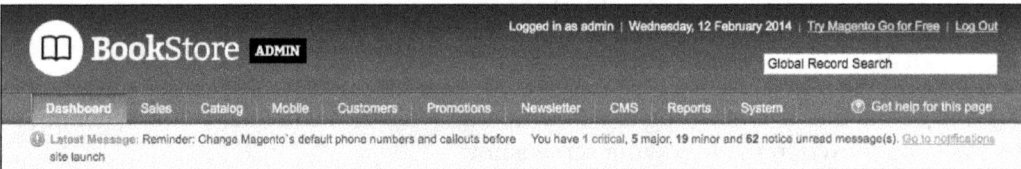

As you can see, we created a white version of the logo to make the admin panel similar to the previous logo, but a little bit different from the frontend.

Using a different logo name or extension

Let's suppose that you want to use a `.png` format logo so that you can have more flexibility while changing and customizing the header.

The logo declaration is in the `header.phtml` file, which is located under `app/design/adminhtml/default/default/template/page/`. Copy it from that folder to the relative folder of the new admin theme, which is under `app/design/adminhtml/default/bookstore/template/page/`. The following is the current path of the logo:

```
<img src="<?php echo $this->getSkinUrl('images/logo.gif) ?>"
alt="<?php echo $this->__('Magento Logo') ?>" class="logo"/>
```

In place of the preceding path, enter the following new path:

```
<img src="<?php echo $this->getSkinUrl('images/logo.png') ?>"
alt="<?php echo $this->__('Magento Logo') ?>" class="logo"/>
```

Now, let's change the header background. We are going to use a gradient background without images to speed up the loading time of the admin.

Creating CSS3 gradients without images

With CSS3, we can add a background gradient in a few seconds and without using images. To create your own gradient, you can use an online service called **Ultimate CSS Gradient Generator**, provided by ColorZilla, and available at `http://www.colorzilla.com/gradient-editor/`. The following screenshot shows you the ColorZilla website:

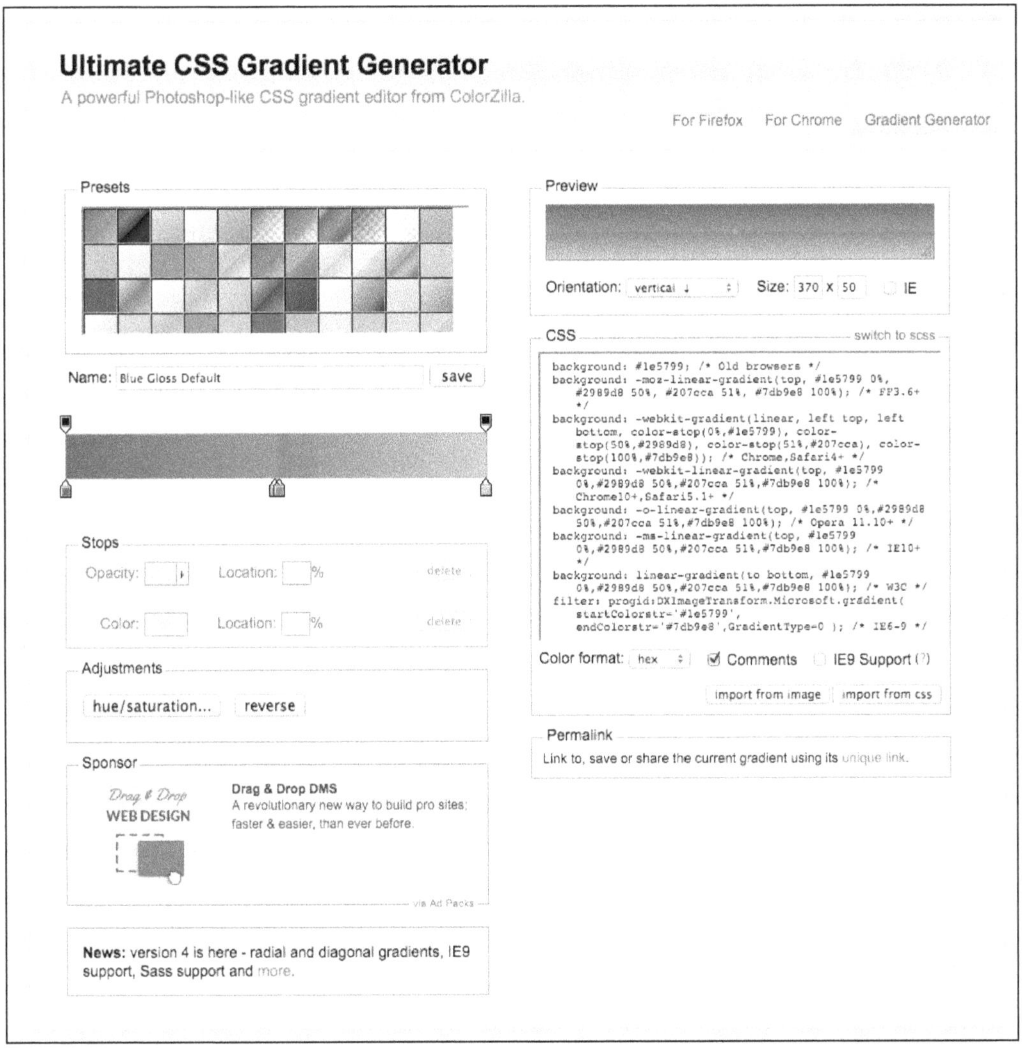

As you can see, the site is very simple and intuitive. You can create your own gradient by uploading an image, or alternatively you can grab one of the existing gradients.

In this case, select the gradient that you like and that better adapts to the logo colors, then copy the code from the right-hand side column and integrate it into your CSS file!

Changing the background color of the header

Once you have selected and copied the text, add the following CSS code into the header:

```
.header {
  /* Old browsers */
  background: #ffa84c;

  /* FF3.6+ */
  background: -moz-linear-gradient(top, #ffa84c 0%, #ff7b0d 100%);

  /* Chrome,Safari4+ */
  background: -webkit-gradient(linear, left top, left bottom,
    color-stop(0%,#ffa84c), color-stop(100%,#ff7b0d));

  /* Chrome10+,Safari5.1+ */
  background: -webkit-linear-gradient(top, #ffa84c 0%,
    #ff7b0d 100%);

  /* Opera 11.10+ */
  background: -o-linear-gradient(top, #ffa84c 0%,#ff7b0d 100%);

  /* IE10+ */
  background: -ms-linear-gradient(top, #ffa84c 0%,#ff7b0d 100%);

  /* W3C */
  background: linear-gradient(to bottom, #ffa84c 0%,#ff7b0d 100%);
  /* IE6-9 */
  filter: progid:DXImageTransform.Microsoft.gradient(
    startColorstr='#ffa84c', endColorstr='#ff7b0d',
      GradientType=0);
}
```

Now refresh the admin. As you can see, we now have a nice and customized background for the header:

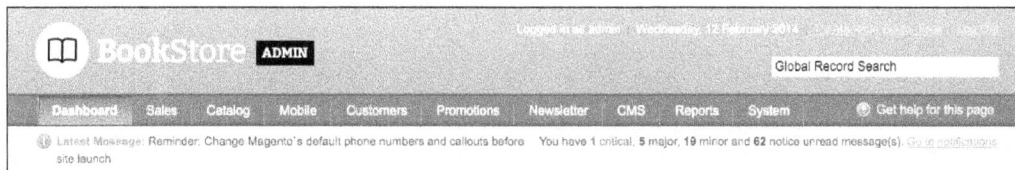

Now, let's customize the right-hand side area of the header a little bit by changing the colors of the **Try Magento Go for Free** and **Log Out** links and styling the search bar with the following CSS code:

```
/* header right */

.header-right {
  float: right;
}
.header-right a, .header-right a:hover {
  color: #000;
}
.header-right .super {
  margin-bottom: 10px;
}


/* Header Search */
.header-right fieldset {
  clear: both;
  display: block;
}
.header-right fieldset input.input-text {
  border: 0 none;
  border-radius: 3px;
  padding: 7px;
  width: 18em;
}
```

The result of the preceding code will be as follows:

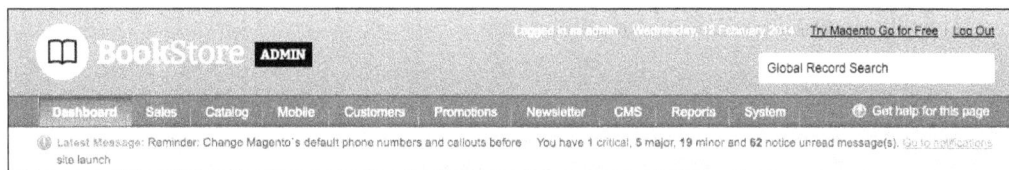

Customizing the navigation

Now, let's customize the navigation, by adding a padding to the navigation bar and changing the color of the active button using the following code:

```
/* navbar */
.nav-bar {
  background: none repeat scroll 0 0 #000000 !important;
  border: 0 none;
  padding: 10px 30px !important;
}
#nav li {
  border-radius: 3px;
}
#nav li.active {
  background: none repeat scroll 0 0 #FF9733 !important;
  color: #FFFFFF !important;
  font-weight: bold !important;
  margin-left: -1px !important;
}
```

The result of the preceding code will be as follows:

Customizing the footer

You can customize the footer by overriding a class on the custom CSS. In this case, we are going to provide a black gradient and white text to the background of the footer using the following CSS code:

```
/* footer */

.footer {

  /* Old browsers */
  background: #45484d;

  /* FF3.6+ */
  background: -moz-linear-gradient(top, #45484d 0%, #000000 100%);
```

```
background: -webkit-gradient(linear, left top, left bottom,
  color-stop(0%, #45484d), color-stop(100%, #000000));

/* Chrome10+,Safari5.1+ */
background: -webkit-linear-gradient(top, #45484d 0%,
  #000000 100%);

/* Opera 11.10+ */
background: -o-linear-gradient(top, #45484d 0%, #000000 100%);

/* IE10+ */
background: -ms-linear-gradient(top, #45484d 0%, #000000 100%);

/* W3C */
background: linear-gradient(to bottom, #45484d 0%,
  #000000 100%);

/* IE6-9 */
filter: progid:DXImageTransform.Microsoft.gradient(
  startColorstr='#45484d', endColorstr='#000000',
    GradientType=0 );

color:#888;
padding: 30px;
}
```

Also, we want to remove the Magento `.gif` icon on the right, which has been highlighted in the following screenshot:

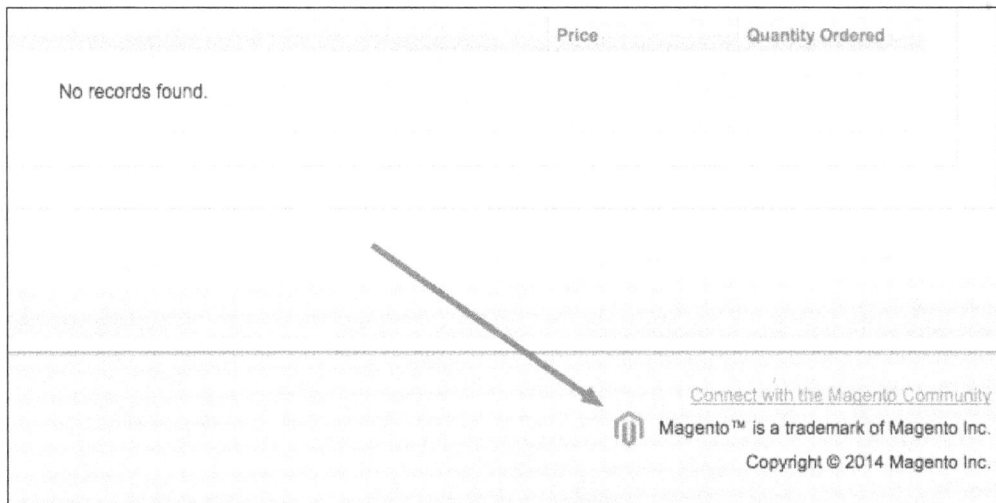

To do so, copy the `footer.phtml` file under app/design/adminhtml/default/ default/template/page/ and paste it under app/design/adminhtml/default/ bookstore/template/page/.

Then remove the following line:

```
<img src="<?php echo $this->getSkinUrl('images/varien_logo.gif')
?>" class="v-middle" alt="" />  
```

After these steps, our new admin footer will look as shown in the following screenshot:

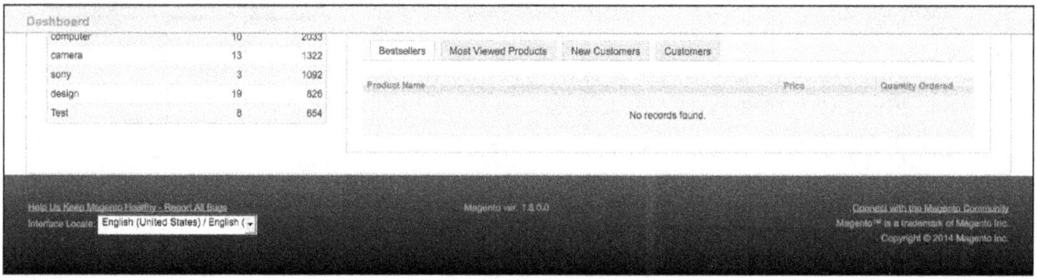

This is an example of what the screen in this program looks like.

Customizing other objects

To customize other objects, you can use **Firebug** — the famous plugin for Firefox — to analyze the content class and create your own style in custom.css.

You can download Firebug into the plugin page from https://addons.mozilla. org/it/firefox/addon/firebug/.

It's pretty simple to add Firebug to your Firefox browser. As you can see in the following screenshot, you only need to click the **Add to Firefox** button and the extension will be installed without the need to restart the browser:

You can make a donation to the developer who developed this great and useful extension that helps us save a lot of time in web development! To make a donation, click on the **Contribute** button and make your offer.

You can change the aspect of the buttons and tables elements using the following code:

```
/* other elements */
button, .form-button {
  font-size: 15px;
  padding: 5px 10px 5px 8px !important;
}
dl.accordion dt, .entry-edit .entry-edit-head {
  background: #333;
  padding: 5px 10px;
}
.content-header h3 {
  color: #000000;
  float: left;
  font-size: 23px;
  font-weight: normal;
}
```

Now, save and refresh the page. The final result of our Magento admin theme customization is shown in the following screenshot:

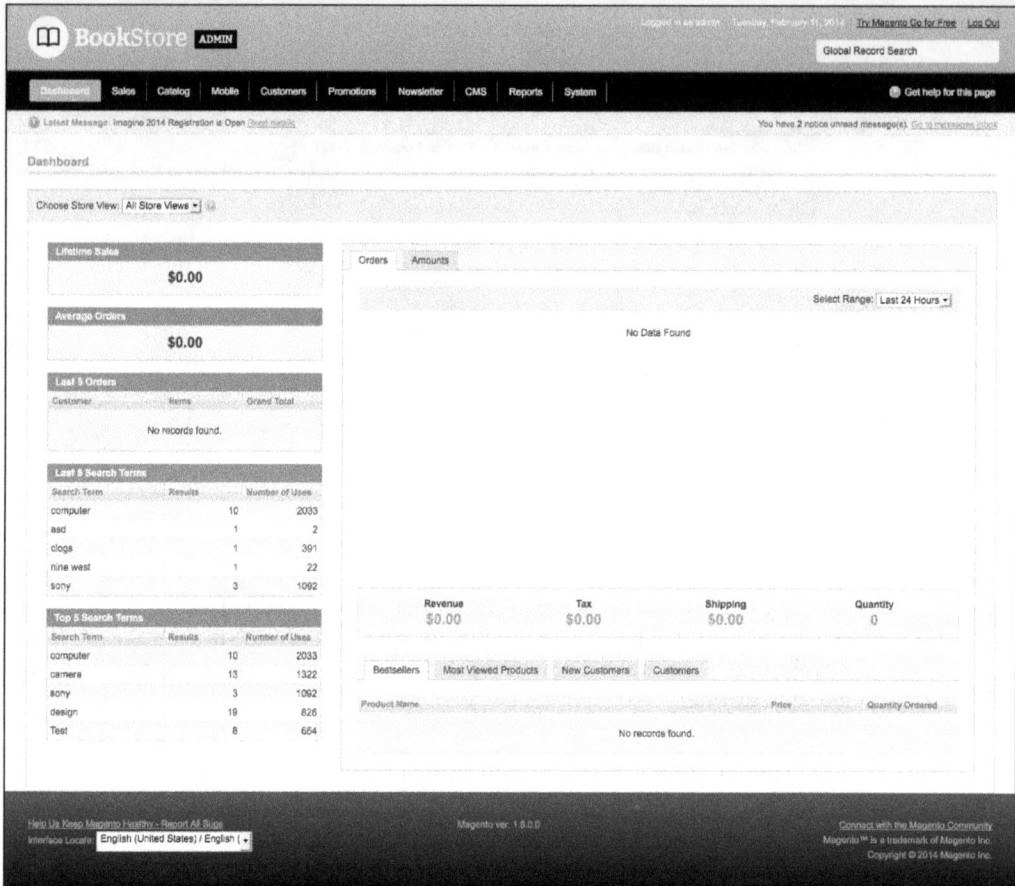

This is an example of what the screen in this program looks like.

Pretty cool, isn't it? Now you can create your own design for the admin panel, adapting it to the theme color, or based on the customer brand identity.

Creating a custom login page

An important section that needs tuning is the admin login form. The default login form, shown in the following section, remembers the style of the Magento admin and replicates it to some degree:

But now that we have customized it, we are going to see how to customize the admin access page with a custom logo and a custom design.

The login file is `login.phmtl`, placed under `app/design/adminhtml/default/default/template/`.

If you take a look at the code of the `login.phtml` file, you can see that its structure is a full HTML document and we have full control of the login page. This means that you can totally customize it, creating your own custom structure. The final result that we are going to reach is shown in the following screenshot, and we will use a custom code structure to make it unique:

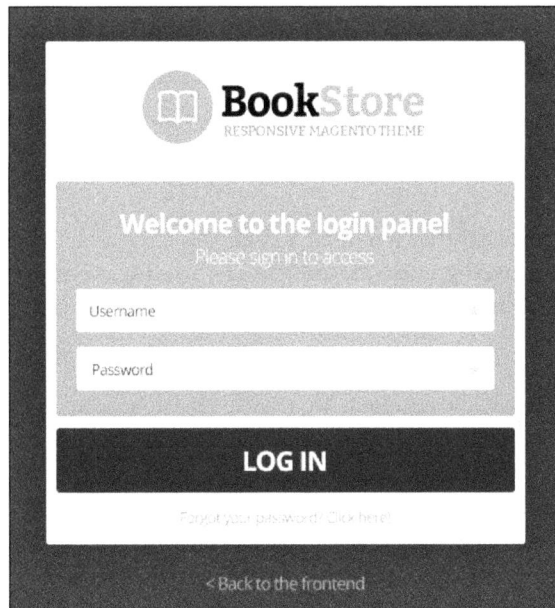

Creating the custom login.phtml file

To create your custom login file, create the `login.phtml` file in your theme admin folder under `app/design/adminhtml/default/bookstore/template`.

We start by creating a basic HTML5 structure using the following code:

```
<!DOCTYPE html>
<html lang="en">
<head>
  <meta charset="utf-8">
  <title><?php echo Mage::helper('adminhtml')->__(
    'Bookstore Admin Login') ?>
  </title>

  <!--[if IE]>
  <script src=
    "http://html5shiv.googlecode.com/svn/trunk/html5.js">
  </script>
  <![endif]-->

</head>

<body id="login_page">
...
</body>
</html>
```

> As you can see, inside the <head> tag, we inserted a conditional script for Internet Explorer to make it HTML5 ready.

To insert our CSS modifications, we need to call the `custom.css` file. This can be done by adding the following code inside the <head> tag, which will take the CSS from the custom `adminhtml` skin folder:

```
<link type="text/css" rel="stylesheet" href="<?php echo $this-
>getSkinUrl('../../default/bookstore/custom.css') ?>" media="all" />
```

Creating the login form

Now, let's create the HTML file of the form container that will include the form with the input, the button to sign in, and the link to retrieve the password.

1. First, we create a container that will include all the elements:

   ```
   <div id="loginContainer">

   </div>
   ```

2. Then, create a logo image named `logo-login.gif`.

3. Inside the `<div id="loginContainer">` tag, create the logo box within the logo image as follows:

   ```
   <div  class="login_logo">
   <img src="<?php echo $this->getSkinUrl('../../default/
   bookstore/images/logo-login.gif') ?>" alt="<?php echo
   Mage::helper('adminhtml')->__('Log into Magento Admin Page') ?>">
   </div>
   <!-- /.login_logo -->
   ```

4. Then, let's create the form with all the elements using the following code:

   ```
   <div class="login_form">

     <form method="post" action="" id="loginForm">

     <div class="form-title">
       <h1>
         <?php echo Mage::helper('adminhtml')->__(
           'Welcome to the login panel') ?>
       </h1>
       <h2>
         <?php echo Mage::helper('adminhtml')->__(
           'Log into Magento Admin Page') ?>
       </h2>
     </div>
     <!-- /.form-title -->

     <div class="input-container">
       <input type="text"
           class="form-control"
             id="login-username"
           name="login[username]"
       placeholder="
         <?php echo Mage::helper('adminhtml')->__(
         'User Name:') ?>" required>
   ```

```
    <input type="password"
        class="form-control"
            id="login-password"
            name="login[password]"
    placeholder="
        <?php echo Mage::helper('adminhtml')->__(
            'Password:') ?>" required>
    </div>
    <!-- /.input-container -->

    <button type="submit"
            id="login-btn"
            class="btn-login">
        <?php echo Mage::helper('adminhtml')->__('Login') ?>
        &raquo;
    </button>

    </form>

    </div>
    <!-- /.login_form -->
```

> As you can see in the preceding code, we added the `required` attribute to the input to avoid a blank form submission.

5. After the form, insert the link to retrieve the password using the following code:

```
<a href="
    <?php echo Mage::helper('adminhtml')->getUrl(
        'adminhtml/index/forgotpassword',
            array('_nosecret' => true)) ?>">
    <?php echo Mage::helper('adminhtml')->__(
        'Forgot your password?') ?>
</a>
```

> We will later see how to customize the **Forgot Password** page as well.

6. Now, at the very bottom of the page, outside `<div id="loginContainer">`, we will add a custom link to go back to the frontend using the following code:

```
<a href="
  <?php echo $this->getBaseUrl() ?>"
  class="link-frontend">
  <?php echo Mage::helper('adminhtml')->__(
    '&laquo; Back to the store') ?>
</a>
```

7. Finally, the script that will make the form work is given as follows:

```
<script type="text/javascript">

var loginForm = new varienForm('loginForm');

</script>
```

Done. The HTML code for the custom login page is finished. But if you refresh the page, we will have a blank form, shown in the following screenshot:

Styling the login form

Now, let's customize the login form with CSS. Open the `custom.css` file and start customizing all the elements as follows:

1. Let's begin with the background and styles of the page; use the following code:

```
/* Login Page */
```

```css
#login_page {
  background: url(images/bg.gif) repeat #000;
  font-family: 'Open Sans', Arial, Helvetica, sans-serif;
}
```

2. Then add simple customization for the heading titles using the following code:

```css
#login_page h1 {
  font-size: 24px;
  margin: 0;
}

#login_page h2 {
  font-size: 14px;
  font-weight: normal;
  margin: 0 0 15px;
}
```

3. We will now customize the login container, styling it with CSS3 features such as a border radius and box shadow using the following code:

```css
#loginContainer {

/* Border Radius */
  -moz-border-radius: 3px;
  -webkit-border-radius: 3px;
  border-radius: 3px;

  /* Box Shadow */
  -moz-box-shadow: 0 0 47px 4px rgba(0,0,0,.24);
  -webkit-box-shadow: 0 0 47px 4px rgba(0,0,0,.24);
  box-shadow: 0 0 47px 4px rgba(0,0,0,.24);

  background-color: #FFFFFF;
  border-radius: 3px;
  box-shadow: 0 0 47px 4px rgba(0, 0, 0, 0.24);
  margin: 100px auto 20px;
  padding: 10px 20px 20px;
  text-align: center;
  width: 460px;
}
```

4. Customize the logo at the top a little bit, positioning it at the center, just above the form, using the following code:

```
#loginContainer .login_logo {
  text-align: center;
  margin: 20px auto;
}
```

5. Finally, customize the login form and all the elements inside it using the following code:

```
#loginContainer .login_form {
  background: none repeat scroll 0 0 #F69235;
  -moz-border-radius: 3px;
  -webkit-border-radius: 3px;
  border-radius: 3px;
  color: #FFFFFF;
  display: block;
  margin-bottom: 15px;
  padding: 20px;
}

#loginContainer .login_form .form-title {
  color: #fff;
  text-align: center;
}

#loginContainer .login_form input {
  border: 0 none;
  display: block;
  margin-bottom: 20px;
  padding: 10px;
  width: 410px;
  -moz-border-radius: 3px;
  -webkit-border-radius: 3px;
  border-radius: 3px;
}
#loginContainer .login_form .btn-login {
  background: none repeat scroll 0 0 #333;
  border: 0 none;
  clear: both;
  color: #FFFFFF;
  cursor: pointer;
  font-weight: bold;
  line-height: 50px;
  width: 100%;
}
#loginContainer .login_form .btn-login:hover {
```

```
    background: #000;
}
```

And in the end, style the link at the bottom

```
#loginContainer a {
  text-align: center;
  color: #fb903d;
  font-size: 12px;
}

#login_page .link-frontend {
  color: #888888;
  display: block;
  font-size: 14px;
  margin: 0 auto;
  padding: 10px;
  text-align: center;
  text-decoration: none;
}
```

6. Refresh the page and the login page should now look like the following screenshot:

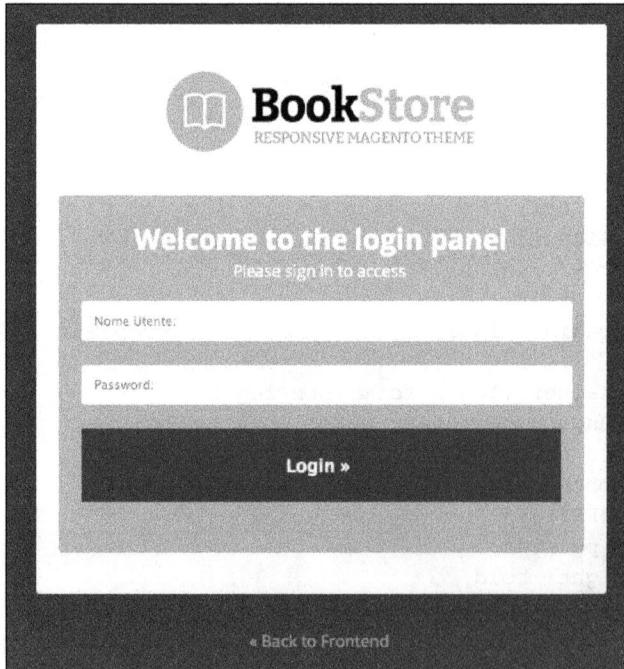

Adding the alert message if the data is incorrect

If a user inserts a wrong combination of username and password, the system returns an alert message. To make it appear in our custom form, you can insert the following code just after the code for the logo image:

```
<?php echo $this->getMessagesBlock()->getGroupedHtml() ?>
```

You can style the preceding code with CSS using the following code:

```
#loginContainer .messages {
  background: none repeat scroll 0 0 #FFEBDA;
  border: 1px solid #FF7C0A;
  color: #DD6700;
  font-size: 15px;
  list-style-type: none;
  margin: 0 0 10px;
  padding: 10px;
  text-transform: uppercase;
}
#loginContainer .messages li {
  list-style-type: none;
}
```

Now try to insert a wrong password, and the following message will appear:

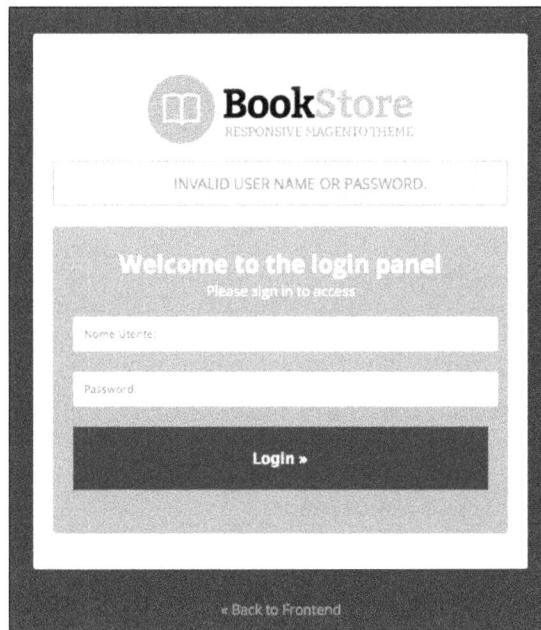

A quick recap of the complete form.phtml file

The final code of the custom login page is as follows. Note that this structure is very important for the next topic:

```html
<!DOCTYPE html>
<html lang="en">
<head>
  <meta charset="utf-8">
  <title>
    <?php echo Mage::helper('adminhtml')->__(
      'Log into Magento Admin Page') ?>
  </title>
  <link type="text/css" rel="stylesheet"
    href="<?php echo $this->getSkinUrl(
      '../../default/bookstore/custom.css') ?>"
  media="all" />
  <!--[if IE]>
    script src=
      "http://html5shiv.googlecode.com/svn/trunk/html5.js">
    </script>
  <![endif]-->
</head>
<body id="login_page">
  <div id="loginContainer">
    <div  class="login_logo">
      <img src="<?php echo $this->getSkinUrl(
        '../../default/bookstore/images/logo-login.gif') ?>"
        alt="<?php echo Mage::helper('adminhtml')->__(
          'Log into Magento Admin Page') ?>">
    <div id="messages">
      <?php echo $this->getMessagesBlock()->getGroupedHtml() ?>
    </div>
  </div>
  <div class="login_form">
    <form method="post" action="" id="loginForm">

      <div class="form-title">
        <h1>Welcome to the login panel</h1>
        <h2>Please sign in to access</h2>
      </div>
      <div class="input-container">
        <input type="text"
              class="form-control"
                id="login-username"
              name="login[username]"
```

```
      placeholder="
        <?php echo Mage::helper('adminhtml')->__(
          'User Name:') ?>" required>

      <input type="password"
            class="form-control"
              id="login-password"
            name="login[password]"
      placeholder="<?php echo Mage::helper(
        'adminhtml')->__('Password:') ?>" required>
    </div>

    <button type="submit"
            id="login-btn"
          class="btn-login">
     <?php echo Mage::helper('adminhtml')->__(
       'Login') ?> &raquo;
    </button>
    <a href="
      <?php echo Mage::helper('adminhtml')->getUrl(
        'adminhtml/index/forgotpassword', array(
          '_nosecret' => true)) ?>">
      <?php echo Mage::helper('adminhtml')->__(
        'Forgot your password?') ?>
    </a>
    </form>
    </div>
  </div>
  <a href="
  <?php echo $this->getBaseUrl() ?>"
    class="link-frontend"> &laquo; Back to Frontend
  </a>
  <script type="text/javascript">
    var loginForm = new varienForm('loginForm');
  </script>
</body>
</html>
```

Customizing the retrieve password form

If you click on the **Forgot your password? Click here!** link, you can see that this page too needs customization:

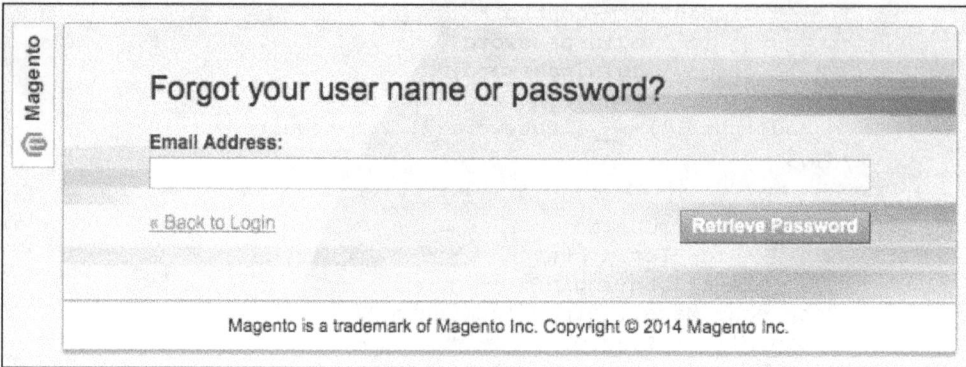

To customize the preceding page, duplicate the file you created for the login page, login.phtml, and name it forgotpassword.phtml in the same bookstore folder under app/design/adminhtml/default/bookstore/template.

What we need to do is only change the title using the following code:

```
<div class="form-title">

  <h1>
    <?php echo Mage::helper('adminhtml')->__(
      'Forgot your user name or password?'); ?>
  </h1>

  <h2><?php echo Mage::helper('adminhtml')->__(
    'Insert your email to restore the password'); ?>
  </h2>

</div>
```

Then, change the content of the form, inserting only the e-mail input as follows:

```
<div class="input-container">

  <input type="text"
          id="email"
        name="email"
       value=" "
       class="required-entry input-text forgot-password
         validate-email" placeholder="
           <?php echo Mage::helper('adminhtml')->__(
             'Email Address:'); ?>" required>

</div>
<!-- /.input-container -->
```

Now, of course, we need to make a change in the button text too:

```
<button type="submit"
         id="login-btn"
      class="btn-login">
  <?php echo Mage::helper('adminhtml')->__(
    'Retrieve Password'); ?> &raquo;
</button>
```

After the form, modify the **Forgot your password? Click here!** link using the following code. Clicking on this link will send you back to the login form:

```
<a class="left" href="
  <?php echo $this->getUrl('adminhtml',
    array('_nosecret' => true)); ?>">&laquo;
  <?php echo Mage::helper('adminhtml')->__('Back to Login'); ?>
</a>
```

Done! Now you don't need to change anything else, because the page action is already set to perform the password reset, which will send an email to the user with the link to change the password or with the new password, depending on the settings.

Refresh the page. You will now see the new design of the pages, made in few simple steps, as shown in the following screenshot:

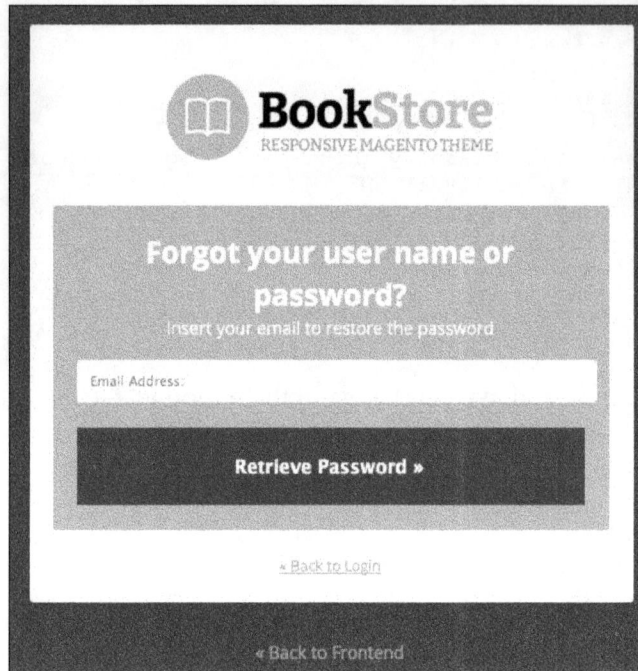

Installing the Magento Go admin theme

As you might know, Magento released a new version called **Magento Go** some time ago; it is a hosted e-commerce solution for small businesses.

If you have tried it, you will know that the admin panel has a custom skin that is very modern and clean, as shown in the following screenshot:

Johan Reinke, a French PHP developer, has created a perfect copy of the Magento Go admin theme and published it for free on GitHub. You can find the full article about this theme on his blog at `http://www.bubblecode.net/en/2012/05/02/give-your-magento-admin-panel-a-facelift/`. An extension is available on GitHub in the master branch at `https://github.com/jreinke/magento-admin-theme`.

The installation is very simple and quick; you only need to download the extension and upload it into your store root by using the following steps:

1. Disable the **Inchoo AdminTheme** extension that may conflict with this module.

2. Download the extension URL from the GitHub repository.

3. Extract the files into your Magento root.

4. Refresh the cache.

Once installed, you can see that a custom Magento login panel is also present, as you can see in the following screenshot:

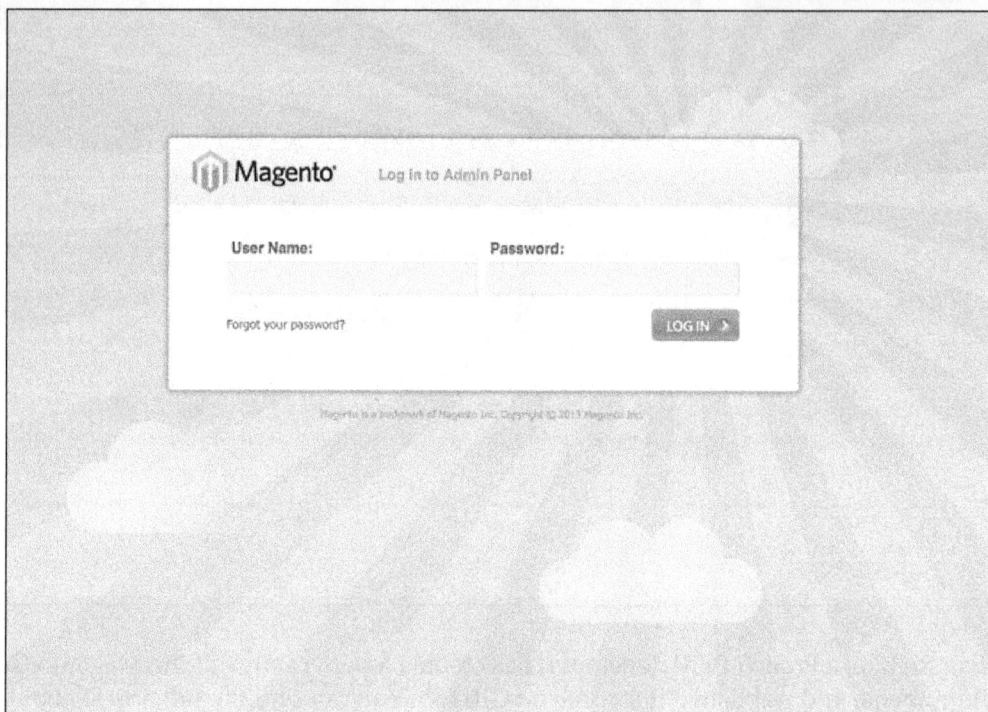

So if you want a better-looking admin panel but don't have time or desire to customize the admin panel for each client, downloading and including the Magento Go admin panel theme extension is a great way to update the look of the Magento admin panel for your end user without consuming too much time or effort on your part.

Summary

In this chapter, you learned how to customize the backend of Magento. By editing the design of the backend, you can give custom style to the administrative area of Magento, creating a unique style and giving added value to the template.

In the next chapter, we will reorganize the whole theme, collecting all the files that we created from the beginning, to create a zip file that is ready to be distributed. We will also see how to sell it on ThemeForest (http://www.themeforest.net), making some extra money at one the most popular theme marketplaces!

10
Packaging and Selling the Theme

Congratulations! Now that you have created the theme and optimized it for all devices, it's time to sell it; if you have created a theme for a customer, it's time to send it with all the necessary files. The path to this point has been long and difficult, but it is not yet done. If you want your effort to translate into money, you must perform a series of operations that are necessary and essential to be able to sell and distribute your theme.

In this chapter, we are going to learn how to create the perfect pack within all theme files and documentation, and how to present it for a live demo preview.

The list of topics that will be covered in the chapter are as follows:

- Collecting and placing all the folders and files under one folder
- Creating the live demo preview
- Creating the theme documentation
- Packing the theme
- Selling the theme on ThemeForest
- Inserting the theme on the **Magento Connect** site
- The support and updates of a theme

Collecting and placing all the folders and files under one folder

The very first thing to do is to collect all the files and the folders created for the theme, and create a folder that is ready to be uploaded or installed by the final user.

Just to remind you, the following diagram is the tree of the folders and the files of our project:

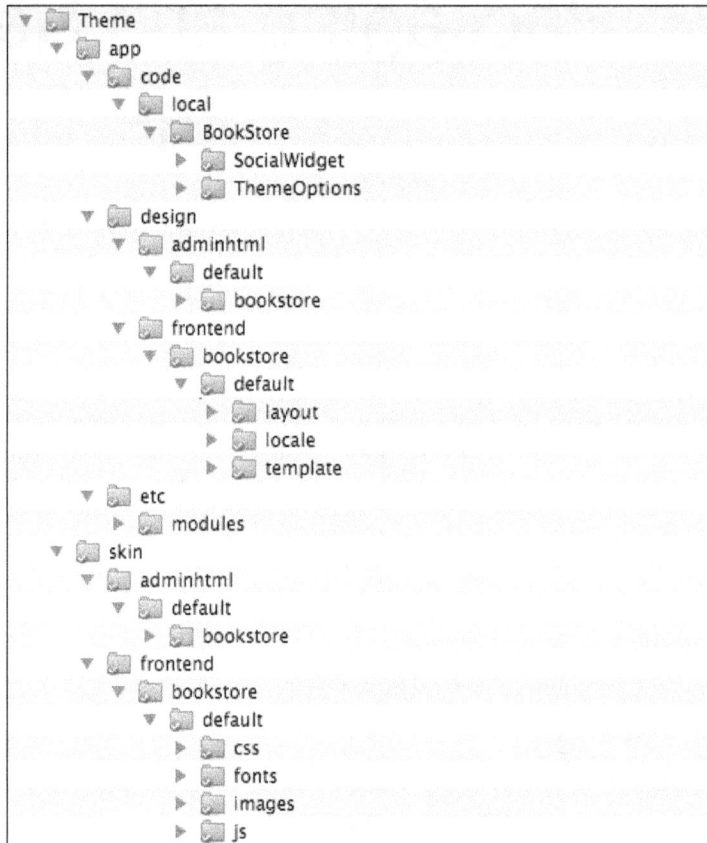

```
▼  📁 Theme
   ▼  📁 app
      ▼  📁 code
         ▼  📁 local
            ▼  📁 BookStore
               ▶  📁 SocialWidget
               ▶  📁 ThemeOptions
      ▼  📁 design
         ▼  📁 adminhtml
            ▼  📁 default
               ▶  📁 bookstore
         ▼  📁 frontend
            ▼  📁 bookstore
               ▼  📁 default
                  ▶  📁 layout
                  ▶  📁 locale
                  ▶  📁 template
      ▼  📁 etc
         ▶  📁 modules
   ▼  📁 skin
      ▼  📁 adminhtml
         ▼  📁 default
            ▶  📁 bookstore
      ▼  📁 frontend
         ▼  📁 bookstore
            ▼  📁 default
               ▶  📁 css
               ▶  📁 fonts
               ▶  📁 images
               ▶  📁 js
```

The `app` folder contains the following folders:

- `code`: This includes the admin theme module and the widgets
- `design`: This includes the design structure of the frontend and the backend
- `etc`: This contains the files needed for the activation of the widget and module

The `skin` folder contains the following folders:

- `frontend`: This includes the images and styles for the frontend theme
- `adminhtml`: This includes the images and styles for the backend theme

Creating the live demo preview

Now you have to test the theme pack by creating a live demo of the theme online, but we will cover this in the next section.

Creating the live demo preview will help you to conduct an additional test on your theme to check if everything is working as expected. If it is, you can proceed to the next step.

The performance of the sever

Please keep in mind that the online demo will be accessed by a large number of visitors, mostly during the initial days after your theme is made available on a marketplace such as ThemeForest. So, make sure that your server is optimized for Magento and has high performance.

To check if the server is compatible with a Magento installation, you can perform the following steps:

1. Download the `magento-check.php` file from `http://www.magentocommerce.com/_media/magento-check.zip`.

2. Extract the file and upload it on your server into the Magento installation folder, for example, `http://www.`**`sitename`**`.com/magento_root/magento_check.php`.

3. Then, open the link and check if everything is working correctly. If the server is optimized as well, you will see the following messages:

> **Congratulations!** Your server meets the requirements for Magento.
>
> - You have **PHP 5.2.0** (or greater)
> - Safe Mode is **off**
> - You have **MySQL 4.1.20** (or greater)
> - You have the **curl** extension
> - You have the **dom** extension
> - You have the **gd** extension
> - You have the **hash** extension
> - You have the **iconv** extension
> - You have the **mcrypt** extension
> - You have the **pcre** extension
> - You have the **pdo** extension
> - You have the **pdo_mysql** extension
> - You have the **simplexml** extension

Sample products

Once you created a live demo, you have to create a product that will highlight all the features and beauty of your new theme. The products you use on the demo are very important, so pay attention to the pictures that you use for the demo products. The pictures you use will have a great impact for the theme, so it is necessary to use pictures that actually represent the products the theme is designed for.

As you know, you can install some sample data with the Magento installation, but the pictures used are not great, and most of the time, not apt for your theme.

In the following screenshot, you can see the default Magento theme with the sample data:

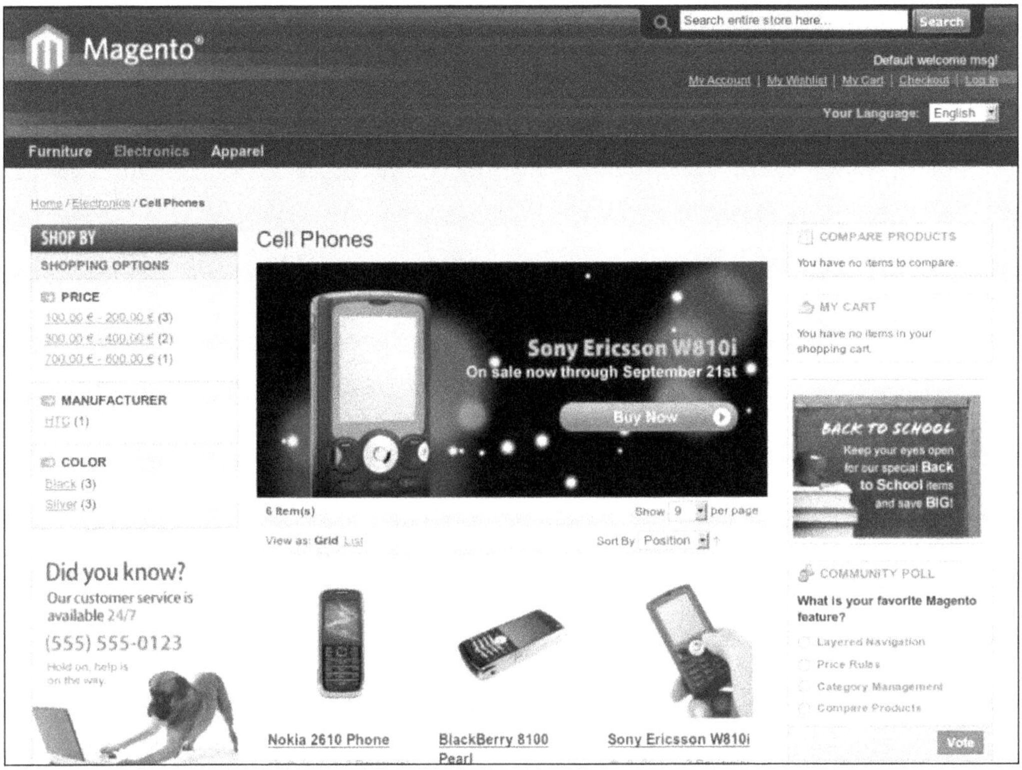

So in our case, for example, the theme is designed for a book store, so we have used some book covers, as you can see in the following screenshot:

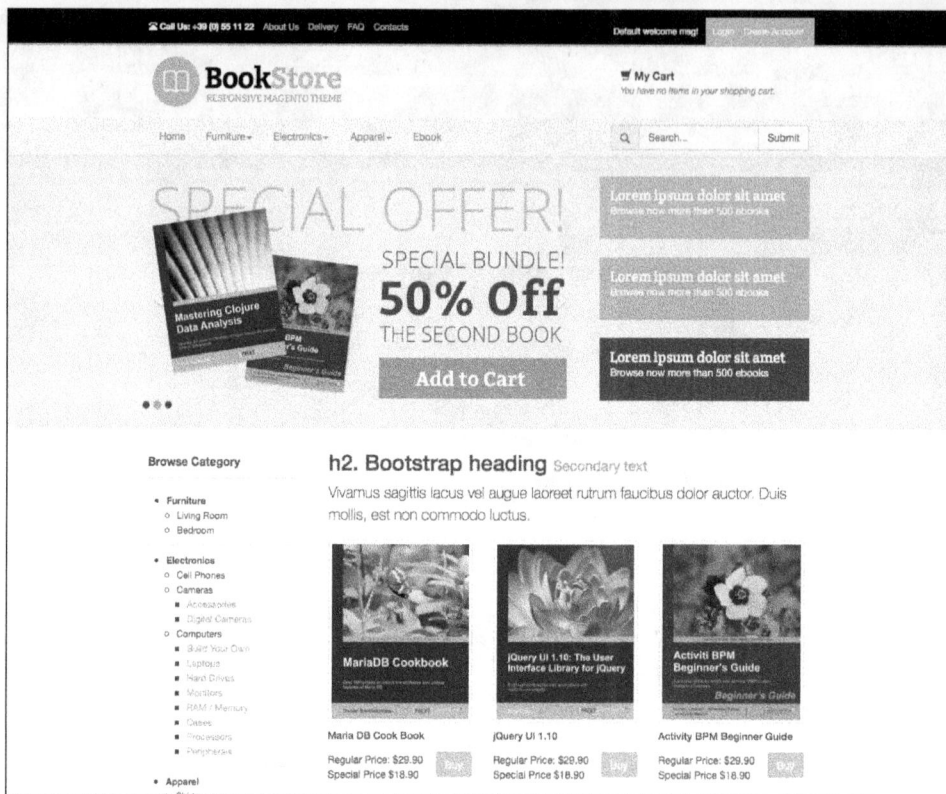

Searching for royalty-free photos for the theme

Where can you find some royalty-free pictures that can be used to create a great eye-catching live demo? If you search on the Internet, you can find a lot of websites. Let's discuss some of the most important ones.

iStock

The **iStock** (`iStockphoto.com`) website is probably one of the most well-known websites to buy photos. The quality of the pictures is very good, but the price of the extended license is very expensive.

The extended license is needed to sell a theme; if you want to invest some extra money to get some eye-catching pictures and illustrations, this is the right site for you.

The following is a screenshot of what the website looks like (`http:/www.istockphotos.com`):

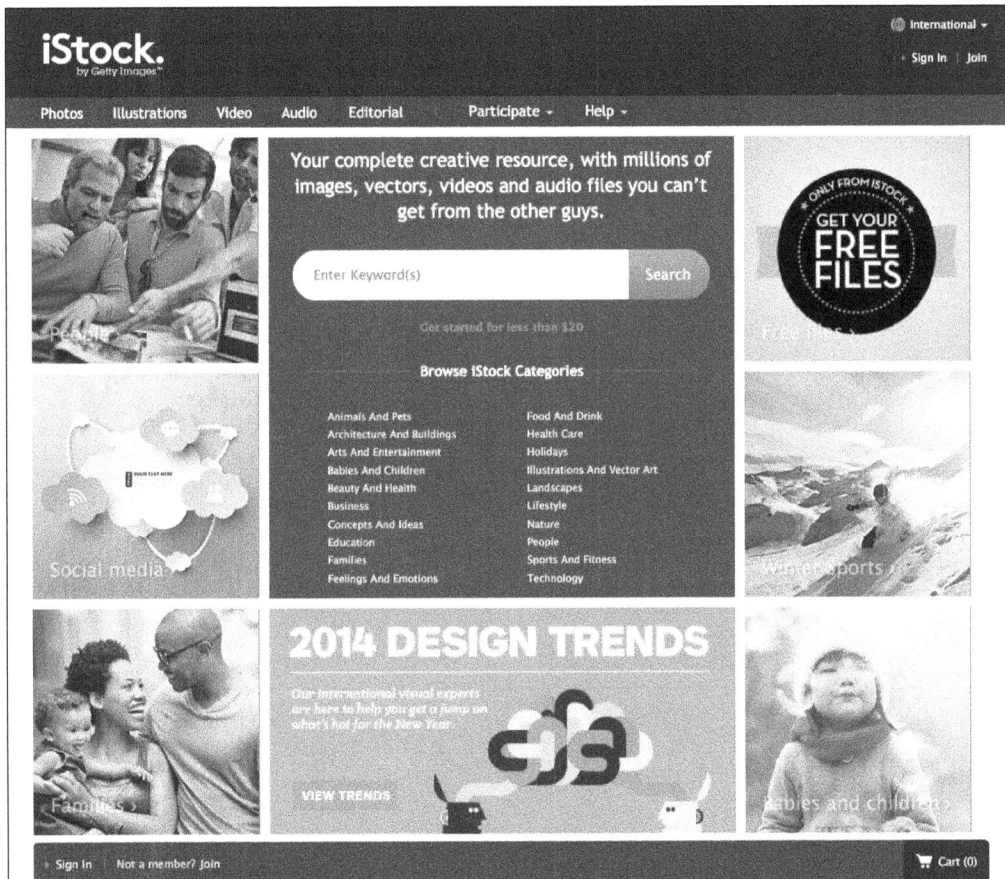

BIGSTOCK

The **BIGSTOCK** website includes a lot of images with licensing for templates. The photos are very good and the price is lower than that of **iStock** photos. You can try it for some days with a limited number of free pictures, or you can opt for a monthly subscription that allows you to download five photos per day.

The site includes not only high-quality photos, but also some great vector files. The following is a screenshot of what the website looks like (`http://www.bigstockphotos.com`):

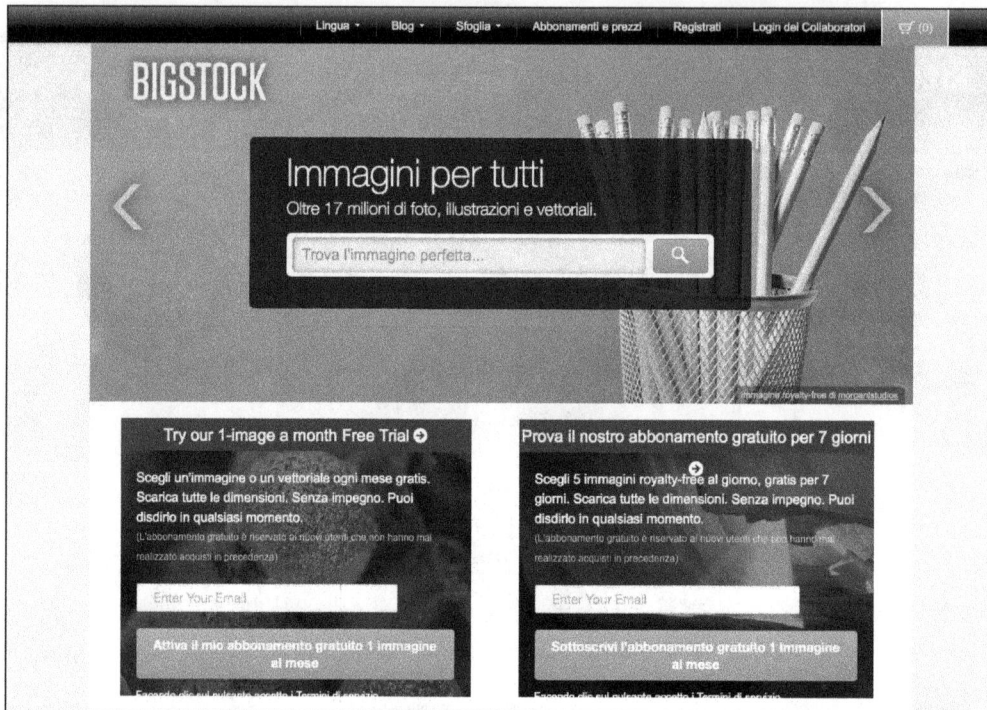

PhotoDune

The **PhotoDune** agency is a part of the **Envato** network, where you can get a lot of pictures at a very low price. The following is a screenshot of what the website looks like (`http://photodune.net/`):

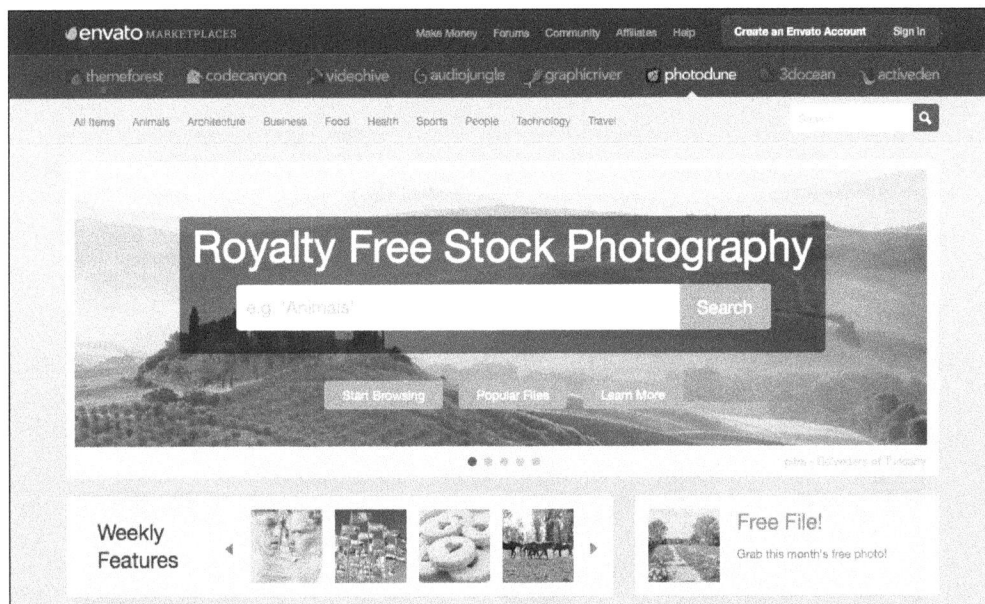

The Envato asset library

On the Envato blog, you can get some tips on where to find photos, and an asset library that includes some free files to be used for your next project.

The following is a screenshot of what the website looks like
(http://themeforest.net/page/asset_library):

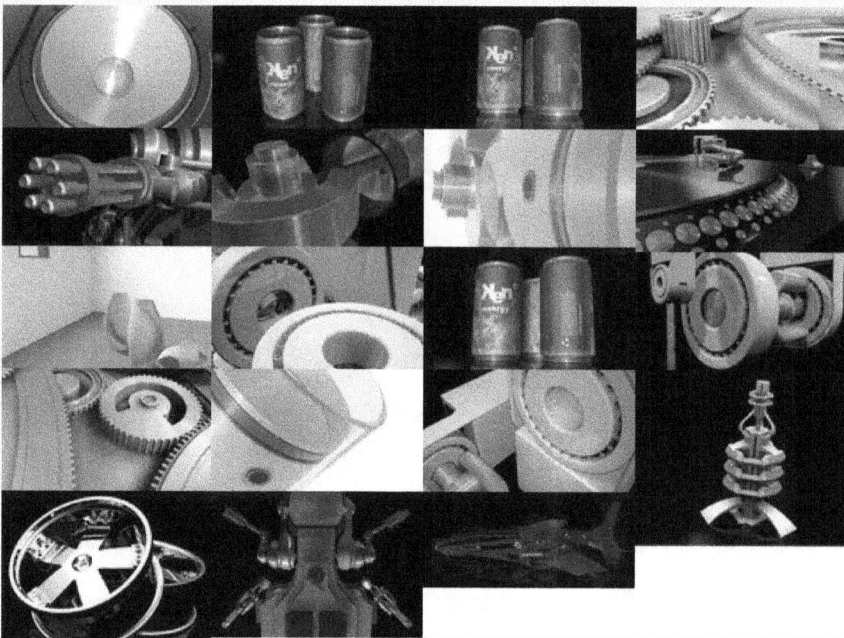

As you can see, there are many images that are grouped by a theme, so you can find pictures in the themes Nature, City, or Portfolio.

Please keep in mind that you must be logged in to the ThemeForest website and that you must agree with the Envato conditions in order to find images on the page.

Creating the documentation of the theme

Now you have a working demo and the theme pack installation ready. Before submitting the theme to be sold, or giving the theme to the final user/customer, it is good practice to send a detailed documentation along with the theme.

The documentation must contain all the instructions to install the theme, the code for the static blocks, and an FAQ section. The documentation is very important and needs to be well written and organized to increase the chances for the theme to be accepted by marketplaces such as ThemeForest. In fact, if the documentation is not good or the theme is not well documented, there are a lot of possibilities of it being rejected.

It is recommended that the designer have an editor or a copyeditor proofread the theme's documentation for a polished, professional end result. Most coders and designers aren't perfect writers, so getting an extra pair of eyes to make sure all the commas and apostrophes are in place would be a good idea.

> If the documentation is accurate and detailed, you will receive less support requests from the users, and the users will be happy to find all the instructions along with the theme.

To create good documentation and make sure the help documentation is in a file format readable by all operating systems and devices, you can create a PDF, HTML, and TXT file that are preferred, say, `.docx`.

To speed up this process, you can use a preset HTML template that will help you write an organized file.

Let us discuss the two different theme documentation files that you can use.

A simple example of the ThemeForest documentation

In ThemeForest, you can find the following useful HTML template at `http://themeforest.s3.amazonaws.com/108_helpFile/Template.zip`.

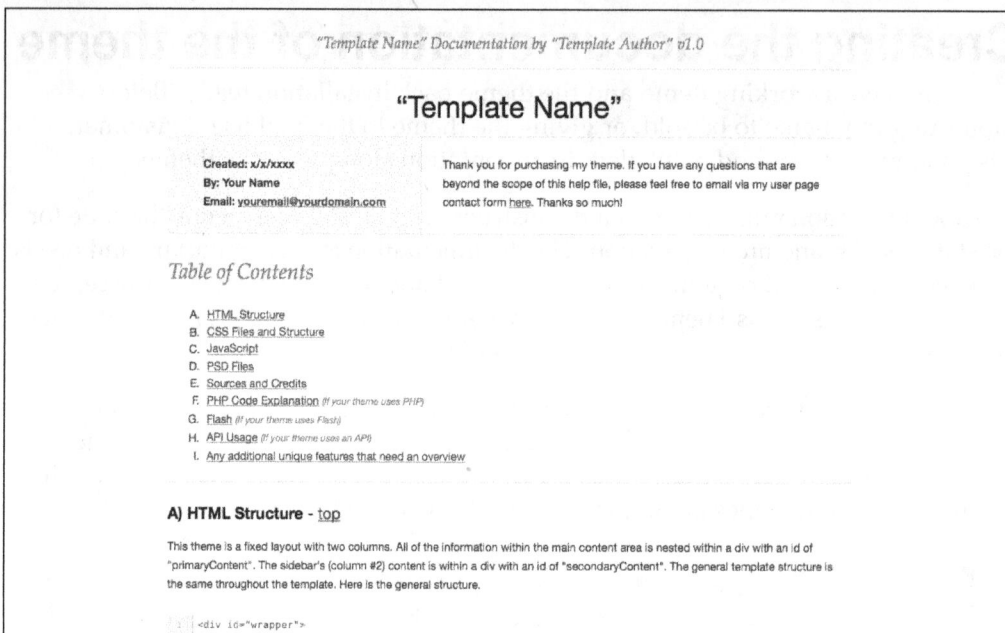

You only need to open and edit all the information of your theme.

The Documenter tool

Documenter is a great tool to generate custom documentation files with the capability of customizing the template and many other features. You can find the tool at `http://revaxarts-themes.com/documenter/` and the following is a screenshot of what the **Documenter** page looks like:

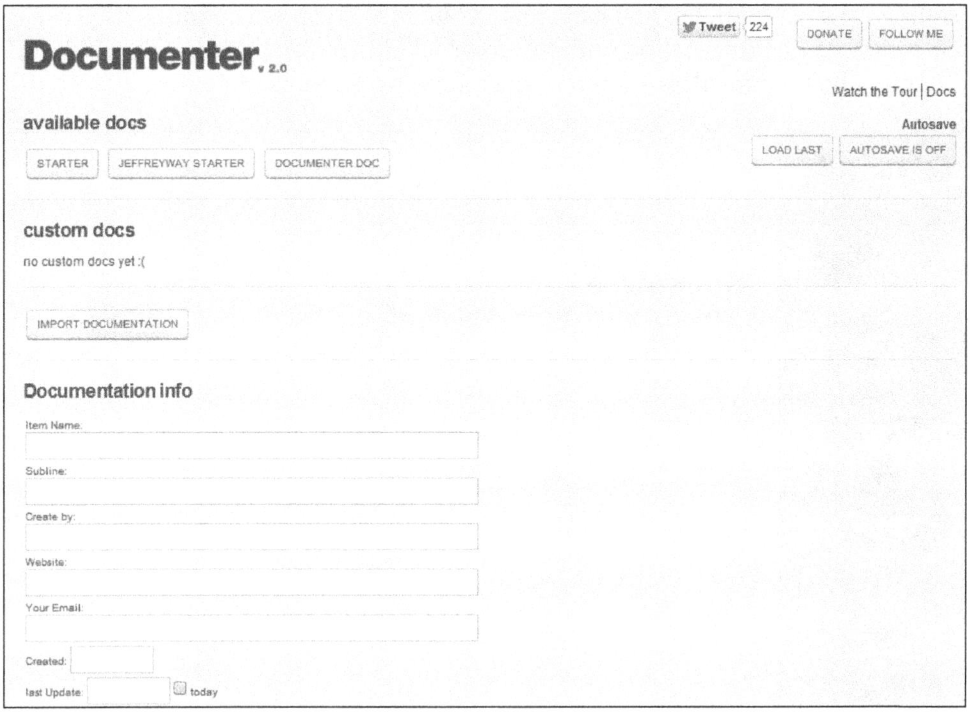

This is an example of what the screen in this program looks like.

Insert all the theme information, as shown in the following screenshot, along with the full documentation on how to install the theme and all the features that are included in the theme:

This is an example of what the screen in this program looks like.

By setting up some options, you can create your own style. For example, you can create a custom documentation with the color scheme of the theme: orange, black, and white. The final result is shown in the following screenshot:

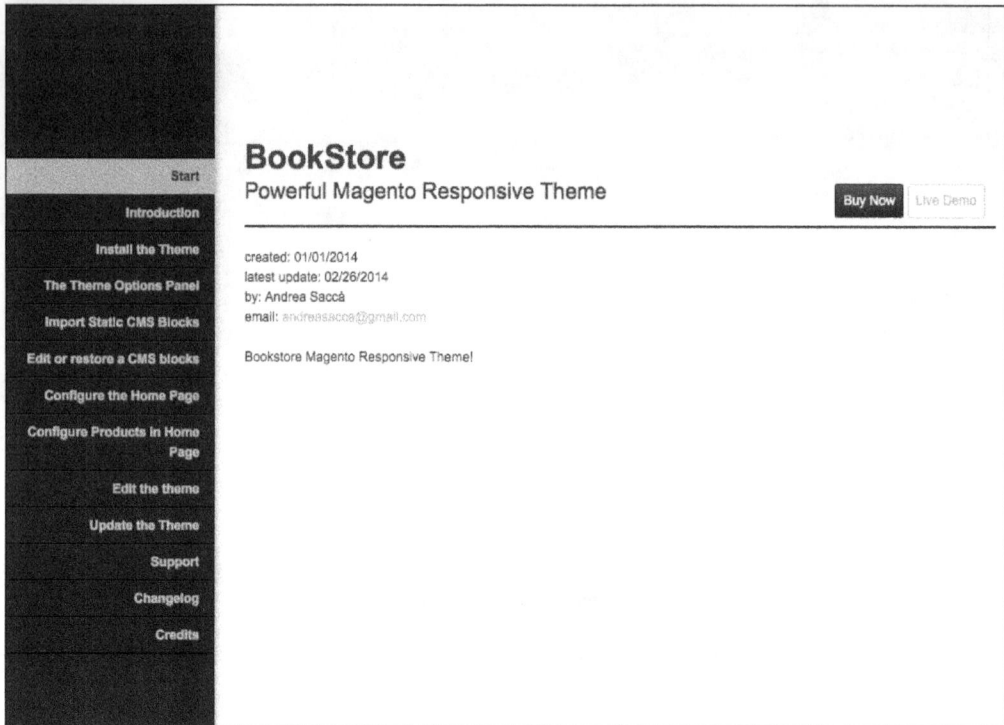

Some tips to write better documentation

After you download the source files, you can open and edit them as you want by adding the section of your choice. The documentation needs to be clear and easy to navigate. You can create a well-organized file by dividing it into the following sections:

- Start
- Introduction
- Installing the theme
- The theme options panel
- Importing static CMS blocks
- Editing or restoring CMS blocks
- Configuring the home page

- Configuring the products in the home page
- Editing the theme
- Updating the Theme
- Support
- Change log
- Credits

Packaging the theme

After you create a well-organized piece of documentation, ZIP everything and the theme is ready to be distributed.

Sometimes, in the pack, you need to insert the mockup of the theme, or if you prefer, only some features such as the product list, the logo, and so on. So, create an additional folder where you can include all the graphics source files.

To complete the pack, name the folder that must be distributed with the theme name and the theme version. This will help to keep you organized with the feature releases of the theme. For example, you can create the folder `BookStore_theme_v1` and you can organize the content with the following folders:

- Theme
- Documentation
- Mockup

Selling the theme on ThemeForest

As you know, ThemeForest is the most popular marketplace where you can sell professional themes and get some extra money. To sell a theme, you need to perform the following simple steps:

1. First, create an account and pass a simple test to check if you understood the conditions of the site.

2. Once you create an account and are ready to sell, open the **Upload** page, as shown in the following screenshot, from your account menu at the top:

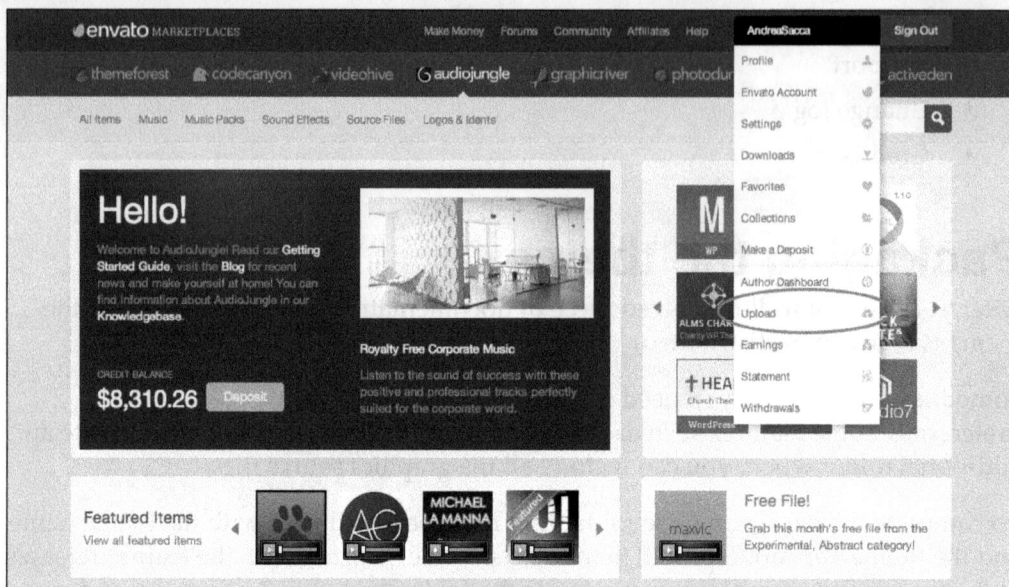

3. On this page, shown as follows, you have to select the category where you want to upload the theme; in our case, we will select the **eCommerce** category:

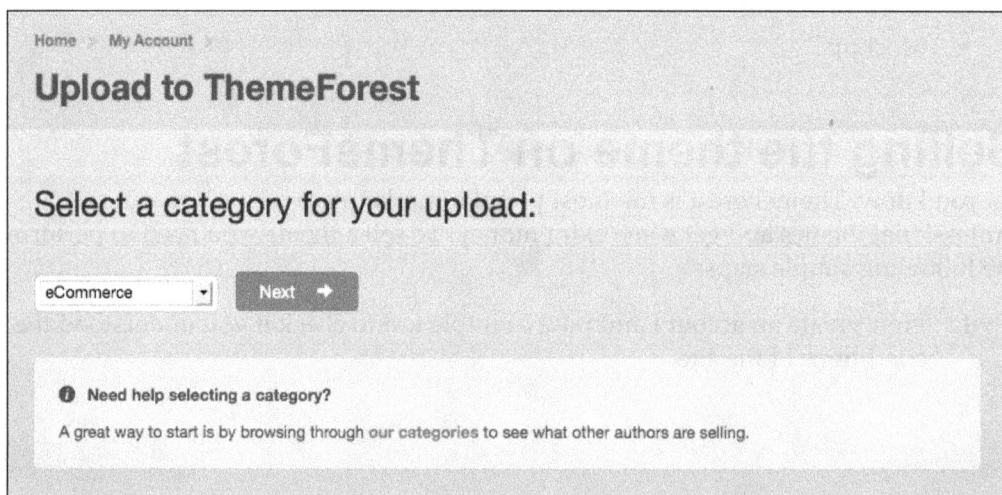

4. In the next step, you need to insert all the theme information, such as the
    Name and **Description**:

Name & Description

Name

Maximum 50 characters. Follow our Item Title Naming Conventions.

Description

This field is used for search, so please be descriptive!

As you can see from the tip, the name of the theme must have maximum 50
characters. You can use a name such as `BookStore Responsive Magento theme`.

You need to think of a name that reassumes the theme concept and the main
features. Think of it with the **SEO (Search Engine Optimization)** techniques
in mind, because the keyword you use will also appear on the search engines.

For example, try to search **Magento Responsive Theme** on Google. Actually,
this was the first theme I created while I was writing this book, which is on
the ThemeForest Marketplace on the first page of Google. This is because I
used some SEO techniques while writing the title and the description.

Emphasis - Multipurpose **Responsive Magento Theme** - ThemeForest
themeforest.net/...**responsive-magento-theme**/5503... ▾ Traduci questa pagina
04/set/2013 - This **Theme** is featured on the Ecommerce Sampler Pack! With the
eCommerce Sampler Pack you Get $240 Worth of Files for Just $20!

The theme is called **Emphasis** and you can find it at `http://themeforest.net/item/emphasis-multipurpose-responsive-magento-theme/5503789`. The following screenshot is of the current theme cover on ThemeForest:

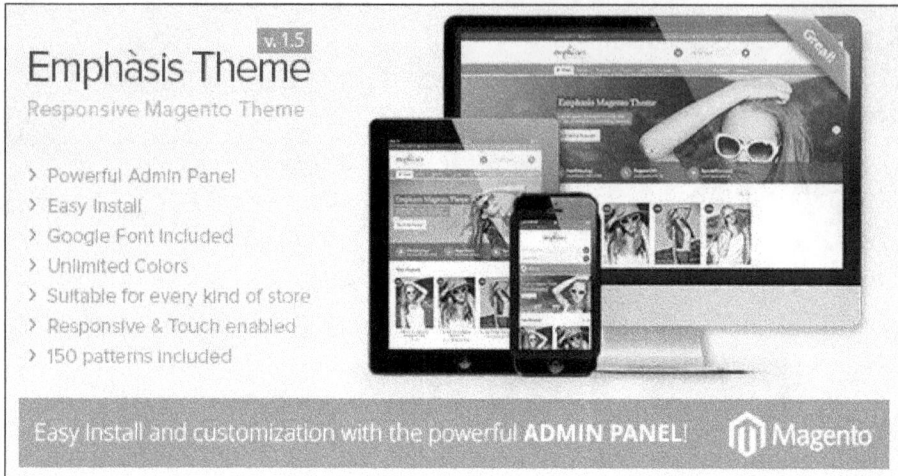

5. In the next section, you need to insert all the files. As you can see in the following screenshot of the theme, you can upload the zip file you created (`Bookstore_Theme_1.zip`):

6. Then, you need to upload all the files including the theme ZIP file and a custom image to represent the theme that will be the cover of the ThemeForest item page. For example, you can create a custom cover to represent the theme features, as shown in the following screenshot:

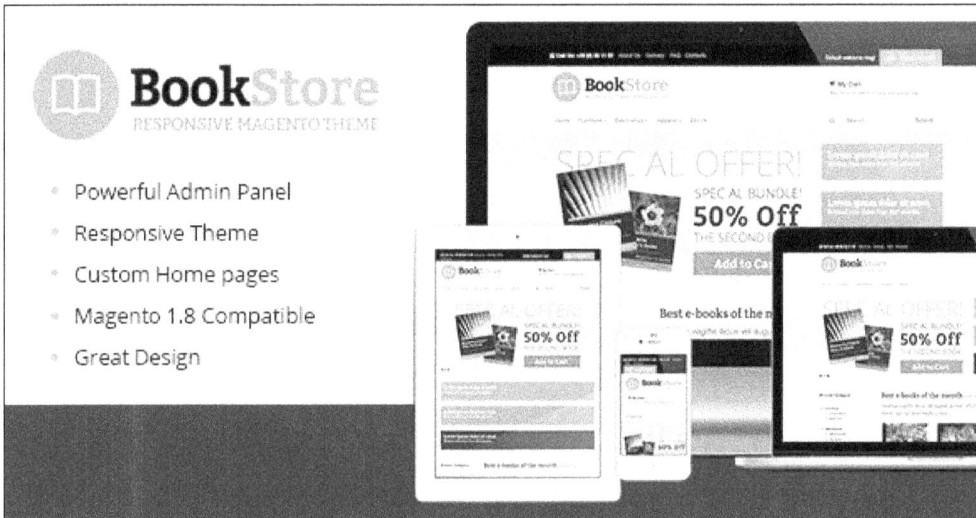

7. Next, you need to insert all the theme specifications. Fill in all the files and select all the options, and finally, submit the theme.

In a few hours, you will get an answer from the ThemeForest team; if everything is done well, the team will accept the theme and you are ready to make money!

My personal experience

I would like to share my personal experience. The first time I sent the theme **Emphasis** to the ThemeForest team, the review team there loved it; however, for some reason, they did not accept it because there were some concerns regarding the copyright issues with the brands used in the theme.

So, I corrected the problems indicated by the team and then submitted the theme again. After those small modifications, my theme was approved. **Emphasis** made 60 sales between October 2013 and March 2014. A good result for the first theme!

A few months after the **Emphasis** theme publication on ThemeForest, the Envato team selected my theme to include it into a special e-commerce bundle pack. This was another very good occasion and I had the opportunity to earn some extra money with that special event.

The eCommerce Sampler Pack included four themes for four of your favorite e-commerce platforms; mine included the following:

- WooCommerce
- Magento
- Opencart
- Prestashop

The **Emphasis** theme was selected to represent the Magento category. I was really surprised with this occasion and I earned a lot of popularity in the marketplace.

The following screenshot shows the banner provided for the eCommerce Sampler Pack, where my theme was featured:

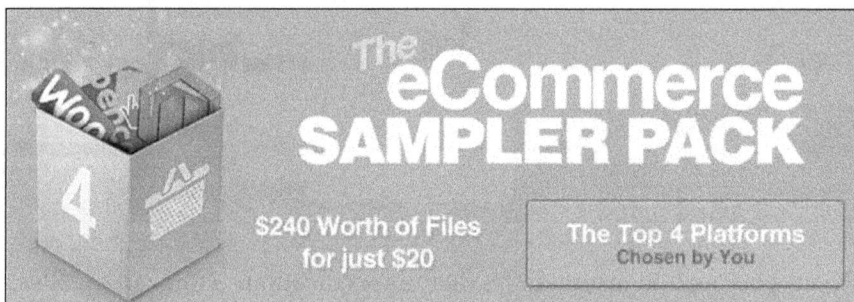

Now the pack is complete; you can see the landing page created for it at `http://go.themeforest.net/the-ecommerce-sampler-pack/`.

This is only to let you understand that sooner or later, the effort you put in to create a theme will be paid for. So if you do a great work, you have a great possibility of gaining a lot with ThemeForest and other marketplaces.

Theme pricing

The theme pricing is decided by the review team. Consider that the pricing of Magento themes start from $80 on ThemeForest and are the most expensive items on the marketplace. Also, consider that you will not earn the full quoted price of the theme; ThemeForest will initially give you a commission of 50 percent that will increase based on the sales. You can see the actual commission rate table at `http://themeforest.net/make_money/become_an_author`.

You can also consider the possibility of selling the theme in other marketplaces too; however, the commission will decrease to 30 percent.

So the more you sell, the more you earn. You may think that this is not very fair, but this is the easiest way to start selling your creations and getting some extra money for your work.

Inserting the theme on the Magento Connect site

Another great channel where you can distribute and publicize the theme is the **Magento Connect** website. This site is the place where you can find free and premium extensions and themes for Magento. The sales will not be through this website, but you have to share the link to the theme page of ThemeForest.

The following screenshot shows what the **Magento Connect** website looks like (`http://www.magentocommerce.com/magento-connect/`):

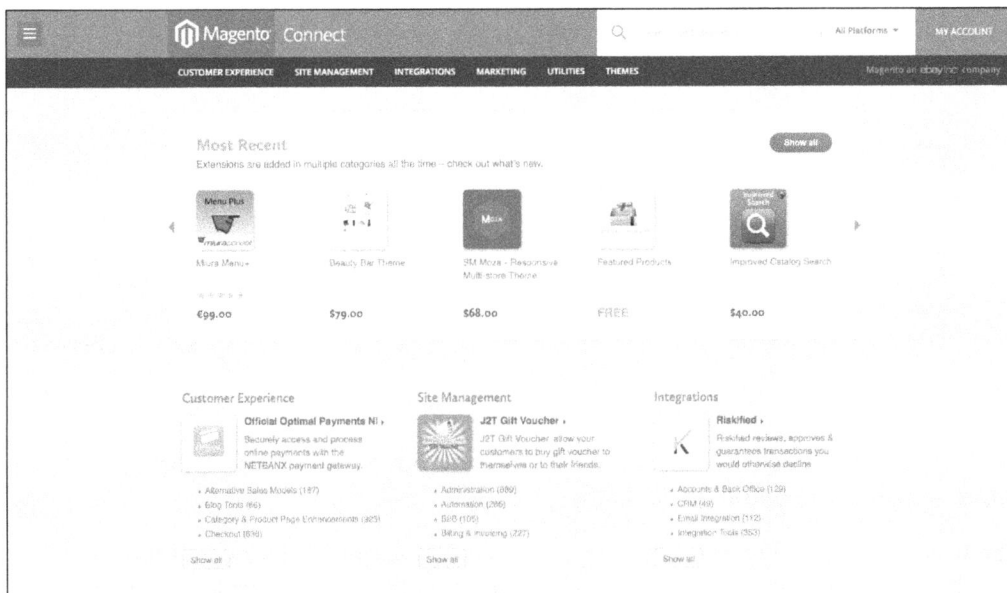

This is an example of what the screen in this program looks like.

Register an account and then you will have the option to upload your extension with all the details using a form similar to the one used by ThemeForest. The item must be approved by the team, and only then can it be found on the website. The approvals take about 48 hours and the price is the cost of the extension that you can find in your theme page. You can also consider selling the theme without going through a marketplace such as ThemeForest; in this case, you can set your own price in **Magento Connect**.

Support and updates

A parenthesis needs to be done on the support and on the updates of the theme. Keep in mind that your theme will be visited and bought by a lot of people. They may find some issues or problems that you can solve or help to solve.

Fixing the bugs and adding new features

Reserve some extra time to collect all the bug fixes and release all the updates for the theme once in a month. This will ensure that the theme is always updated and that users can rely on your products and services.

To do this, you can collect some bugs and fix them in the current version of the theme; once fixed, repackage the files and resubmit the new ZIP file in the marketplace.

To maintain a report of the modifications you make for each version, you can create a file called `changelog.txt` and add all the fixes or the new features in the following manner:

```
Version 1.1 (September 6, 2013)
- FIX: Minor Css bugs fixed
- FIX: Top Cart Background fix
- FIX: Responsive Menu
- FIX: Fixed bug in Google font selector
- FIX: Mobile Account links made like Flags and currency dropdown
- NEW: Animated Scroll to top on top Cart click for better user
experience
- NEW: Animated Scroll to top on Menu click for better user experience

Version 1.0 (September 1, 2013) - Initial release
```

Through this file, both the final user and you will have a report of all the improvements you make to the theme.

The update approval of ThemeForest usually takes about 24 hours, and the users who buy the theme can choose to be notified when the theme is uploaded through their account. In this way, the users will be notified once the theme is updated.

Supporting final users

You have to also consider the possibility of helping the users who buy the theme with the theme installation or to fix some problems. Some of the people who buy the theme already know how to install it and how to work with it, but many people don't know how to install it on Magento (even if you provide documentation). In this case, many of them will contact you to ask if you are available to support them during the installation phase. You can provide this service for an additional cost, or you may choose to not provide the support. However, keep in mind that good support is very important and will provide confidence to the people, who will probably come back to buy your products if they are satisfied.

Summary

Now you have the key to start creating a powerful theme for the most-used e-commerce CMS of the world. You can create a theme from scratch with the powerful framework Bootstrap and make it responsive.

You also learned how to distribute it on the most important marketplaces, and now, I hope that you can test and create your very own theme for your customer or sell it on the marketplace and become one of the best Magento theme designers!

In the appendix that follows, you will find all the references and resources used in the theme.

Thank you for reading and keep designing and coding!

Conclusions and Credits

We are done! Thank you for reading this book. I hope you can get the most out of all the information provided in all the chapters and benefit from the creation of Magento custom themes.

To end this book, here is a list of useful links used to create this book where you can find a lot of information to learn more about Magento design.

The resources are divided in the following way for quick and easy consultation and reference:

- Official Magento resources
- Useful websites on Magento
- Free resources for design, UI, and web design

Official Magento resources

Magento is the core of this book. The following are a few places you can visit to to to deepen your knowledge about it:

- Magento commerce website
- Magento design guide
- Magento front end developer certification
- Magento 2

The Magento commerce website

You can access the official website of Magento commerce at

```
http://magento.com/.
```

Consider the following screenshot:

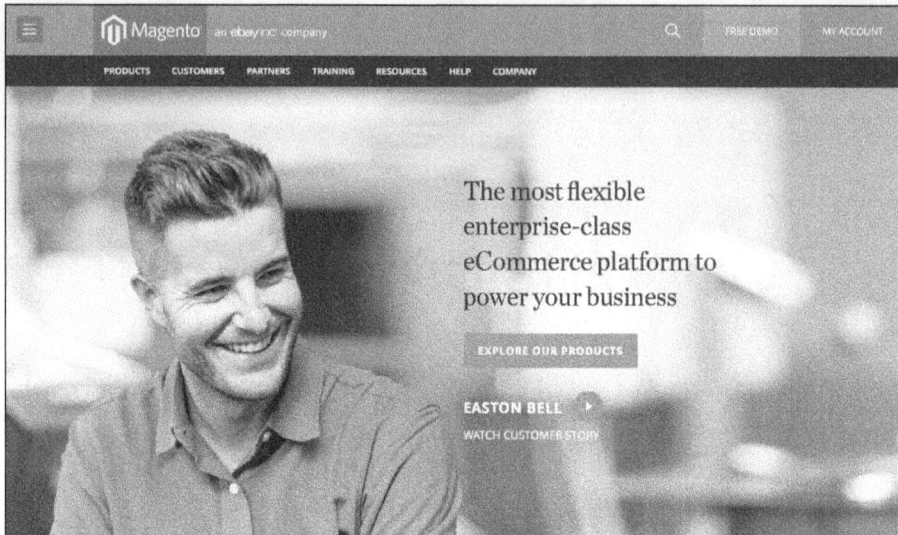

The Magento design guide

You can learn more about Magento design basics with the official Magento design guide that you can find at

`http://www.magentocommerce.com/resources/magento-user-guide.`

Consider the following screenshot:

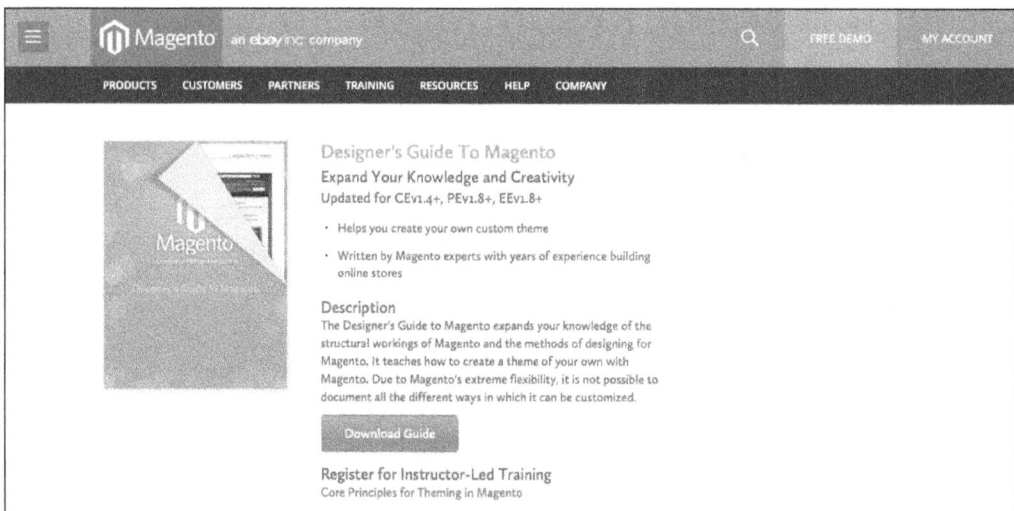

Magento Front End certification

Do you know that Magento has also introduced the Front End Developer certification? The following is the logo of Magento Front End Developer certification:

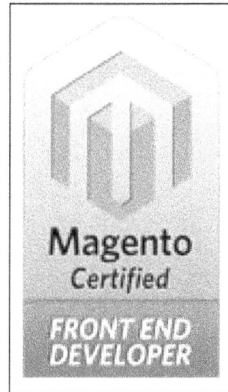

This certification is aimed at all the frontend developers with a good knowledge of the Magento front end, whose main focus is on modifying the **user interface** (**UI**) of existing themes or on creating new themes.

To become a certified frontend Magento developer, you have to register on the Magento web site at `http://www.magentocommerce.com/certification/front-end-developer`.

The certification voucher costs 260 USD and you can take the exam at a specific center nearest to you.

I obtained the certification here in Rome, and you can see my profile at

`http://www.magentocommerce.com/certification/directory/dev/76379/`.

Consider the following screenshot:

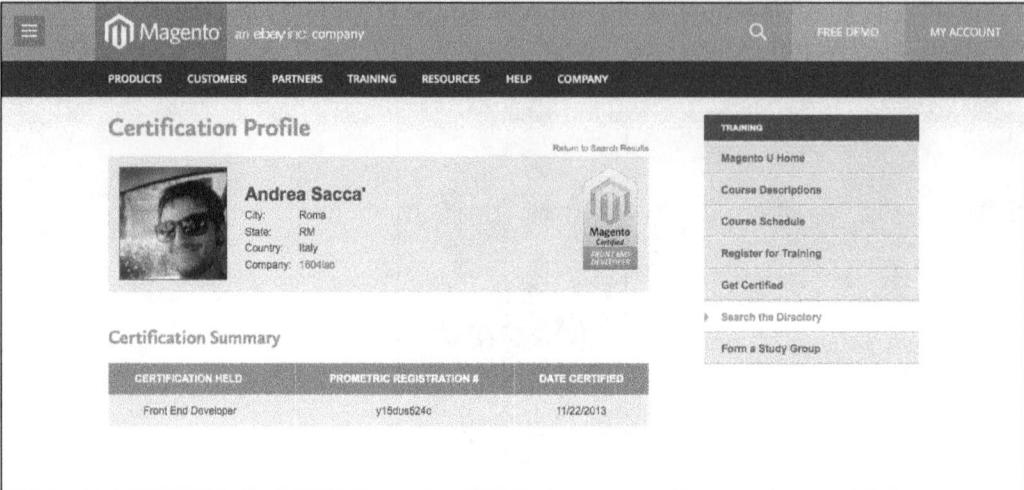

After I took this certification, many companies contacted me for professional services to create custom Magento themes or to improve their stores.

Thanks to the certification, you can assure your customers and the agency you work with that you have all the capabilities and a full understanding of Magento theming.

Magento 2

What's next? If you haven't ever heard, the Magento platform is growing and work is in progress on Magento 2 Version.

The following is a preview of how it will look:

This is an example of what the screen in this program looks like.

This version was expected to be released in 2013, but it may be released this year.

Keep in mind that the new core structure and the front end is going to be a little bit different from now, and if you want to keep yourself updated, you can follow the Magento 2 development on GitHub at `https://github.com/magento/magento2`.

You can find all the Magento releases at

`http://www.magentocommerce.com/download/release_notes`.

You can find a very useful Wiki section on the Magento website at

`https://wiki.magento.com/display/MAGE2DOC/`.

Useful websites on Magento

In this section, you can find a lot of interesting articles about Magento development, Magento design, and free extensions.

Excellence Magento blog

This is the blog of Manish Prakash, a Magento and mobile app developer. His blog is full of interesting tutorials and articles on Magento development.

Check out at `http://excellencemagentoblog.com`. Consider the following screenshot:

Fabrizio Branca blog

Fabrizio Branca is a certified developer, and he released a number of free extensions to boost up your Magento, especially the cache.

You can find all the free extensions he created at

`http://www.fabrizio-branca.de/magento-modules.html.`

You can even read interesting Magento articles at

`http://www.fabrizio-branca.de/magento.html.`

Consider the following screenshot:

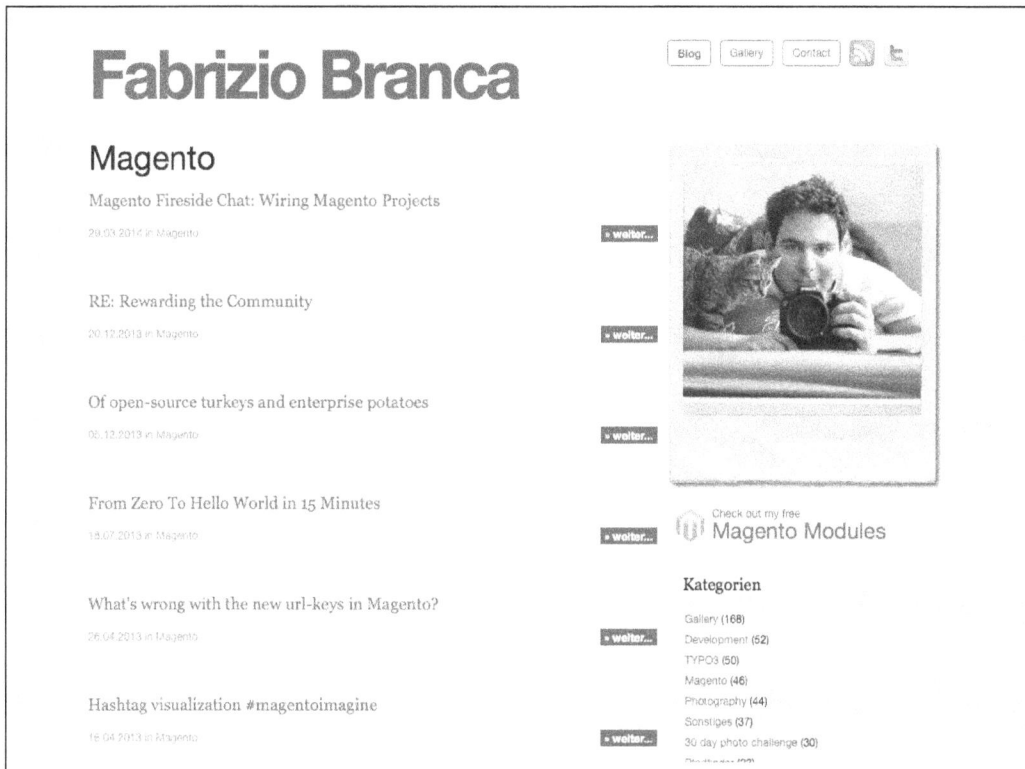

Bubble codes by Johann Reinke

In this website blog, you can find interesting articles and resources related to Magento as well as the free Magento Go admin theme.

You can check this out at `http://www.bubblecode.net/en`. Consider the following screenshot:

Inchoo's blog

Inchoo is a web company specialized in Magento and they own a blog full of useful information, tips, and free modules that you can use for your project and to understand a lot of things about Magento development, e-commerce-related marketing, and Magento custom free and useful extensions.

You can find the blog at `http://inchoo.net/blog`. Consider the following screenshot:

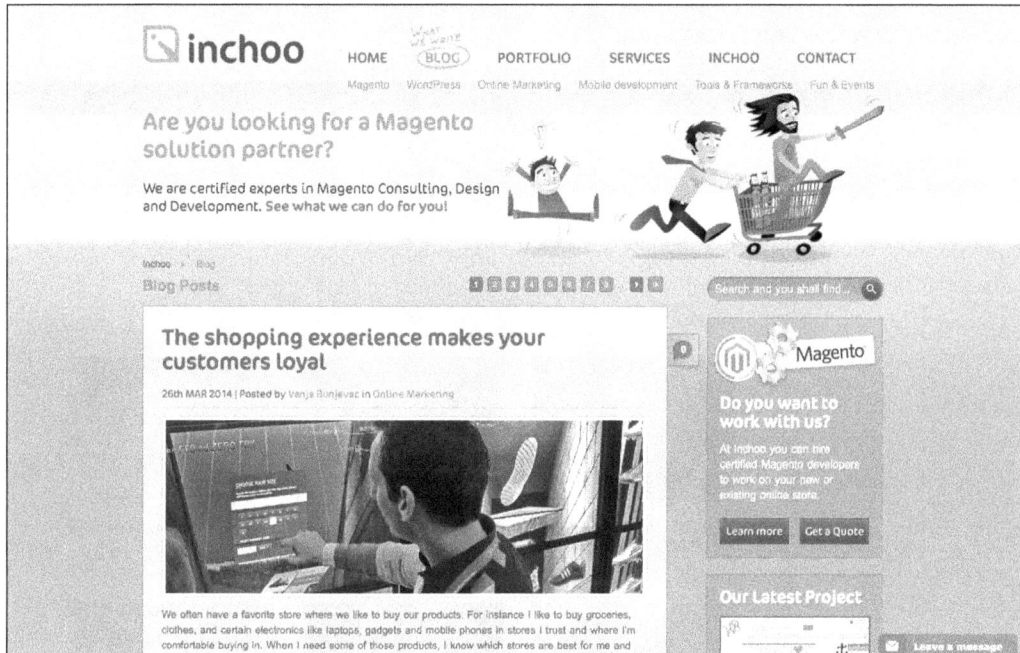

Tuts plus Magento tutorials

If you are looking for some other neat, simple tutorials on Magento and Magento design, you can find some interesting articles when you go to the Tuts plus website and search for Magento.

You can access all the Magento articles at

```
http://code.tutsplus.com/search?utf8=%E2%9C%93&view=&search[keywods]=
magento&button=.
```

Consider the following screenshot:

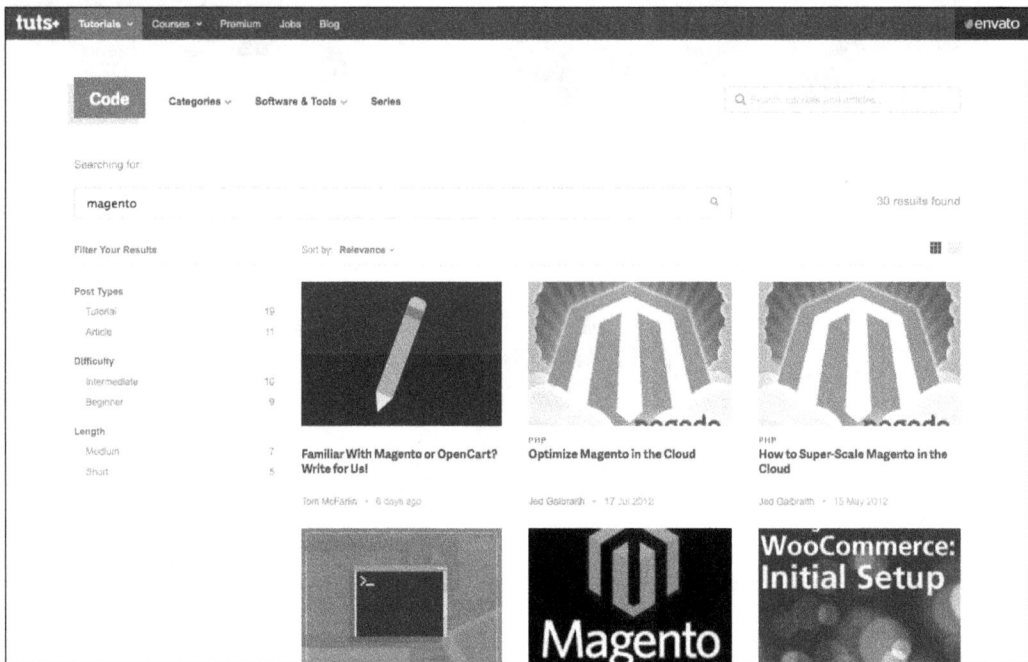

This is an example of what the screen in this program looks like.

Smashing magazine

Smashing magazine is an online magazine for web designers and developers.

Here too, you can find a lot of articles about Magento. You can access this at `http://coding.smashingmagazine.com/tag/magento/`. Consider the following screenshot:

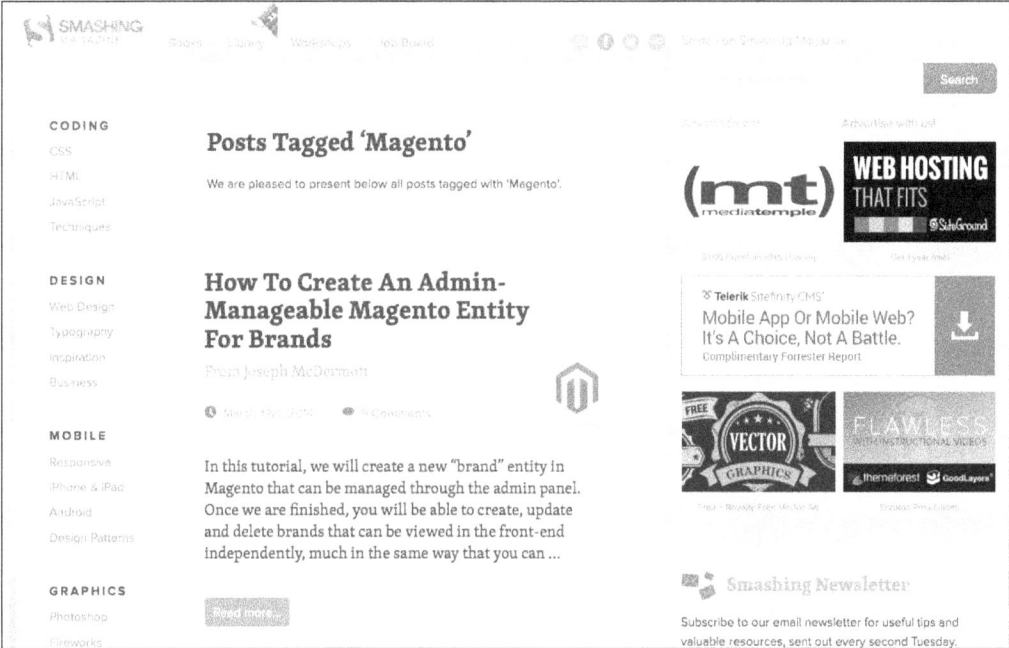

Free resources for design, UI, and web design

And now a few links about design, responsive design, and other interesting topics that you may want to delve deeper into to improve your knowledge on designing.

Responsive design

In this section, you can find some useful links about the resources used and other tutorials that can be useful for reference:

- Bootstrap: `http://getbootstrap.com/`
- Responsive test Viewport Resizer: `http://lab.maltewassermann.com/viewport-resizer/`
- CSS3 media queries: `http://www.w3.org/TR/css3-mediaqueries/` and `http://css-tricks.com/snippets/css/media-queries-for-standard-devices/`

UI – UIX resources

The following are some useful links that can be used for reference:

- Ux news: `http://uxmag.com/topics/e-commerce`
- Magento successful stories: `http://www.magentocommerce.com/customer-success-stories/user-experience-design/`
- Smashing magazine UX section: `http://uxdesign.smashingmagazine.com/`

Animations

The following are some useful links that can be used for reference:

- jQuery: `http://jquery.com/`
- CSS3 animations & transitions: `http://www.w3schools.com/css/css3_transitions.asp`
- `http://css-tricks.com/almanac/properties/t/transition/`

Fonts

The following are some useful links that can be used for reference:

- Google fonts: `https://www.google.com/fonts`
- Font Squirrel: `http://www.fontsquirrel.com/`
- Font Awesome: `http://fortawesome.github.io/Font-Awesome/`
- Typekit: `https://typekit.com/fonts`

Social media

The following is a useful link that can be used for reference:

- AddThis social media: `http://www.addthis.com`

Photo stocks resources

The following are some useful links that can be used for reference:

- iStockPhotos: `http://www.istockphoto.com`
- BigStock Photos: `http://www.bigstockphoto.com/`
- PhotoDune: `http://photodune.net`
- Envato Asset Library: `http://themeforest.net/page/asset_library`

Free resources

The following are some useful links that can be used for reference:

- Free mockup to present your theme: `http://line25.com/articles/40-free-mockup-templates-to-present-your-ui-designs`
- Freebies bug: `http://freebiesbug.com/`
- Pixeden: `http://www.pixeden.com/`

Selling your theme

The following is a useful link that can be used for reference:

- ThemeForest: `http://themeforest.net/`

Conclusions

In this book, we have seen how to create and develop a responsive Magento theme with custom widgets and the custom admin theme panel. We have also seen how to customize the admin theme to make it look better and similar to the front end.

The responsive web design is very important, especially during a time like this, when mobile devices are constantly developing and being disseminated, and purchases via smartphones are increasing. If you improve and learn how to do this in the better way, you can offer very high quality services to your clients.

I hope you found this guide useful and that it has offered you the fundamental knowledge to be able to continue your work and realize some fantastic Magento themes.

Thank you

Thank you for reading and keep in touch if you wish to!

You can find more information about my work and the projects I created on my website and portfolio at `http://andreasacca.it/`.

If you wish, you can also follow me on Twitter for the latest news about design, web tips, and other web stuff at `http://twitter.com/andreasacca`.

Index

Symbols

+ button
  integrating in, product page 153, 154
.js files
  declaring, in local.xml 36

A

admin panel
  CMS home page, creating from 70-72
  customizing, AdminTheme module used
     216
  design, overviewing 214, 215
  widgets, adding in 172, 173
admin panel, customizing
  AdminTheme module, installing to change
     folder path 216-218
admin panel interface
  conditional options 198
  creating 196
  frontend, customizing 197
  input text field value, obtaining 197, 198
  uploaded image file, obtaining 199-201
  Yes/No dropdown option, accessing 198
AdminTheme module
  installing, to change folder path 216-218
  used, for customizing admin panel 216
admin theme options panel
  advanced admin options panel, creating
     191
  advanced options features 201
  creating 175
  interfacing, with theme 196
  System.xml fields, overviewing 186, 187

theme options module, creating 175
  visual color picker, creating 205
Adobe TypeKit
  about 111, 112
  URL 112
advanced admin options panel
  creating 191-194
  custom dropdown field, creating 194-196
advanced options features
  dependent field, creating 201-203
  JavaScripts, adding in comment tag 204
alert message
  adding, for incorrect data 237
animated cart
  content, styling with CSS 95, 96
  creating, in header 92
  CSS, customizing 94
  top.phtml file, customizing 93
app directory
  folders, creating in 22
  layout subdirectory 10-12
  locale folder 13, 14
  template files 12
  translatable entries, creating 14

B

background color, header
  changing 222, 223
banners
  CMS block, creating for 68, 69
BIGSTOCK
  about 252
  URL 252
block-title attribute 92

M

visual color picker, admin panel
  creating 205-207
  default values, defining for options fields
    209
  options, validating 208

W

Web-safe font sources
  Adobe TypeKit 111, 112
  Font Squirrel 111

Google fonts 110, 111
websites, Magento
  Bubble codes by Johann Reinke 276, 277
  Excellence Magento blog 274
  Fabrizio Branca blog 275
  Inchoo blog 277
  Smashing magazine 279
  Tuts plus Magento tutorials 278
widget.xml file
  options, adding to 168-170
WYSIWYG editor
  disabling 30

Thank you for buying
Mastering Magento Theme Design

About Packt Publishing

Packt, pronounced 'packed', published its first book "*Mastering phpMyAdmin for Effective MySQL Management*" in April 2004 and subsequently continued to specialize in publishing highly focused books on specific technologies and solutions.

Our books and publications share the experiences of your fellow IT professionals in adapting and customizing today's systems, applications, and frameworks. Our solution based books give you the knowledge and power to customize the software and technologies you're using to get the job done. Packt books are more specific and less general than the IT books you have seen in the past. Our unique business model allows us to bring you more focused information, giving you more of what you need to know, and less of what you don't.

Packt is a modern, yet unique publishing company, which focuses on producing quality, cutting-edge books for communities of developers, administrators, and newbies alike. For more information, please visit our website: www.packtpub.com.

About Packt Open Source

In 2010, Packt launched two new brands, Packt Open Source and Packt Enterprise, in order to continue its focus on specialization. This book is part of the Packt Open Source brand, home to books published on software built around Open Source licences, and offering information to anybody from advanced developers to budding web designers. The Open Source brand also runs Packt's Open Source Royalty Scheme, by which Packt gives a royalty to each Open Source project about whose software a book is sold.

Writing for Packt

We welcome all inquiries from people who are interested in authoring. Book proposals should be sent to author@packtpub.com. If your book idea is still at an early stage and you would like to discuss it first before writing a formal book proposal, contact us; one of our commissioning editors will get in touch with you.

We're not just looking for published authors; if you have strong technical skills but no writing experience, our experienced editors can help you develop a writing career, or simply get some additional reward for your expertise.

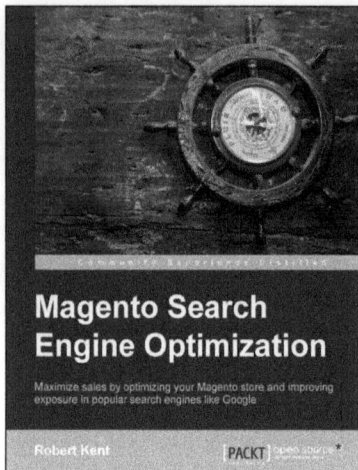

Magento Search Engine Optimization

ISBN: 978-1-78328-857-1   Paperback: 132 pages

Maximize sales by optimizing your Magento store and improving exposure in popular search engines like Google

1. Optimize your store for search engines in other countries and languages.

2. Enhance your product and category pages.

3. Resolve common SEO issues within Magento.

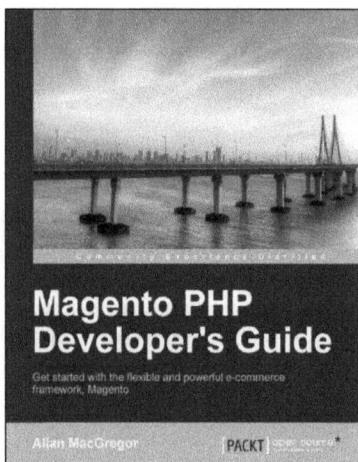

Magento PHP Developer's Guide

ISBN: 978-1-78216-306-0   Paperback: 256 pages

Get started with the flexible and powerful e-commerce framework, Magento

1. Build your first Magento extension, step by step.

2. Extend core Magento functionality, such as the API.

3. Learn how to test your Magento code.

Please check **www.PacktPub.com** for information on our titles

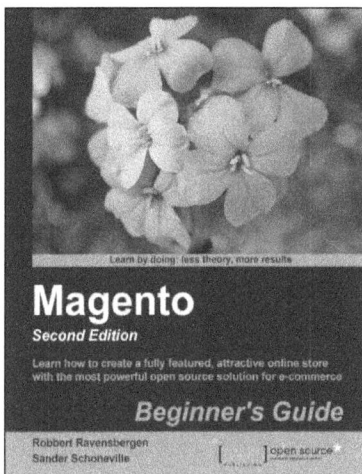

Magento Beginner's Guide

Second Edition

ISBN: 978-1-78216-270-4   Paperback: 320 pages

Learn how to create a fully featured, attractive online store with the most powerful open source solution for e-commerce

1. Install, configure, and manage your own e-commerce store.

2. Extend and customize your store to reflect your brand and personality.

3. Handle tax, shipping, and custom orders.

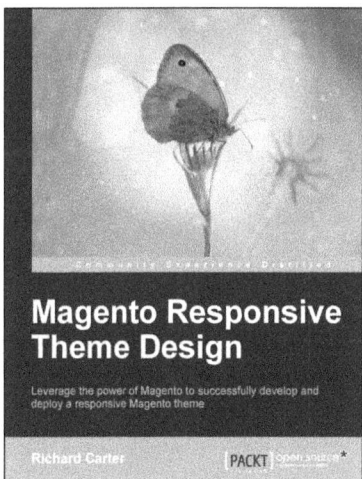

Magento Responsive Theme Design

ISBN: 978-1-78398-036-9   Paperback: 110 pages

Leverage the power of Magento to successfully develop and deploy a responsive Magento theme

1. Build a mobile-, tablet-, and desktop-friendly e-commerce site.

2. Refine your Magento store's product and category pages for mobile.

3. Easy-to-follow, step-by-step guide on how to get up and running with Magento.

Please check **www.PacktPub.com** for information on our titles

www.ingramcontent.com/pod-product-compliance
Lightning Source LLC
Chambersburg PA
CBHW080936220326

41598CB00034B/5795